I say unto **you**

OSHO is a registered trademark of OSHO International Foundation
www.osho.com/trademarks

This book is a series of original talks by Osho, given to a live audience. All of
Osho's talks have been published in full as books, and are also available as
original audio recordings. Audio recordings and the complete text archive can
be found via the online OSHO Library at www.osho.com/library

Osho comments in this work on excerpts from: The Holy Bible (The Authorized
King James Version, "Red Letter Edition")

OSHO MEDIA INTERNATIONAL
New York • Zurich • Mumbai
an imprint of
OSHO INTERNATIONAL
www.osho.com/oshointernational

Distributed by Publishers Group Worldwide
www.pgw.com

Library of Congress Catalog-In-Publication Data is available

Printed in India by Manipal Technologies Limited, Karnataka

ISBN-13: 978-1-938755-00-2
This title is also available in eBook format ISBN-13: 978-0-88050-992-3

contents

preface

When I talk to you about Jesus, it is not *about* Jesus. I am not a theologian, not a Christian, not a scholar. Theologians talk "about." They go round and round, they beat around the bush. I am not going to talk about Jesus, I am going to talk Jesus. And when I talk about Jesus, it is not that I am talking about him, rather, he talks himself. I give him way, I become a passage. All that I do is that I don't hinder him. That is the only way to talk about Jesus or Buddha or Krishna. And when I will talk Jesus I will not talk about Christ. Jesus is real, Christ is a principle. Jesus is concrete, Christ is abstract. Jesus is a man like you and me, of blood and bone. His heart beats. He laughs, he cries, he loves, he lives.

Christ is a dead concept, bloodless; there is no heart beating there. Christianity is concerned with Christ, I am not concerned with Christ. The word *christ* is beautiful, but corrupted, contaminated, polluted. The whole beauty of it has been destroyed. Whenever a word is used by theologians it loses meaning and purity and innocence – then it is no longer virgin. Jesus is still virgin, Christ is corrupted. Christ is a concept; Jesus is reality, concrete reality.

Osho
Come Follow to You

CHAPTER 1

be a nobody and have all

Matthew 5

And seeing the multitudes, he went up into a mountain: and when he was set, his disciples came unto him:

And he opened his mouth, and taught them, saying,

Blessed are the poor in spirit: for theirs is the kingdom of heaven.

Blessed are they that mourn: for they shall be comforted.

Blessed are the meek: for they shall inherit the earth.

Blessed are they which do hunger and thirst after righteousness: for they shall be filled.

Blessed are the merciful: for they shall obtain mercy.

Blessed are the pure in heart: for they shall see God.

The body is like grapes, the grapes will have to go. You cannot keep grapes for long – they will go rotten. But you can create wine out of the grapes, that's why it is also called "spirit." You can create spirit, a wine, in your being. Grapes cannot be accumulated, they are temporary, momentary. But wine can stay forever. In fact, the older it becomes the more precious and valuable it is. It has a non-temporal duration; it is something of eternity. The body is like the grapes, and if you use it rightly you can create the wine in you. The body is going to disappear, but the wine can remain, the spirit can remain.

Jesus has done many miracles. One of the miracles is that of transforming water into wine. These are metaphors – don't take them literally. If you take them literally, you destroy their meaning, their significance. And if you start proving that they are historical facts, you are stupid, and with you Jesus also looks stupid. They are metaphors of the inner world. The inner world cannot be expressed literally, but symbolically – only symbolically. Turning water into wine simply means creating the eternal from time, creating that which remains from that which cannot remain.

If you keep water, sooner or later it will start stinking. But you can keep wine for ages, for centuries. And the longer it is there the better it becomes, the more powerful, the more potent it becomes. Wine is a metaphor for the eternal. Jesus is transformed through his sacrifice. Nobody is ever transformed without sacrifice. You have to pay for it; the cross is the price that you pay. You have to die to be reborn; you have to lose all to gain godliness.

Jesus begat himself. That phenomenon happened on the cross. He hesitated for a time, he was very puzzled – it was natural. For a single moment he could not see God anywhere. All was lost, he was losing all; he was going to die and there seemed to be no possibility... That happens to every seed. When you put the seed into the earth, a moment comes when the seed is losing itself, and there must be hesitation – the same hesitation that happened to Jesus on the cross. The seed is dying, and the seed must cling to the past. It wants to survive – nobody wants to die. And the seed cannot imagine that this is not death, that soon it will be resurrected in a thousand-fold way, that soon it will start growing as a sprout.

The death of the seed will be the birth of the tree. There will be great foliage and flowering and fruits, and birds will come and sit on the branches and make their nests, and people will sit under the shade of the tree. And the tree will talk to the clouds and the stars in the night, and will play with the sky, and will dance in the winds; and there will be great rejoicing. But how can this be known to the poor seed which has never been anything else? It is inconceivable. That's why God is inconceivable.

It cannot be proved to the seed that it is going to happen, because if the seed asks, "Then let me see what you are going to do," you cannot make it available, you cannot make visible to the seed what is going to happen. It is going to happen in the future, and when it happens, the seed will be gone. The seed will never meet the tree. Man never meets God. When the man is gone, God descends.

Jesus hesitated, was worried, bewildered. He shouted, almost shouted against the sky: "Why have you forsaken me? Why? Why this torture for me? What wrong have I done to you?" A thousand and one things must have crossed his mind.

The seed is dying, and the seed is completely oblivious to what is going to happen next. It is not possible for the seed to conceive of that next step; hence faith, hence trust is needed. The seed has to trust that the tree will be born. With all the hesitation, with all kinds of fear, insecurities, with all kinds of anguish, anxiety – in spite of all of them – the seed has to trust that the tree will happen, that the tree is going to happen. It is a leap into faith. That leap happened to Jesus: he relaxed on the cross and he said, "Thy kingdom come. Thy will be done..." His heart was palpitating. It is natural. Your heart will also palpitate, you will also be afraid when that moment of death comes to you, when that moment comes when your self disappears and you are losing yourself into a kind of nothingness, and there seems to be no way to survive, and you have to surrender.

You can surrender in two ways: you can surrender reluctantly, then you will miss the real point of it, you will simply die and be born again. If you can relax in deep acceptance, trust, if you can sur-render without any resistance... That's what Jesus did, that is the greatest miracle. To me that is the miracle – not that he gave health to somebody who was ill, or eyes to somebody who was blind, or cured the leprosy of somebody; or even helped Lazarus to revive, to come back to life after he had died. No, these are not real miracles. To me, they are all parables, metaphors. Every master has given eyes to those who are blind, and ears to those who are deaf. Each master has brought people out of their death that they call life, has called them out of their graves. These are metaphors. But the real miracle is when Jesus – in spite of all of his hesitations, worries, doubts, suspicions – relaxes, surrenders, and says, "Thy will be done." That moment Jesus disappears, Christ is born.

Teilhard de Chardin calls it "Christogenesis": Jesus begetting Christ. Through Christogenesis man becomes that which he really is; he loses that which he is not and becomes that which he is: man becomes "Christified." Be Christified, never become a Christian. The Christian is one who follows the Christian dogma. *Christified* means one who dies as a seed and becomes a tree. *Christified* means that you drop the ego, you disappear as yourself and you start appearing on another plane in a kind of transfiguration, a resurrection. *Christified* means you are no longer alone: existence is in you and you are in existence.

This is the paradox of christ consciousness. Christ calls himself many times the son of man, and many times the son of God. He is both: the son of man as far as the body is concerned, the son of man as far as mind is concerned; the son of God as far as spirit is concerned, the son of God as far as consciousness is concerned. Mind is the mechanism of consciousness, just as the body is the abode of the spirit. Mind belongs to body, consciousness belongs to spirit. Jesus is the paradox: on the one hand man, on the other hand God. And when God and man work together, then if miracles happen there is nothing to be surprised about. Miracles happen only when God and man function together in cooperation.

Leo Tolstoy has said, "Christ is God and man working together, walking together, dancing together." St. Augustine says, "Without God, man cannot; without man, God will not." Christ is the combined operation – the meeting of the finite with the infinite, time and eternity meeting and merging into each other.

An old gardener was digging his plot as the priest came along. "George," said the priest, "it is wonderful what God and man working together can do."

"Yes sir," replied George, "but you should have seen this garden last year when he had it all to himself!"

Yes, that is true. Man alone is impotent. God also cannot work alone. God alone is potent but has no instrument. Man alone is a hollow bamboo – nobody to create a song on it, nobody to fill it with music, harmony, melody. God alone has the capacity to create a melody but has no hollow bamboo to create a flute. Christ is the flute on God's lips. So whatsoever has come from Christ is *godspel,* is gospel.

Fourteen generations passed between David and Jesus. That too is very symbolic. Books like the Bible are not written by ordinary people, they are what George Gurdjieff used to call "objective art." The Bible is one of the representative objective works of art in the world. It is not like a book written by a George Bernard Shaw or a Kalidas. These people create subjective art. They write something, they write beautifully, they have the aesthetic sense, but they are as unconscious as any other human being. They have a nose for beauty, but they are as sleepy as anybody else. Their works of art are subjective; they express themselves.

But books like the Vedas, the Koran, the Bible, the Upanishads, are not written by people who are asleep, they are not written as beautiful poetry or prose; they are written by people who know what truth is, who have awakened themselves to truth. Then whatsoever they write is almost like a map. You have to decipher it, you have to decode it; otherwise you will go on missing it.

Why fourteen generations? No scholar has asked, no biblical scholar has asked. Why only fourteen? Why not fifteen? Why not thirteen? I am giving you this as an example of objective art. It is fourteen for a certain reason. It has to be decoded. The spirit matures just like the body matures. The body matures in fourteen years – it becomes sexually mature, it can reproduce sexually. At fourteen years the body is ripe as far as sexual reproduction is concerned: the boy can become a father, the girl can become a mother; they can reproduce replicas of themselves.

In exactly the same way the spirit also matures. Just as it takes fourteen years for the body to mature sexually, it takes fourteen generations for the spirit to mature spiritually. That is the meaning of four-teen generations: from Abraham to David, from David to the exile in Babylon, and from the exile in Babylon to Jesus. When the spirit has come to its maturity, when the fruit is ripe it falls from the tree. Unripe, it clings to the tree. Unripe, it has to cling – if it falls unripe, then it will never become sweet; it will remain bitter, sour. It will be useless. To ripen, it needs to cling. Clinging simply shows, "I am not yet ready to leave you." Whenever somebody is ripe, that very ripeness becomes freedom, then clinging disappears.

Jesus disappears into existence, Jesus disappears from this tree of life: the fruit is ripe. That's what we in the East say, that whenever a man has become perfect – perfect in the sense that he has grown all that he could grow on this earth, in this situation – he will not return again. He crosses to the beyond, he passes beyond the point of no return and he never comes back. We call him a buddha, or a *jina*.

Jews used to call that state, christ: one who has gone beyond and will be here only for a time. The fruit is ripe and waiting to drop any moment – any small breeze and the fruit will be gone forever, and it will disappear into existence. Hence, the tree stops at Jesus; he remains unmarried, he does not reproduce. This celibacy has nothing to do with ordinary, repressed celibacy. He is not against love, he is not against sex, he is not a puritan, he is not a moralist.

I was reading the other night that Dostoevsky has said that moralists are always very miserable people. This seems to be an absolutely true observation. Moralists are miserable people. In fact only miserable people become moralists. They are so miserable that they would like to make everybody else also miserable, and the best way to make people feel miserable is to make them feel guilty.

Jesus is not a moralist. His *brahmacharya,* his celibacy, has a totally different quality to it. It simply says that he is no longer interested in reproducing on the physical plane, he is interested in reproducing on the spiritual plane. He does not give birth to children, he gives birth to disciples. He creates more abodes in the world for godliness to descend into. He does not create bodies, he creates souls. He is a miracle master; he created many enlightened people on the earth – he had that magic touch, and he created them out of nobodies.

Buddha created many enlightened people, but they were very, very grown-up souls. A Sariputra was already a very grown-up soul; the fruit was ripe. My own feeling is that even if Buddha had not come into the life of Sariputra, he would have become enlightened sooner or later; Buddha was not very essential. He helped, he speeded up things, but was not very essential. If Sariputra had not met him, maybe in one life or two lives he would have come around the corner by himself; he was already coming, he was just on the verge. So was Mahakashyapa, so was Maudgalyan, and so were Buddha's other disciples.

But Jesus really did miracles. He touched ordinary stones and transformed them into diamonds. He moved among very ordinary people: a fisherman throwing his net. Jesus comes, stands behind him, puts his hand on his shoulder and says, "Look into my eyes. How long are you going to catch fish? I can make you a catcher of men. Look into my eyes." The poor, ordinary fisherman – uneducated, unsophisticated, uncultured, has never heard about anything, may not have ever been interested in spiritual growth; was contented with catching fish and selling them, and was happy in his day-to-day life – looks into the eyes of Jesus, throws away his net and follows him. This fisherman – or a farmer, or a tax-collector, or even a prostitute, Mary Magdalene – becomes an enlightened person. Jesus transforms ordinary metal into gold. He is really the philosopher's stone. His touch is magical: wherever he touches, suddenly the spirit arises.

Buddha enlightened many people, but those people were already on the path. Buddha moved with sophisticated people, learned, virtuous, special. Jesus moved with very ordinary people: downtrodden, oppressed, poor. This was one of the crimes against him put by the priests: "He moves with gamblers, with drunkards, with prostitutes. He stays with prostitutes, he stays with anybody, he eats with anybody. He is a fallen man." And on the surface, to all appearances, he looked like a fallen man. But he was falling only with those people to help them rise; he was going to the lowest to turn them into the highest, and there is a reason.

The lowest may be unsophisticated, uncultured, but he has a purity of heart; he has more love in him. Now you will be able to understand the difference. Buddha's path is of intelligence. He cannot go to a fisherman and say, "Come to me and I will make you enlightened." This is not possible for him. His path is that of awareness, intelligence, understanding. The fisherman will not even understand his language; it is too far above him, it is beyond his grasp.

The path of Jesus is the path of love, and the poor people have more love than the rich. Maybe that is why they are poor, because when you have much love you cannot accumulate much money – they don't go together. When you have much love you share. A rich man cannot be a loving man because love will always be dangerous to his riches. If he loves people then he will have to share.

I used to live in a family for seven years. The man was very rich, and he was interested in my ideas – that's why he invited me to stay with him. He had made all the arrangements for me in a beautiful way. He had provided a big bungalow and a big garden. He came to live with me with his family, just to be with me. I was surprised; I had never seen him talking to his wife or to his children. When we had become more and more accustomed to each other, one day I asked him, "I never see you sitting with your wife or with your children. I never see you talking to anybody in your family. What is the matter?"

He said, "If I talk to my wife, she immediately starts demanding, 'There is a beautiful ornament in the shop,' or, 'Better saris have come,' or this and that. Immediately she jumps on my pocket. If I talk to my children, their hands start groping into my pocket. I have learnt that it is better to keep quiet, remain stiff and have a hard face. It protects you. Then nobody asks for anything."

I understood his idea. It is the idea of all the rich people in the world. The person who becomes too obsessed with money is really obsessed with money because he cannot love. Money becomes a substitute love. He starts hoarding money because he thinks there is no other thing to be happy about: "Hoard money, then at least you have the money and you can purchase everything." He even believes that he can purchase love with his money. He can purchase sex but not love. But then many people think that sex is love.

He can purchase bodies, but he cannot have any intimacy with a person. Many people think that to have the body of the other, to possess the body of the other is enough. "What more is needed? Why bother about anything more?" Many people are interested only in casual sex, not in intimacy, not in going into depth, not moving into a deep dialogue. They are afraid of the deep dialogue because then there is commitment, and commitment brings responsibility. Then they have to be very sensitive, alive. "Who bothers? Just casual sex is good, and casual sex can be purchased, it is available in the market-place." The man who is after money thinks that all can be purchased through the money. "So why bother about anything else? You can have the most beautiful woman, you can have the most beautiful house, you can have this and that..." He thinks that this is going to satisfy him. This never satisfies. Only love satisfies, no substitute can ever satisfy. A substitute is a substitute; it is pseudo.

Poor people have more love, because poor people have not grown their heads, so their whole energy revolves around the heart. These are the two centers: either the energy moves into the heart or the energy moves into the head. It is very rare to find a balanced being whose energy moves into both or who is capable of moving energy wherever it is needed – diverting it. When he wants to have intelligence, he moves, channels his energy into the head. When he wants to love, he channels his energy, his whole energy, into his heart. This is the perfect man. But ordinarily people are not so perfect. Either they are hung-up in the head or they are available to the heart.

Jesus' path is of love; hence he worked miracles on poor people, on ordinary people whose intelligence was not yet very developed. But that opportunity could be used; their energy was raw and yet in the heart. They were more like children.

Just as the body matures in fourteen years, so the spirit matures in fourteen generations; that is the minimum limit. It depends on you. It may not grow even in one hundred and forty generations – you can be very lazy or you can remain unaware, then you can go on and on for millions of lives and it may not grow. But fourteen generations is a natural time limit; that much is needed.

The spirit is not a seasonal flower: it is like a great cedar of Lebanon. It takes time – fourteen generations for the tree to grow, to reach to the sky. It is not a seasonal flower that comes within weeks but is gone within weeks too. The spirit means the eternal; the eternal needs time, patience. These fourteen generations are just a symbolic number. Jesus cannot be born before fourteen generations. This state is possible only after a time – after a few steps have been crossed, and that is so in other dimensions too.

For example, the caveman could not have given us the Platonic Dialogues or the symphonies of Beethoven or the paintings of Leonardo da Vinci or the poetry of Rabindranath Tagore. It was not possible for the caveman to give these things. The caveman could not have given us an Albert Einstein either, or a Dostoevsky or a Picasso. The caveman could not have given us a Buddha or a Lao Tzu or a Jesus. It needs time and it needs preparation, and it needs a certain milieu in which to grow, only then is Jesus possible. For

Jesus to exist many things are needed; he can only exist in these circumstances. For Jesus to say what he wants to say, a certain kind of person is needed who can understand it.

What I am saying to you can only be said now. It can only be said now, not before; it was not possible before. And what I will be saying to you tomorrow will only be possible tomorrow, not today. You have to become receptive, you have to grow. If you are not in a certain state to receive it, it cannot be uttered.

Jesus is the culmination of the whole Jewish consciousness, and the strange thing is that the Jews rejected him. That has always been happening. Buddha was the culmination of Hindu conscious-ness, and the Hindus rejected him. Socrates was the culmination of the Greek consciousness, and the Greeks killed him. This is very strange, but this has always been happening. Why can we not accept our own culmination? What goes wrong? Why could the Jews not accept Jesus? They had been waiting for Jesus, they had been waiting for the Messiah, for Christ to come. They are still waiting, and the Messiah has already come and gone too. They helped him to go, and they are still waiting for him.

What went wrong? What always goes wrong? Jesus is the culmi-nation of the Jewish consciousness. All the prophets of the Jews that had preceded Jesus were preparing the ground for him to come. That's what John the Baptist was saying to the people: "I am nothing compared to the person for whom I am preparing the way. I am just a sweeper. I am simply cleaning the path for him to come. The one higher than me is going to come." John the Baptist and the other prophets were simply preparing the way for this ultimate cul-mination, for this peak, this Everest. And then the Everest comes, and something goes wrong. What goes wrong? – the other peaks start feeling small.

They have all helped. Just think: Everest cannot stand alone if the other peaks of the Himalayas disappear. Everest cannot stand alone; it needs the whole Himalaya to support it, to be there. It cannot rise so high alone – no peak can rise so high alone. It will need the support of thousands of other peaks: smaller, bigger, and all kinds. But once the peak has come up, the other peaks start feeling hurt. Their egos ache; it is very painful. They have supported it – this is the paradox. They have supported the happening of this peak. It could not have happened without them, and now that it has happened, they are feeling very low, depressed. If all the peaks of the Himalayas were to conspire against Everest, it would be very logical. If they crucified Everest, it would be very logical.

That's what happened to Jesus. Once he was there, the Jews, the rabbis, the religious leaders, the priests, started feeling very offended. His very presence was offensive – not that he offended anybody, not that he hurt anybody. How could he hurt them? But his very presence, that Everest-like height, that plenitude, that height... Everybody looked low and small.

Now Everest cannot do anything about it. It is not arrogant, it is not egoistic, but it is high – that is certainly so. And every other peak is hurt, feels pained, wants to take revenge. Hence Jesus was cruci- fied. So Buddha was rejected – thrown out of this country completely. He became a foreigner in his own land. This has been so down the ages, it is so, still. It seems this is going to remain so forever because man is, after all, man. In his sleep, in his egoistic attitudes, this is how he functions.

Jesus' Beatitudes are God's songs through him. Remember, he is just a medium. He is not the author of these Gospels, he is just a messenger. He is simply giving you that which he is receiving.

Now, let us go into these Beatitudes:

And seeing the multitudes, he went up into a mountain: and when he was set, his disciples came unto him...

I would like you to go into each word very silently, very sympa- thetically. *And seeing the multitudes* – the crowd, the mass – *he went up into a mountain...* These are ways of saying certain psycho- logical things. The multitude is the lowest state of consciousness: the mass, the crowd. It is a dense darkness. It is very dark there, and a very deep sleep. When you move in the multitude, if you want to connect and relate with the multitude, you have to come to their level. That is why whenever you go into a crowd, you feel a little bit lost. You start feeling a little bit suffocated. That feeling of suffocation is not only physical – it is not just that people are around you, no. The suffocation is more psychological, because when you are with people who are very low in their consciousness, you cannot remain an Everest; they pull you down. Whenever you go to the masses you lose something. Hence the need arises for aloneness, for meditation.

And in Jesus' life you will find that many times he moves in the multitude – his work was there, that was his field – but again and again,
after a few months, he goes to the mountains; he goes away from the
multitude, and the crowd, and the crowd-mind, to be with God.

When you are alone you are with God. You can be with God only
when you are absolutely alone. And when you are with God you start
flying in the sky. The very presence of God takes you up and up. And
the presence of the crowds takes you down and down. Only with God
can you fly into the sky, can you have wings. With the crowds, your
wings are cut off. Even your hands and your legs are cut off – what to
say about wings? You become a cripple, because they are all crip-
ples. You become paralyzed, because they are all paralyzed. And
they will never forgive you if you don't live according to them when
you are with them. If you want to work with them, if you want to help
them, you will have to move in their world, according to them. This is
tiring and very exhausting.

And seeing the multitudes, he went up into a mountain... He was
staying in a village doing his magical work of transforming people –
blind people were given eyes, and deaf people were given ears. And
those who could not walk, who could not grow were made whole,
and those who had become dead and dull were again rejuvenated,
revitalized. But this whole work... Many more people were coming,
and a great crowd was surrounding him; he became exhausted, he
became tired, hence the need to go up into a mountain. Going out is
going down, going in is going up. In the inner world, up and in mean
the same; out and down mean the same. When you have to relate
with people you have to go out, and when you have to relate with
people who are very low in consciousness you have to bend low. That
is very tiring.

Jesus, Buddha or Mahavira, all move to the mountains. They go
into a lonely place just to regain their height, just to regain their purity,
just to regain their own state; just to spread their limbs again, just to
be themselves and just to be with God. With God, they start soaring
high. With God, you become a seagull, you start soaring high. There
is no limit to it. Again you are vital, again you are full of godliness,
again you are like a cloud full of rainwater and you would like to
shower. You come back to the multitude where people are thirsty.

People ask me what I go on doing in my room alone. That is my
mountain. That is where I can soar high. I need not think about you,

I need not commune with you. I need not function through the body and through the mind. I can forget the body, I can forget the mind. I can forget you; I can forget all. In that moment of utter forgetfulness of all, one is. And that *isness* is immense. That *isness* has a splendor to it. It is freshness, it is vitality, because it is the very source of life.

But once you are full of that life, you have to share. So every morning I am back with you, every evening I am back with you. I go on from my mountain to the multitude continuously! Going to a mountain does not mean really going to a mountain, it simply means going to inner height. Whether Jesus went to a real mountain or not is irrelevant; it has nothing to do with the Gospel. He may have gone to the mountain, because it was almost impossible in those days to live the way I live. It was impossible.

For fifteen years I also lived like Jesus, moving in the multitude, and it was impossible to get even a single moment alone. I had to go back again and again to my place where I used to live in Jabalpur and I kept myself absolutely alone. Jabalpur was very unfortunate... I would go around the country and everywhere I would meet people – but not in Jabalpur. That was my mountain. And when I would come to Mumbai, or to Delhi, or to Pune, people would ask me why I unnecessarily traveled back to Jabalpur again and again. Fifteen, twenty days... I would have to go back to Jabalpur for three or four days, and then I would start again. It was unnecessary. I could have gone from Pune to Mumbai, from Mumbai to Delhi, from Delhi to Amritsar, from Amritsar to Sri Nagar. Why should I go to Jabalpur first, and then again after a few days?

Jabalpur was my mountain. There I kept myself absolutely alone. When it became impossible to be alone even there, and the multitude started coming there, then I had to leave that place. Alone in my room I am doing exactly what Jesus did.

And seeing the multitudes, he went up into a mountain: and when he was set, his disciples came unto him... To talk to disciples is a different matter. To talk to the multitude is a different matter. That's why I had to stop talking to the crowds. I had to create a special class of my own sannyasins with whom I could have a communion of the heart.

When you are talking to the multitudes, first, they are very indifferent to what you are saying – you have to shout unnecessarily. Second, if they are not indifferent, then they are against – antagonistic, always afraid and protecting their ideas, always resisting, arguing. That is unnecessary work. And these things that I am talking about or Jesus was talking about are not things that can be argued. No proof is possible – only trust. If you can trust me, these things can be explained to you. But trust has to have a very, very basic thing to it. If you don't trust me, there is no way to prove anything. Then it is simply a waste of my time and your time.

To talk to disciples is a different thing. To talk to disciples means that the other side is receptive – not only receptive but immensely welcoming. You are welcome, the other side wants you to come in, the other side wants to become a host to whatsoever you are saying. The doors are open, the windows are open for you to become a breeze, or sunlight, and enter into their beings. They are not afraid, they are not defending, they are not arguing; they are ready to go with you wholeheartedly to any unknown dimension. To talk to disciples is not a kind of discussion or debate; it is a dialogue. It is as much a dialogue as it is when two lovers talk to each other. The disciple is in love with the master, the master is in love with the disciple. There is deep love flowing. That love becomes the bridge, and then great truths can be explained, conveyed, almost materialized.

...and when he was set, his disciples came unto him:

And he opened his mouth, and taught them, saying...

He has escaped from the multitude, but not from the disciples. He is available to the disciples. He can fly with existence and the disciples can fly with him. Maybe they are not so expert at flying, but their readiness is there, and that is the only thing that is needed, the most essential. Maybe they cannot go to the very heights alone; but trusting the master they can follow, they can follow to any length, they can go to any extreme. The master flies with God, the disciple flies with the master. The disciple cannot see God yet but he can see the master, and through the master he can feel God. That's why the master becomes almost a God to the disciple. He is. By and by, the closer the disciple comes to the master, the more and more he will see that the master is an emptiness, or a mirror in which God is reflected. Sooner or later, he himself will become an emptiness, a mirror, and will be able, in his turn, to help others.

...he opened his mouth, and taught them, saying,

Blessed are the poor in spirit: for theirs is the kingdom of heaven.

This is one of the most fundamental statements ever made. Many other Beatitudes will follow, but nothing to be compared to this. It is exceptional, it is extraordinary. And the beauty is: *Blessed are the poor in spirit: for theirs is the kingdom of God.* In other Beatitudes he will say *...they shall inherit the earth.* But in this he says *...for theirs is the kingdom of God.*

The *...poor in spirit...* means exactly what Buddha was saying to Sariputra: nothingness. Ego makes you feel that you are rich, that you are somebody, this and that. When the ego disappears and you are a nobody... That's what Jesus means by *...poor in spirit...*

Buddha's word is more sophisticated, philosophical.

> Therefore, O Sariputra,
> Form is nothingness,
> Nothingness is form.

Jesus' words are simple, unsophisticated. And it is natural. Buddha was the son of a great king, Jesus is the son of a carpenter. For many years he was just working in his father's workshop bringing wood, cutting wood. He knows the ways of the simple people, the woodcutters, the carpenters.

He says: *Blessed are the poor in spirit...* Those who know that they are nothing, those who know that their inside is just empty; there is no self, no ego, no claim, no word, no knowledge, no scripture – just emptiness, pure sky, spaciousness. *Blessed are the poor in spirit: for theirs is the kingdom of God.* It is theirs right now! It is not said that they will have, there is no postponement, there is no time element involved. If you are nothing, this very moment you are God. If you are nothing, you are God. Between nothingness and God, there is no gap to be crossed – there is no gap. From one side it is nothingness, poverty of spirit, from the other side it is the kingdom of God.

A very paradoxical statement: Those who are poor will become kings; and those who think they are kings will remain poor. Lose if you want to gain; gain if you want to lose. Possess if you want to remain a beggar; dispossess if you want to become a king. Don't possess anything at all – not even yourself. That's what is meant by ...*poor in spirit*... Theirs is the kingdom of God here and now, right away. It is not a promise for the future, it is a simple statement of truth.

The other Beatitudes are not so deep. If this is understood, then there is no need to read ahead. If this is not understood – and this must not have been understood, that's why Jesus continues – then he makes the truth more diluted, understandable.

He says:

Blessed are they that mourn: for they shall be comforted.

Now the future comes in. The disciples have missed, otherwise there would have only been one Beatitude because it contains all. There is no need to elaborate on it. Jesus has said everything. This is his ultimate sutra. But he must have looked around into the eyes of the disciples, and he must have seen that they had not been able to understand it – it is too high. He has to come a little lower, he has to bring the future in.

The mind can understand the future, the mind cannot understand the present. The mind is absolutely incapable of understanding the present. If I say to you, "Right now you are buddhas and christs." You listen to me but you say: "What are you saying? I – and a buddha? And just last night I was gambling. And, Osho, you don't know me, I am a smoker. Or sometimes I even take hashish. You don't know me, I am a sinner. And what are you talking about? I know myself better. I am not a buddha, I am the worst sinner in the world." So you can listen to me if I say, "You are a buddha right now. Nothing is missing, nothing is lacking." You listen out of politeness, but deep down you say, "Nonsense!"

Jesus has said the ultimate: *Blessed are the poor in spirit: for theirs is the kingdom of heaven.* This can be compared to the sutra Buddha gave to Sariputra, when he said, "This is the unique mantra, this is the incomparable mantra. There is no other mantra higher than this: *Gate, gate, paragate, parasamgate, bodhi svaha.* Gone, gone, gone beyond, gone altogether beyond. What ecstasy! Alleluia!" He says this is all, condensed into one small mantra.

This mantra is just like that: *Blessed are the poor in spirit: for theirs is the kingdom of heaven.* Right now, here-now, this very moment – be a nobody and have all. Be a beggar and become an emperor. Lose and possess.

He must have looked around – the arrow had not reached the target. The disciples had saved their hearts. They just went out of the way of the arrow; it passed them by. It went above their heads. Jesus had to come low – he brings in the future.

The future means bringing the mind in. The mind can understand means and ends, the mind can understand cause and effect: do this and this will happen. But remember, it *will* happen – it will be in the future. You put the seed in the soil and one day it will become a tree. "Perfectly true," the mind says. "I can understand it. There is a process: step by step the tree will come up." If you say, "Put the seed there, and look, behold, the tree is there!" It will say, "Are you a magician or what? Only magicians can do that."

The first statement is very magical, the mind cannot figure it out; it cannot reckon what it is. The mind can understand division, duality, cause and effect, past and future, this and that, here and there. The mind divides – and then the mind is at ease. It says, "Perfectly okay. Be righteous, and you will get that. But there is going to be a time gap, and you have to prepare, and you have to do many things." The mind is a doer.

Blessed are they that mourn: for they shall be comforted. Jesus says, "Okay, then be like small children who are helpless." The child just cries and weeps for the mother, and the mother runs to the child. When the child is in misery, the mother comes to comfort. So mourn, let your prayers be cries of helplessness. Remember, the definition of a prayer is meditation through tears, meditation with tears. When the tears are your meditation, it is prayerfulness. When meditation is with love, and you think about yourself as a lost, small child, and existence is a mother or a father... That's Jesus' approach. He says, "Then pray, cry out of your helplessness and the help will come and you will be comforted."

Blessed are the meek: for they shall inherit the earth.

And become simple, humble, meek, don't be arrogant. Now listen to the difference. The first was *...poor in spirit...* It does not say be humble, because in humbleness a subtle ego remains. You have the idea, "I am humble" – the "I" is there. First you were thinking, "I am very great," now you think, "I am very meek." But "I am" is still there; the "I" still continues. *Blessed are the meek: for they shall inherit the earth.* So, a little barrier, that's why it is in the future. You cannot be right now. That small barrier of humbleness, meekness will go on surrounding you, and will go on dividing you from the truth.

Blessed are they which do hunger and thirst after righteousness: for they shall be filled.

Now do good works, be virtuous and God will come and fill you.

Blessed are the merciful: for they shall obtain mercy.

Be merciful, be compassionate. Whatsoever you want God to give to you, you give to the world – to God's world. That's the law.

Blessed are the pure in heart, for they shall see God.

Even with purity some distance. Poverty is ultimate; in purity, there is still some ego: "I am pure, holy, sacred, holier-than-thou," and things like that continue. The sinner is one who claims the ego, gross ego. The saint is one who claims the subtle ego: holiness. And the sage is one who claims not. The sage is one who simply says, "I am nobody, a nothingness." It is not just a saying, he knows it; existentially, he knows it.

Blessed are the peacemakers: for they shall be called the children of God.

Blessed are they which are persecuted for righteousness' sake: for theirs is the kingdom of heaven.

Rejoice, and be exceeding glad: for great is your reward in heaven: for so persecuted they the prophets which were before you.

Ye are the salt of the earth...

Jesus says: *Rejoice...* But this rejoicing is not the ultimate rejoicing, it is a desire, because great will be the result in heaven. There is a desire to attain something, to achieve something. If you don't have any desire – not even the desire for God, not even the desire for heaven – then right now you are kings, right now the kingdom of God is yours.

And Jesus says to his disciples: *Ye are the salt of the earth...* Now it is very absurd, looks absurd. These are poor people. Somebody has been a carpenter, somebody has been a shoemaker, somebody has been a fisherman – people like that. And Jesus says to them: *Ye are the salt of the earth...* And he is right, although he looks absurd. They were not kings, great emperors, viceroys, lords, rich people – they were not. But why does he say, *Ye are the salt of the earth...?* – because whosoever knows a little bit of God is the salt. It is because of these few people that the earth remains meaningful, that there remains some significance, that there is some taste in life and some joy.

And the same I say to you: you are the salt of the earth, because whosoever has started moving towards godliness has started moving towards joy. And when you move towards joy, you help the whole world to move towards joy, because you are the world. *Rejoice, and be exceeding glad...* Because:

> *Ye are the salt of the earth: but if the salt have lost his savor,*
> *wherewith shall it be salted? it is thenceforth good for nothing, but*
> *be cast out, and to be trodden under foot of men.*

I say unto you too: you are the salt of the earth. You are the spearhead of the future evolution of man. You sannyasins are carrying the seeds of the future. Rejoice! And become more and more salty, more and more full of godliness.

Enough for today.

CHAPTER 2

come out of your mind

The first question:

Osho,
What am I to do with the Jesus I thought I knew and loved for so long?

The question is from Chintana, who has been a nun. She has suffered enough by being a nun, and suffered for sins she has never committed. To be a nun is a kind of masochism, a kind of self-torture inflicted upon oneself in the name of Jesus, in the name of Buddha – only the names differ, the torture is the same. And when you are torturing yourself, your relationship with Jesus or Buddha or Mahavira is going to be pathological.

Relationship is healthy only when there is joy, when there is celebration, when there is full acceptance of life and all that it brings.

When there is denial, rejection, when you are restricting your vital parts and you are destroying yourself, the relationship is not really a relationship. You are in love with your misery, and you call your misery Jesus. Never be in love with your misery. If you are in love with your misery, then wherever you are, you will be in hell. To be healthy means to be in love with joy. Even if sometimes misery happens, it is unnatural. It has to be lived, but it is accidental, it is not natural. Joy is natural.

All kinds of pathological people have gathered together around Christ down the ages. In fact they are not in love with Jesus, they are in love with the cross. That's why I call Christianity "crossianity." It has nothing to do with Christ – Christ is just a symbol – the real thing is the cross, the death, the suffering that Jesus went through. You are in love with that. But the mind is very cunning; it can always rationalize its prejudices. It can always find arguments, reasons to support its own prejudices.

Now, about poor Chintana... I feel sorry for her; she is in a kind of turmoil here. It is bound to be so. Here, the whole message is "Alleluia"; the whole message is of ecstasy, love, joy; *celebration* is the key word here. And for many years she has been a nun, so her whole past is against the present. But if she goes on thinking that she has been in love with Jesus, then it will be very difficult for her to drop her misery, because how to drop Jesus? And Jesus is so beautiful, how can one gather courage to drop Jesus?

There is no need. I am bringing you a healthy Jesus. I am bringing you the real Jesus. The real Jesus was never on the cross, only the body was on the cross. The real Jesus never died, the real Jesus cannot die. You cannot die, nothing ever dies. That which dies was not really part of you. The nonessential dies, the essential continues. Nobody can kill you – I mean you, not your body. Your body can be killed. But you are so identified with the body that when you see Jesus on the cross, you think Jesus *is* on the cross.

Not for a single moment was Jesus on the cross. He cannot be – he knows himself. There is no way to crucify him. That is the hidden meaning of the phenomenon of resurrection: he resurrects because in the first place he has never died. If he had died, then there would have been no possibility of resurrection. Only the body, the outermost shell, has been killed. But because of this – this cross, this death, this suffering, this martyrdom – Christianity became obsessed with death, became very morbid about death. And people are very afraid of death, frightened, scared. The more afraid they are, the more frightened they are, the more the cross becomes very significant.

A Krishna playing his flute does not look real. Who can play the flute in this ugly life, on this miserable earth where people are killing each other, exploiting, oppressing? Where human beings exist only in the dictionary, in language? Just the other day I was reading about Adolf Hitler's concentration camps. In one concentration camp forty-five lakh people were killed, murdered, gassed. But they made a good profit out of it. That was the real thing with it. The hair was sold, the bones were sold to the glue factories, the eyes were sold, everything was sold. Papers have been found, correspondence has been found in which factories were haggling over the price. The officers were haggling about human beings' hair – how much they were going to ask. "When they are killed, how much are you ready to pay for their bones?" Hitler was doing business with death, through death. It was a good, going concern. They were giving almost nothing to the prisoners to eat. It was very cheap, and within two weeks the prisoner would be gone. They had to wait just two weeks. So the cost was very low and the price was very good. The hair was going to the wig-makers, the bones were going to the glue factories, and so on and so forth.

How can one play the flute here where Adolf Hitlers exist, where Hiroshimas happen? Krishna looks like a dream. Christ looks very real. But let me tell you, Christ was also playing on his flute when he was on the cross. The flute continues – it makes no difference whether in life or in death. The flute is eternal. Let me tell you, Krishna is more real. And the Christ that you have created is more or less a figment of your mind. You don't know the real Christ. So listening to me is going to be difficult for you, because I will be revealing a totally different Christ that you are not acquainted with. You have a Christ preached to you by the priests. You have a Christ painted by the Vatican. You have the Christ visualized by so many hysterical saints.

There has been a long tradition of pathology in Christianity. Christians say Jesus never laughed. Now this is utter nonsense. I say to you that Christ laughed his whole life – only he could laugh, who else? But Christians say he never laughed. They want to depict him as very sad, very burdened. They project their sadness onto Jesus, they project their misery onto Jesus. Jesus becomes a screen, and you go on projecting your mind onto him. Jesus laughed, enjoyed, loved. If you go into the Gospels without your prejudices, you will find it. How can you think otherwise about a man who was having parties, eating well, moving with women, drinking – yes, wine was not unknown to him, he loved it. He was a very, very happy man. It is impossible to conceive that a man who drinks, eats well, loves eating, loves friends, never laughed. But Christians have depicted Jesus according to their own projection. The projection is of their misery. And then Jesus becomes just an excuse to be sad, to be miserable. That's why in the church there is no laughter, no joy, no celebration.

Churches have become graveyards. It is not accidental that the cross has become the symbol. It should not be the symbol. I can understand your difficulty, particularly Chintana's difficulty. She says, "What am I to do with the Jesus I thought I knew and loved for so long?" You have not known Jesus.

Through me there is a possibility to know Jesus. If you are courageous enough, you can know Jesus for the first time. Because you can know Jesus only through a man who has attained to christ consciousness. A Krishna can be known only through a man who has attained to krishna consciousness. And they are the same thing: krishna consciousness, christ consciousness, buddha consciousness – the transcendental.

You cannot understand Jesus through a priest. He himself has not known. He has read, he has thought, he has contemplated, he has speculated, philosophized. Yes, he has a very cultivated mind, he knows the scriptures. But to know the scriptures is not to know Jesus. To know Jesus you will have to know your innermost nothing-ness. Without knowing it you cannot make anybody else acquainted with Jesus. You have an opportunity here to come in contact with the reality that was there two thousand years before. The window is open again and you can enter – you can have a glimpse at least. But if you go on carrying your ideas about Jesus, then it will be difficult. Rather than entering through me and coming to know Jesus, you will start condemning me and you will remain surrounded by your own ideas, and you can always find reasons.

It happened in Montreal – it can happen only in Montreal...

Two nice looking men were walking down the street, hand in hand. There was a married couple in front of them, arguing. One of the men squeezed the other's hand and said, "See, dear, I told you mixed marriages don't work."

You can always find an argument. Now the marriage between a

man and a woman is a "mixed marriage." How can it work? Marriage between a man and a woman can work; it is homogeneous. The homosexual can find that argument. If you have a certain prejudice in the mind you can always find support. The world is so big that it supports all kinds of things. And what can your idea of God, or Christ, or Krishna be? You don't even know yourself, Chintana. Not knowing yourself, how can you know Jesus? And whatsoever you know is going to be wrong. It will be more or less guesswork, and guesswork done in immense ignorance.

It is like painting a picture of Jesus on a dark night when there is no light. You have never seen him, and you have never touched colors, and you don't know how to paint, and the night is dark and not even a single candle is there. You go on painting, and you don't know how to paint, and you don't know how to keep the brush in your hand, and you don't know how to mix the colors, and you cannot see which color is which – the night is so dark. You go on painting, and in the morning when you see it, you say, "This is Jesus."

It is all guesswork, in deep ignorance. Whatsoever man has thought of God is just guesswork. If you are honest you will not be interested in any guesswork. God cannot be guessed at – he can be known but not guessed at. How can you guess at God? How can you imagine God? There is no way to do it. Whatsoever you do is going to be wrong. The best way is not to guess but to drop all prejudices that you have been taught and conditioned with. Become a pure nothingness, a mirror, that's what meditation is all about. In that nothingness your eyes open for the first time. You start seeing that which is.

Two goldfish were swimming around and around in a glass bowl. One announced crankily that he had become an atheist.

"Fine, fine," scoffed the other. "Now just explain to me who changed the water in this bowl!"

Now, a goldfish in a bowl thinks that God changes the water. Your guesswork about God cannot be more than that. That's why if you say to people that there is no God, they say, "What are you talking about? Then who created the world? Who changed the water?" Stupid ideas because God is not the cause, and the world is not the effect. God has not created the world. If he has created this world, then that is enough proof that he is absolutely mad; it will prove only that, nothing else.

God has not created the world. God is not really a creator. It will be far better to say that God is the world. God is not the creator but the creativity. The flower opening is God. Not that God is standing there and opening it – not separate from the flower and forcing the petals to open. God is the flowering, the star shining in the night. Not that God is pouring oil into it, or some fuel, and running it and managing it somehow; God is that light. Not that God has created you; you are that. The Upanishads say, "Tattvamasi: Thou art that." They are far closer to the truth. In the East we have always depicted God as a dancer, not as a creator – God as Nataraj, the master dancer. Why? There is something immensely meaningful in that concept.

God is not a painter, because when a painter does a painting, the painting becomes separate from the painter. When the painter has finished with the painting, the painting has its own existence. The painter may die, the painting can live. And when the painter has finished the painting, it may be beautiful but it is dead because the painter cannot put his breath into it. It is not possible. He cannot pour his vitality into it, his life into it. The painting may be beautiful but a painting is a painting – it is dead.

God is not a painter, God is not a potter; God is a dancer. What is the meaning of it? In dance, the dancer and the dance are one, they can never be separated. That is the beauty of the dancer. The poet is separate from the poetry, the potter is separate from his pottery, the painter is separate from his painting, the sculptor is different, separate, from his creation, and so on and so forth. Only the dancer is not separate. The dancer is the dance. And when the dancer is really in the dance, there is no dancer in him, all disappears. It is just pure, vibrant energy, it is just pure energy dancing. There is no ego in it. The dance comes to perfection when the dancer dissolves into it. But the moment the dance stops, you cannot find the dance anywhere, it is not separate from the dancer.

One thing more: the dance cannot exist separate from the dancer, and the dancer too cannot exist separate from the dance. When you say that this is a dancer, if he is not dancing, your description is not right. A dancer is only a dancer while in dance, otherwise he is no longer a dancer. Then it is a linguistic fallacy that you go on calling him a dancer because he was dancing yesterday. Then yesterday he was a dancer. Or tomorrow he will dance again. Then tomorrow he will be a dancer again, but right now if he is not dancing, then he must be somebody else. If he is walking, he is a walker; if he is running, he is a runner; if he is sitting, he is a sitter – but not a dancer.

Dancer and dance exist together. In fact, they are not separate. God is not the creator of the world. God is its creativity, its very soul. He is in the trees, and in the rocks, in you, in me – he is everywhere, he is all. But to know this God you will have to drop guessing, because when he is inside you what is the point of guessing? Why don't you go in? Why don't you close your eyes and travel inwards? Come to a point where no thought exists and you will know what God is. And to know God is to become Christ. And by becoming Christ, you will know what Christ is. By tasting christhood, you will know what Christ is. How can you have any idea of Jesus? That idea will be Catholic, will be Protestant, will be this or that. That will be your idea and your idea is the barrier – beware of it. All your ideas have to disappear. Your mind has to cease for Christ to be.

So it will look very paradoxical. I am saying if you are not a Christian, not a Hindu, not a Jaina, not a Buddhist, only then will you know what truth is. By being a Christian, how can you know Christ? Your very Christianity will be a barrier. By being a Buddhist you cannot know Buddha. Your ideology will function as a wall, a Wall of China. Drop all ideologies, and don't be a nun.

She has now become a sannyasin; she is no longer a nun, but deep inside she still is. When she comes to me, I can see two personalities together, split. When she comes to me, a part of her being is with me – she has taken the jump and become a sannyasin – but I can see the Christian is still there and very strong. And there is every fear that when she goes back to Australia, she may again get into the old nonsense. I am not yet certain about her, because the Christian is very strong there. She has devoted her life in a certain way; she has lived in a certain way with very wrong notions. She has been anti-life, and now I am trying to bring her back to life. I am calling to her just as Jesus called to Lazarus, "Come out, Lazarus!" – and he was dead. But Lazarus was a beautiful man – he came out.

People always think Jesus did the miracle. My idea is that Lazarus did the miracle. Anybody can call – that is not the point. The point is that Lazarus came out. He had been dead for four days, and nobody believed that it was possible. When Lazarus died, Jesus was not in that town. But Lazarus was a follower, and his two sisters were Jesus' followers, so the two sisters sent a message: "Come as quickly as possible. Your beloved disciple is dead. You can save him, you can still bring him back." Jesus came in his own leisurely way – not with the American rush – he came easily, the way he was to come. He took four days. He was not very far, maybe just in the neighborhood, the other village. He came. The sisters had become very, very depressed. And when he came, the body had started stinking. They had put it in a cave, because the message had come that Jesus was coming: "So wait. Don't bury the body, keep it."

When Jesus came, the two sisters started crying and weeping and they said, "You are late. Too late. Now what can be done? The body has started deteriorating. It is stinking. Nobody can go near the body. Now it is so difficult. How to bury it? – because nobody wants to go into the cave and take the body out. Even from outside it is stinking."

Jesus said, "Don't be worried. Let me go to the cave." They went, and the whole town gathered, and the body must have been stinking because Jesus also did not enter.

He called from the outside. Is this a way to call? Somebody is dead and from the outside you are calling, "Lazarus, come out?" Lazarus was a miracle man. He came out; he said, "Yes sir, I am here."

This is a parable; it is not a historical fact. This is how the master calls the disciple – out of your death, out of your stinking cave where you are just rotting and rotting and deteriorating, deteriorating every day. He calls you out of your death. So I call to Chintana, "Come out of your mind," because mind is death, because mind is time. If you live in the mind, you live in death. If you drop the mind, you live in eternity, deathlessness. And that's what religion is all about. Christianity, Hinduism, Buddhism are just names for the same process. A great opportunity is here. Chintana can drop her life-negative attitudes. To be a nun means to be against life. And to be against life means to be against God, because life is God. To be against love is to be against God. To be against your body is to be against God, because it is God's body. It is his temple, his shrine; he has chosen to reside in it. Don't destroy it, don't be against it.

My approach is absolutely life-affirmative. And I call this religious approach, yes-saying – saying yes to all. Jesus was able to say yes even to death, and you are not even able to say yes to your life. Learn first to say yes to life, then one day that pinnacle, that consummation, that fulfillment also happens when you can say yes to death too – because you have learned to say yes, and you have enjoyed saying yes, and you have seen how beautiful it is to go on saying yes.

Remember, the ego always says no. The no is the way of the ego. That's why when children start saying no, know well they are starting to become egoistic. At a certain stage the child starts saying no, and starts enjoying saying no. Whatsoever you say, he says, "No!" No-saying comes easily at a certain stage. Why does he say no? – because he has to create the ego. Only through the no is the ego created. Say no more often, and more ego is created. Say yes more, and ego starts dispersing. If you have uttered a deep yes to your total life – with no reservations – then the ego disappears. In that yes is your prayerfulness. But first one has to learn to say yes to life, only then can you say yes to death. How will you be able to say yes to death if you cannot even say yes to life and joy?

Never be a nun, and never be a so-called monk. This is an ugly state, pathological, neurotic, hysterical. But why has it been chosen down the ages? There is a certain trick in it, a strategy. The nun is taught to say no to her body, no to her sex, no to her love, no to all relationships, so all doors are closed. She cannot say yes to any life experience. Then, naturally, her yes-saying heart feels very suffocated, prevented from every door and window. In that state of suffocation she starts saying yes to Christ, because one has to say yes. But this is a pathological yes, this is not real. It is coercion, it is violence.

Do you follow me? When you don't say yes to anything, it is as if you are in a desert. You are lost and you cannot see any oasis anywhere, and for days you have been thirsty and thirsty and thirsty, and the thirst becomes absolute. Then you can even drink your own urine. People are known to have done that. They can drink the urine of the camel. They can kill the camel and drink the water that he reserves in his body. Nauseating, but it can be done. When there is no possibility of any other water, and you are thirsty and the thirst goes on becoming fiery, intense, then you can drink anything – the dirtiest water – and you can drink it as if it were the water of life.

You need not be a Morarji Desai. You can drink your urine without being a Morarji Desai if you are in a desert. Then you will understand his idea that urine is "the water of life" – but only in a desert, unless you are neurotic. Now he is trying to do two things in India. One he has started: that is prohibition. First the country has to go through prohibition. And the next step – logical step – will be to start forcing people to drink their urine, because that is the water of life. You need not be a Morarji Desai. If you are lost in a desert you will start drinking anything. When you are hungry and you cannot get food, you will eat anything. Then you cannot and will not be very choosy. You cannot say, "Where is the menu?" – those things will look like non-sense. If you are hungry in a desert, you don't ask for the menu. You will jump on whatsoever is available – whatsoever!

That is the trick: say no to sex, so that you are sex-starved – sex goes on accumulating in you. You want to love somebody and that is not possible. Love is not possible. You cannot love any human being – that door is closed. And your love capacity is just like a thirst: it goes on accumulating. You start loving Christ, and then it is patholog-ical. Nuns have been known to report that Christ comes in the night and makes love to them, that he comes and fondles their breasts. Nuns have been known to have become pregnant because Christ made love to them. Of course their pregnancy was nothing but hot air, but the stomach... It was found to be a false pregnancy, but the idea... These are pathological states.

When your love is starved, naturally only one direction is left open. It is as if all the doors of the house are closed, only one hole is left open, and the house is on fire. Then you will not think of pro-priety, you will not think whether it is proper to get out of the house through this hole. You will get out of the house. Any hole will do. This is the situation that has been created for monks and nuns. Starve their love, and their love has to become focused on Jesus. But this is coercion. This is not conversion. This is not transforma-tion. This is a very ugly state of affairs.

My own approach is just the opposite. I say: "Make love as much as possible." Make it a celebration as much as possible. Let Jesus enter from joy. You love a woman, you love a man; you love so deeply that suddenly one day you start feeling the depth of the man or the woman. That depth will be the door of Jesus, or Krishna – or whatsoever name you want to give to it. Love deeply, so deeply that the body of the beloved disappears, that the mind of the beloved dis-appears, that even the self disappears. Love so deeply, go so deeply

into each other, that one day you are just two skies, utterly clean and
virgin, interpenetrating each other. In that very moment you will
know that your beloved has become the door.

Celebrate! Let God come through celebration, and then you will
have a health, a wholeness. I call that holy.

Nuns and monks are unholy people. They need psychiatric treatment; their minds are not in harmony. They cannot be in harmony
because they have taken such an ugly course, unnatural, perverted.
So listening to me, this question is going to come to you again and
again. Let it be very clear from the beginning. I am bringing to you a
totally new Jesus, a far truer Jesus than the Vatican has given to you.
And I want Jesus to come to you through life, through love, through
light – not through perversion, not through repression.

The second question:

Osho,
The Gospels provide no techniques for developing a loving heart.
The Gospels are also too difficult for ordinary people. Perhaps this
is why the Christian message has always seemed less practical
than, say, Buddha's.

The question is from Nirvan.

First, love is not based on any techniques. The path of love
knows no technique; that's why in the Gospels no techniques are
given for developing your love.

The path of intelligence, Gyana Yoga, the path of knowing, of
course has many techniques. Meditation is a technique. Intelligence
moves though techniques. Intelligence always creates technology. If
intelligence goes into science, then it creates technology. If it goes into
spirituality, it creates Yoga, Tantra – they are also technologies for the
inner being. Intelligence is technological. It always finds ways, short-
cuts, how to do things more efficiently. Wherever you apply intelligence you will find better ways to reach the goal – faster, speedier,
with less inconvenience, with less cost – that's what intelligence is.

But the path of love, Bhakti Yoga – and Jesus is a bhakta, a
devotee – knows no techniques. Love is not a technique. Please
remember, love is not a technique and cannot be a technique, and
if you bring technique into love, you will destroy it. That's what is

happening in the West. There are many love techniques available in the West. Everybody is learning from books how to make love, and how to make love more efficiently, more skillfully, and how to have greater orgasms, and all that. Now, all these things – many books are available – are making people incapable of being in love.

There is a problem to be understood. If you are too interested in technique, you will not achieve orgasm. Impossible! Your whole concern will be the technique – how to do it. If you become too interested in Vatsyayana and his love postures, then you will be doing a kind of gymnastics, exercises. But love will disappear.

Love needs no technique. Can't you see? Animals love, birds love, trees love, and if you have eyes to see, the whole existence is love energy. But there is no technique. It is natural, it is spontaneous. Technique is against spontaneity. Love is spontaneity, not a technique. It needs only that you drop your being into the heart. Through the head there is no way towards love, it is through the heart. And remember that the heart is capable of moving into love from the very beginning. It is just like a roseflower opening. You need not open it, it has the capacity to open. That capacity is built-in, it is intrinsic. The roseflower opens of its own accord – so opens the heart. The heart needs no training. If you give training to it you will destroy it, because through training you will destroy the spontaneity.

That's why in the Gospels no techniques are given. Techniques cannot exist on that path. Buddha appeals to you. Every day Buddha is gaining more and more followers in the West, because the West has become very, very mind-oriented. Intelligence has become predominant in the West. The West has become technological about everything. So, when you read about Buddha or Patanjali or Vatsayana, it has immense appeal; it simply fits with you. Your whole being says, "Yes, it must be so!" You are ready to accept Buddha, Patanjali, Mahavira.

The grip of Christ is lessening on the West. The reason is that the West no longer goes through the heart; it bypasses the heart. People are Christian because they are born Christians, but every day the appeal of Christ is becoming less and less and less. Buddha will fit better. Patanjali even more. Immediate appeal will be there because there is logic, there is intelligence, and there is a clear-cut path – what has to be done.

Love is not a doing. It is a happening; it is a trust, not a technique.

Jesus says, "Love God." If you can love, then there is no problem. If you cannot love, then Jesus is not the way for you. Then you will have to search for Buddha. On the path of Buddha, love is non-existent; emotion, sentiment, love are non-existent. Buddha says, "Those who are very, very emotional and loving have to find other ways. My way is not their way."

Do you know that for many years Buddha was very resistant to initiating women? He rejected it again and again. Many times appeals were made to him, "Why don't you initiate women?" And he would say, "No. My path is the path of intelligence, not of love, and if women are allowed to enter it, they will destroy my whole thing." When too much pressure was put on him – he was a very, very democratic man and he understood that it was not right to deprive women – he finally, but very reluctantly, agreed. The day he initiated women he declared, "My path was going to remain pure for at least five thousand years, but now I can only hope for five hundred years, not more than that." And that's exactly how it happened.

Through the entry of the woman, Buddhism started changing its character, because the woman brings love. Once Buddha had gone, the whole quality of Buddhism changed; it became absolutely the opposite. If Buddha comes back he will not be able to recognize the Buddhism that is prevalent in China, Burma, Thailand. He will not be able to recognize it, because its whole quality has changed. Now Buddha is thought to be God, and people are praying to him – and his whole life he was saying that prayer is nonsense, only meditation will do. He was utterly on the path of intelligence; prayer was meaningless. And he was saying, "There is no God, so to whom are you praying? It is crazy." And he was saying, "Nobody can help you except yourself."

The last message on his deathbed was... Ananda, his chief disciple asked, "Bhagwan, give us your last message." And he said, "Ananda, *appa dipo bhava*: Become a light unto yourself." There is no other light, so don't look into the sky, don't look at me. There is no other light. Be a light unto yourself. Your own intelligence has to become your light, depend utterly upon yourself – no other dependence, no shelter anywhere, no refuge.

He was one of the most intelligent persons born on the earth, but soon, once he had gone, the quality started changing. And it is a surprise of history that Buddhism became the source of Tantra, the source of love techniques. Buddhism became the source of love techniques. It is utterly against Buddha. There is no relationship between them, but it had to be so. Once women entered – they came in great crowds, and they have very loving hearts so they can fall into anything very easily – soon the proportion between men and women was one to four. One man to four women – they predominated. And with them came love, tenderness, softness, femininity, receptivity. With them came everything that Buddha was holding out against. The quality changed: Buddha became a God, was worshipped and prayed to. Temples were erected, images were built, and all that which Buddha had been saying was not possible on his path, entered and bloomed.

I am not saying that something went wrong. Nothing went wrong, because so many people attain through love. But Buddha's purity was lost. His absolute grip on intelligence was lost. The path became more and more the meeting of the opposites.

To me, it is very good. Nothing like this has happened on Jesus' path. Nobody has come on Jesus' path who would bring intelligence and the path of intelligence into it, no. Nothing has happened like that. Jesus' path has remained purer in that way. It is the path of prayer, of love: love of the whole existence, love of God – God simply means the whole. You will not find any techniques there. If you are looking for techniques in the Gospels, you are looking in the wrong place. Look for techniques in Patanjali's *Yoga Sutras,* look for techniques in *Vigyan Bhairav Tantra*: look for techniques somewhere else. Jesus is a lover. If you can love, nothing else is needed. If you cannot love, you cannot be helped on that path. Then forget about it, it is not for you.

The problem is arising... Nirvan wants to love and cannot love, so he wants to find some techniques. But love never happens through techniques, so you are asking for the impossible. Follow the path of intelligence. If Buddha appeals to you, there is no problem. Forget about Jesus. Buddha will do.

"The Gospels provide no techniques for developing a loving heart" – because there are none. "The Gospels are also too difficult for ordinary people." There, you are absolutely wrong. The Gospels are difficult only for intellectuals, not for ordinary people. Jesus moved with ordinary people; he was very much against intellectuals. He was all for the ordinary people. His whole disciplehood came from very ordinary people, because the ordinary people have a purer heart, naturally. The intellectuals lose their hearts; they become hung-up in the head. They think about love but they cannot love. Even sometimes when they say that they are in love, they only think that they are in love.

Love is not possible through the head. It is as impossible as somebody trying to see through the ears, or to listen through the eyes. You cannot listen through the eyes, and you cannot see through the ears, because they are not meant for it. Intelligence is not meant for love. For that a different faculty exists in you: the heart. The intellectual is trained for the head; the schools, the colleges, the universities all train for the head. The more and more clever, intelligent, calculating you become, the more and more difficult it becomes to love. That's why Jesus moved with ordinary people, because ordinary people are extraordinarily loving people. The so-called extraordinary intellectuals are very ordinary lovers.

So how can it be that you say the Gospels are also too difficult for ordinary people? No, sir, they are not. If they are difficult for you it simply shows that you are difficult for them, that you are too much in the head. The Gospels cannot be approached from the head. Through tears, yes – through logic, no. Through dancing, yes; through singing, yes; through chanting, yes – but through argumentation, no. You must be approaching in the wrong way. You must be bringing your head into the Gospels.

They are very simple phenomena – like flowers, like rivers. Jesus lived with ordinary people. He is the past master of how to relate to ordinary people. Buddha lived with extraordinary people: great scholars, great intelligent people, poets, philosophers; his atmosphere was that of intelligence. Jesus walked with the fisherman, with the woodcutter, with the shoemaker. These Gospels are those dialogues. They were between Jesus and very ordinary people. In fact, he himself was very ordinary. He was not the son of a king but a carpenter's son. He could not say anything that could not be understood by ordinary people.

But I understand your problem. It is difficult for you. Then it is not for you. Don't be unnecessarily worried about it. Look for something that is for you. There are a thousand and one doors; the door is irrelevant. The real question is to get into God; by what door you enter will not make any difference. Enter – that is significant. So let Buddha be your door.

"Perhaps this is why the Christian message has always seemed less practical than, say, Buddha's." It depends. If you are a very, very intellectual person, Buddha's approach will look very practical and Jesus' approach will look impractical. If you are a loving person, Buddha's will look impractical and Jesus' will look very practical. It depends. It depends more on you how it looks. If something suits you, it is practical for you. If something does not suit you, it is impractical. And there is no need to remain hooked with the impractical.

The third question:

Osho,
Why is Jesus thought to be born out of a virgin mother?

There are a few points to be understood...

One: Jesus can be born *only* out of a virgin woman. But remember, virginity has nothing to do with celibacy – not, at least, for me. Virginity is something immensely different. Don't reduce it to sex.

Sex can be virgin, and celibacy may not be virgin. Things are very complicated. If a man is celibate and thinks constantly of sex, he is not virgin. On the other hand, if a man makes love to a woman, or the woman makes love to a man, and there is no thought of sex – no sexuality in the head, no cerebral sex – it is virgin. Virgin means pure. Virgin means uncontaminated. Virgin means spontaneous. Virgin means simple, innocent.

Now, sex is not the problem. Sexuality is the problem. There are people who are continually thinking of sex. And the more you try to enforce some celibacy on yourself – you become a nun or a monk – the more you think of sex. In fact, you don't think about anything else, you only think of sex because that is your starved part. It takes revenge, it becomes very aggressive. It comes again and again, bubbles up, surfaces in the head. You go on saying prayers to keep it repressed, and you go on doing this and that – a thousand and one things. But whenever there is rest, it is there. You go to sleep and it is there. It becomes your dream, it becomes your fantasy. If you repress it too much, it then starts coming through different symbols. They may not be sexual on the surface but deep down they are sexual.

Sexuality means that sex has entered into the head, but why has sex entered into the head in the first place? It enters into the head if you repress it. Anything repressed enters into the head. Try for three days: go on a fast, and the thought of food will enter into the head. For seven days don't take a bath... I am not talking about hippies. If you are a hippie, then this won't do. For seven days don't take a bath, and that will enter into your head. For three, four days don't sleep, and that will enter in your head. Then you will be continuously thinking of sleep, sleep will be continuously coming and you will be yawning. Whatsoever is starved enters the head, and when something enters the head your whole being becomes polluted with it.

By virginity, I mean that Mary must have been in a very, very non-sexual state. She must have been a very innocent woman. She must not have been thinking about sex; she must have made love, but that love was innocent. There was no idea in it; the mind was not interfering. It was completely uncontaminated by the mind, uninterfered with by the mind. That's what we in Tantra say is real love.

Ordinarily what do you do? You see a woman, a beautiful woman, and you start fantasizing. "A beautiful woman... How to take her to bed?" Now you start planning. Now there is great turmoil and calculation inside – how to introduce yourself to her, and how to "make it." On the surface you don't show that; it continues inside: calculation, thinking, planning, designing. When you talk to her you don't show any indication that you are sexually interested in her – because she may feel offended. Things may go wrong from the very beginning. You talk about other things – poetry, literature – and you are not concerned with poetry and literature at all. You are concerned somehow with how to jump into bed. You are planning inside, but on the surface you are showing interest in art, in music, you are praising the music that is on. But deep down, you are waiting for something else. This is non-virginity.

You meet a woman, you don't think about sex at all. Only pathological people think about sex, healthy people don't think about sex. There is no need. You enjoy the beauty of the woman – her face, her eyes, her proportion – you are simply thrilled by her being. There is no idea to do anything to her, there is no idea to exploit, there is no idea to possess. You are immensely interested, but very innocently. There is no planning in your mind, there is no future, then it is a virgin relationship. One day love can happen. One day listening to music, dancing together, love can possess you both: you can make love to each other. But even while making love, there is no idea – there is no mind in it. It is innocent of mind, then it is a virgin relationship.

If you ask me, then this is what I mean by virgin. Jesus cannot be born in the way Christians say – that is absurd, stupid. But why do they say that he was born out of a virgin mother? They are too obsessed with sex, and to them it seems degrading that Jesus should come out of sex, out of an ordinary love relationship. That looks very, very disturbing to them. Their God, their master, their savior coming through the ordinary passage of sex? No, it is not possible. If Jesus can come through sex, then how will they condemn sex? Then how will they tell their nuns and their monks, "Don't ever go into sex. It is ugly, it is the greatest sin there is"? If Jesus himself enters the world through natural love, it will be difficult to condemn it. Then a nun can say, "Who knows, maybe Jesus wants to come through me?" Or a monk can say, "Who knows? Joseph never knew. Who knows maybe Jesus wants to come through me?"

If Jesus can come through love, love is enhanced, enthroned. Then love becomes a great value. If Jesus comes through love, then love will have a splendor to it, and that is difficult for the pathological people. They condemn sex, because through condemning sex they can control people, they can make them feel guilty – that is their strategy. Make people feel guilty, and they become slaves and serfs. Make them feel guilty and they are always crawling. Make them feel guilty and you can exploit them. Make them feel guilty and they will come crawling to the churches and to the mosques and to the temples, and they will never be rebellious. They will be so afraid – they are sinners, they have to be saved. Create the idea in them that they are sinners, then certainly they will start searching and seeking how to be saved. Then you can trap them into the church. You can say to them, "This is the only way to be saved – only those who go through Jesus will be saved."

The more they are trembling, the more they are afraid, the closer death is coming, the more they will start coming to the church, and the more they will believe in any nonsense that you say. This has been used by the priest and the politician to exploit people, to repress people, to oppress people, to dominate people. They cannot say that Jesus comes through ordinary love; they want to make it special. And this tendency exists in all the religions. Somehow they want to make their master special. Jainas say that Mahavira's perspiration does not smell – in fact, he does not perspire. He does not defecate – he's not an ordinary human being. Defecation, urinating, are very ordinary things – Mahavira does not do that.

Now, that seems to be the longest case in the history of constipation: forty-two years. I have heard about the record; the record is one hundred and twelve days. The greatest record known to medical science is one hundred and twelve days. One man retained that long. But Mahavira: forty-two years. Now you cannot compete with Mahavira. This is absurd, this is foolish, but that's how things go.

Every religion tries to make something special of the master, and the masters are the most ordinary people, because they are non-egos. They are very simple people. But the disciple's ego is in trouble, the disciple's ego wants to find something which is special – so special that nobody else can claim it. Christians have found it through this idea of virginity. They say that Jesus was born out of the Virgin Mary through the Holy Ghost. But why can't the Holy Ghost come in the usual way through Joseph – as he always comes? Why did he get lost? Why did he go astray?

I have heard...

The problems of the world were weighing heavily on God's shoulders and he confessed the need for a rest.

"Why don't you take a short vacation, Boss?" suggested the archangel Gabriel.

"Yes, but where?"

"How about the little place, Earth? You haven't been there for a good while."

"No, no. It's a world of busybodies," shuddered God. "I was there two thousand years ago and that's enough. I had an affair with a little Jewish girl, and they're still talking about it."

Christians are obsessed. This is a very ill state of affairs.

To me, virginity means innocence. And naturally, Jesus can only come out of innocence. Such a flower can only bloom in innocence. Mary must have been a virgin – virgin in my sense. She must have been pure love. She must have been as innocent as the animals. She must have been a perfect animal – that is the meaning – like a cow. Look into the eyes of a cow. Those eyes must have been the eyes of Mary. Jesus can only come through such simplicity, such innocence.

The fourth question:

Osho,
If somebody kills you... Then?

Then somebody kills me. So what?
I don't see any problem in it. Life is good, so is death.

All is good; you need not choose. Choice brings conflict. If you choose life against death you are creating a dichotomy in your being. If somebody kills me, he kills me. There is nothing more to it.

Life is good, so death is going to be good. And death is going to happen, whether somebody kills or not. Death is the culmination of life, the fulfillment of life. Death is not against life, death is the crescendo, the greatest peak of life. Death is the greatest orgasm. That's why I say that even on the cross Jesus was laughing. He must have been enjoying the whole joke.

The last question:

Osho,
Why did you end up your talk yesterday abruptly? Hot date?
Anyhow I'm caught in the words of this series. Would you explain the Beautitude about those who are persecuted for righteousness' sake.

There was nothing esoteric about it. Just my bladder was hurting and it is hurting again. I am not a Mahavira, so I will not be answering it.

Enough for today.

CHAPTER 3

first be reconciled

Matthew 5

Jesus said unto his disciples:

Therefore if thou bring thy gift to the altar, and there rememberest that thy brother hath ought against thee;

Leave there thy gift before the altar, and go thy way; first be reconciled to thy brother, and then come and offer thy gift.

Ye have heard that it was said by them of old time, Thou shalt not commit adultery:

But I say unto you, that whosoever looketh on a woman to lust after her hath committed adultery already in his heart.

And if thy right eye offend thee, pluck it out, and cast it from thee: for it is profitable for thee that one of thy members should perish, and not that thy whole body should be cast into hell.

Ye have heard that it hath been said, An eye for an eye, and a tooth for a tooth:

But I say unto you, That ye resist not evil: but whosoever shall smite thee on thy right cheek, turn to him the other also.

Ye have heard that it hath been said, Thou shalt love thy neighbor, and hate thine enemy.

But I say unto you, Love your enemies, bless them that curse you, do good to them that hate you, and pray for them which despitefully use you, and persecute you;

That ye may be the children of your Father which is in heaven: for he maketh his sun to rise on the evil and on the good, and sendeth rain on the just and on the unjust.

For if ye love them which love you, what reward have ye? do not even the publicans the same?

Be ye therefore perfect, even as your Father which is in heaven is perfect.

Moses brought law to the world; Jesus brings love. Moses is a must before Jesus can be possible. Law is enforced love; love is spontaneous law. Law is from the outside; love is from the inside. Law is without; love is within. Love can happen only when a certain order, a certain discipline, a certain law, exists. Love cannot exist in the jungle. Moses civilizes man; Jesus spiritualizes man. That's why Jesus says again and again, "I have come not to destroy, but to fulfill."

Moses gives commandments, Jesus gives insight into those commandments. One can follow the commandments on a formal, superficial level. One can become a righteous person, a puritan, a moralist, and deep down nothing changes: all remains the same. The old darkness is still there, the old unconsciousness is still there. Nothing has really changed; you have just painted your surface. Now you are wearing a beautiful mask. Nothing wrong in wearing a beautiful mask – if you have an ugly face it is better not to show it to others. Why be so hard on others? If you have an ugly face, wear a mask – at least it will save others from seeing you. But the mask cannot change your ugly face. Never forget for a single moment that the mask is not your face. You have to transform your face too.

Moses gave a very crude discipline to society. He could not have done better – there was no way. Human consciousness existed in a very, very primitive way. A little bit of civilization was more than one could expect. But Moses prepared the way, and Jesus is the fulfillment. What Moses started, Jesus completes. Moses has laid the foundation; Jesus raises the whole temple. Those stones in the foundation have to be crude and ugly. Only on those crude and ugly stones can a beautiful marble temple be built. Always remember this: Jesus is not against Moses. But the Jews misunderstood him, because Moses talks about law and Jesus talks about love.

To the Jews, particularly the priests, the politicians, it appeared that the law would be destroyed by Jesus; hence they were angry. And they were right too. The law would be destroyed in a sense, because a higher law would be coming in. The lower law would have to go. The lower has to cease for the higher to come.

Law depends on fear, law depends on greed, law punishes you. The central idea of law is justice, but justice is not enough, because justice is crude and hard, violent. Only compassion can allow your being to bloom, can help you come to your highest peak – not justice. Law is better than lawlessness, but compared to love, law itself is lawlessness – compared to love. It is relative, because law depends on the same evils against which it fights.

Somebody murders, then the law murders him. Now, it is the same thing you are doing to the person that he has done to somebody else. It is not higher, although it is just. But it is not religious, it has no spirituality in it; it is mathematical. He has killed somebody and the law kills him. But if killing is wrong, then how can the law be right? If killing in itself is wrong, then the law is very much lacking. It depends on the same evil – remember it.

When Jesus started talking about love, the people who had been law-abiding became very much afraid. Because they knew that if the law was dropped, then the animal hidden inside them would come up, and would tear down the whole society. They knew that their faces were only beautiful on the surface – deep down, great ugliness. And when Jesus said, "Drop all masks," they became afraid, they

became angry: "This man is dangerous, this man has to be pun-
ished and destroyed before he destroys the whole society."

But they misunderstood. Jesus was not saying just to drop the
mask. He was saying: "I have brought you an alchemy, so that your
real face can be beautiful. Why carry the mask? Why this weight?
Why this false plastic thing? I can give you a higher law that needs
no fear, that needs no greed, that needs no enforcement from the
outside but arises in your being because of understanding, not
because of fear." Remember, that is the difference: out of fear is law;
out of understanding is love.

Moses is a must, but Moses must go also. Moses has done
his work, he has prepared the ground. When Jesus appears, Moses'
work is fulfilled. But the Jews were angry. It is very difficult for people
to stop clinging to their past. Moses had become very, very central to
the Jewish mind. They thought Jesus was against Moses. And this
has been so down the ages: the misunderstanding.

Hindus thought that Buddha was against the Vedas – the same
problem, exactly the same. Buddha is not against the Vedas – in a
sense, yes, but only in a sense. He is bringing something from the
depth, and once that depth becomes available to you, the Vedas
will not be needed. So he looks like he is against: he makes the
Vedas meaningless. And that is the whole purpose of Jesus: to fulfill
Moses and still to make Moses meaningless. The new dispensation
has come in.

Jesus was a man of love, of immense love. He loved this earth,
he loved the smell of this earth. He loved the trees, he loved the
people. He loved the creatures because that is the only way to love
the creator. If you cannot praise the painting, how can you praise the
painter? If you cannot praise the poetry, how can you praise the poet?

Jesus is very affirmative, yea-saying. And he knows one very significant fact which he brings into his sayings again and again: "God is
an abstraction; you cannot stand face to face with God." God is as
much an abstraction as humanity is. Whenever you come across, you
come across human beings, never across humanity. You meet this
human being, that human being, but never humanity. You always
come across the concrete. You will never come across the abstract
God, because he will not have any face. He will be facelessness. You
will not be able to recognize him. Then where to find him?

Look into each eye that you come across, look into each being

that you come across. This is God in concrete form, God materialized. Everybody here is an incarnation of God – the rocks and the
trees and the people and all. Love these people, love these trees,
these stars, and through that love you will start feeling the immen-
sity of being. But you will have to go through the small door of a
particular being.

Jesus has been very much misunderstood. He was misunderstood by the Jews, and he was the climax of their intelligence for
which they had waited for ages. When he came he was rejected.
And he has been even more misunderstood by the Christians. A
great yea-sayer has been converted into a no-sayer. Christians have
depicted Jesus as very sad, with a long face, in great misery as if he
is being tortured. This is false; it is not true about Jesus. It cannot be
true about Jesus. Otherwise who else will laugh, and who else will
love, and who else will celebrate? Jesus is a celebration of being,
and the highest celebration possible. Remember it, only then will
you be able to understand these sutras.

An immensely beautiful anecdote:

Jesus was on the cross, and below St. Patrick was praying for
his soul, as soon his master would die.

Jesus called down to St. Patrick, "Patrick, come up here. There
is something I must tell you."

Patrick, not looking up, replied, "Lord, to be sure oi cannot for oi
am praying fer yer soul, that oi am."

Jesus then calls – a little louder, with a hint of urgency: "Patrick,
for Christ's sake stop this nonsense and come up, it is very important what I must tell you."

"Lord, oi cannot. Have not oi told you oi'm prayin' fer yer soul,
bejabbers!"

Jesus again, almost shouting, "Patrick, for the last time I say,
come up here! It is of utmost urgency, you cannot afford to miss."

Patrick reluctantly relents, and says under his breath, "God-
dam-mit! This man is a fool. Asking me to go up there when oi am
busy praying for his soul!" – goes off to fetch a ladder. He puts up
the ladder against the cross and with slow, deliberate reluctance
climbs rung after rung till he reaches the top. "Well, master, here oi
am. Now will yer tell me what it is that you brought me all the way
up here for?"

"Look Patrick," Jesus says, "over beyond those trees you can see our house."

Jesus is dying on the cross and he says, "Look beyond those trees. Can you see our house?" He was immensely in love with this earth. That is the only way to be in love with God; there is no other way.

If you deny existence, you are intrinsically denying God. If you say no to life, you have said no to God, because it is God's life. Always remember God has no lips of his own; he kisses you through somebody else's lips. He has no hands of his own; he embraces you through somebody else's hands. He has no eyes of his own, because all eyes are his; he looks at you through somebody's eyes. He sees you through somebody's eyes and he is seen by your eyes, and he goes on seeing through your eyes.

Quakers rightly say that God has nothing else but you, only you – that's what God has. This insight has to penetrate deeply, only then will you be able to understand the sayings of Jesus; otherwise you will miss – as Christians have been missing down the ages. Let this become the very foundation stone: that life is God. And then things will become very, very simple. Then you will have the right perspective. Say yes, and suddenly you feel a kind of prayer arising in you.

Have you tried it? Sitting silently, doing nothing, start swaying in a kind of inner dance and start saying, "Yes, yes..." Go into it. Let it come from your very heart. Let it spread over your whole being. Let it throb in your heartbeat, let it pulsate in your blood. Let this yes electrify you and you will be surprised: for the first time you have tasted what prayerfulness is.

The English word *yes* can become a great mantra. It is. The very sound of it is yea-saying; the very sound of it creates an affirmation in the heart. Say no – try the polar opposite sometimes – sitting silently, say "No, no..." Go into it. Let your whole being say no, and you will see the difference. When you say no you will be angry. When you go on saying no you will become enraged. When you go on saying no you will feel that you are cut off from existence, separate, isolated, alienated – the bridge has disappeared. And particularly the modern mind is a no-saying mind. Descartes, the French philosopher, has said: "*Cogito ergo sum*: I think therefore I am." The modern mind says: "I say no therefore I am." It is a no-saying mind, it goes on saying no. No creates the ego. You cannot create the ego without saying no. You can create the ego only by saying no, more and more.

Ego separates, ego makes you irreligious, because ego takes you away from the whole, and you start thinking you are a whole unto yourself. You forget that you exist in an immense complexity, that you are part of a vast universe, that you are not an island – "No man is an island…" We are all parts of an infinite continent. Yes-saying bridges you with the continent. Yes-saying bridges you with God. Say yes more and you will become more religious. Let yes be your church, your temple. And Jesus is a yes-sayer.

Even dying on the cross, he says, "Look beyond those trees. Can you see our house?" And this is his last moment. But his love for existence, for life is still there, radiantly there. In the last moment he prays to God: "Father, forgive these people because they don't know what they are doing."

They knew exactly what they were doing. They knew they were killing. But that is not the point. When Jesus says: "They don't know what they are doing," he is saying: "They are so asleep, so confined in their egos, they have lost their eyes, Father. They don't have any consciousness. I can see great darkness in their heart. Forgive them, they are not responsible." This is the voice of love. He is not condemning them. Ordinarily he would have prayed: "Destroy all these people. They are destroying your only begotten son. Kill them immediately, right now! Come like a thunderbolt! Shower like fire; burn them here and now. Show them what they are doing to your son." That may have been just, but that was not right for Jesus.

Jesus does not exist at the level of justice, he exists at the level of compassion. Compassion forgives, justice punishes, and when you punish you create in the other's mind great anger. He will watch for his own time to take revenge – and with a vengeance. Only love creates reconciliation because love does not create any chain. Anger, fear, violence, aggression, punishment – all create ugly chains. And one thing leads still into deeper darkness, into deeper gloom.

Jesus' whole message is yes. He says yes to his own death, accepts it, welcomes it because it is the will of his God: "Then let it be so." He relaxes into it. You are not relaxed even in life, and he relaxes into death too. That was the last test, and he passed through it victoriously.

Death is the only criterion, the only touchstone where a man is really known: what he is, of what mettle he is made. It is very easy to talk about love; it is difficult to love, because love is a cross. It is very easy to talk about compassion, but to be committed to compassion one has to lose all.

Just the other day I was reading this anecdote:

Uncle Si and Aunt Rose were on in years, but they still prayed every night. Their prayer was always, "Lord, when you're ready for us, take us. We are ready."

A group of playful boys heard their prayers and decided to have a little fun. They got on top of the house and talked down the chimney, in a deep voice, Si, Si..."

Aunt Rose asked, "What do you want?"

The voice answered, "I want Si."

"Who are you?"

"I'm from the Lord and I've come for Si."

"Well, he ain't here, he's gone."

"Well, I'll just have to take you, Aunt Rose, instead of Si, if he's not there."

"Get out from under that bed, Si," said Aunt Rose sharply. "You know he knows you are there."

When death comes, one forgets everything. For years they have been praying, "Lord, we are ready whenever you are ready." And now that the Lord is ready, Aunt Rose is not ready to go.

I have heard an old Sufi parable:

An old man was coming from the forest – he was a woodcutter. He was carrying a big load of wood, and he was really old – seventy, eighty, tired of life. Many times he would say to the sky, "Where is death? Why don't you come to me? I have nothing left to live for here, I am just dragging on. Do you want me to commit suicide? That will be a sin. Why can't you come easily?" Again and again he would pray, "Death, come and take me, I am finished." And, in fact, there was nothing to live for. He was an old man and had nobody to look after him, no money left. Every day he would have to go to the forest, cut wood and sell it, and somehow manage for his bread and butter.

That day it happened that death was passing by. Suddenly he

asked – he threw down his load of wood – and shouted to the sky, "Death! Where are you? You come to everybody. I have seen so many people dying. Why are you so angry with me? Why don't you come to me? Come on! I am ready!"

And, by chance, death was passing by, so death came. It appeared before him and said, "Okay, so what do you want?"

And he started trembling. He said, "Nothing much, it's just that I am an old man and I am unable to put this load onto my head, and there is nobody else to support me. Please, just help me to put this load on my head. Thank you."

For years he had been praying for death. In fact, he was not praying for death; he was not aware of what he was doing.

Jesus is fully aware, and yet for a moment he wavers. So what to say of other people? For a moment he wavers on the cross, and he says to God, "Why have you forsaken me? Why? What wrong have I committed? Why are you so far away? Why is this being done to me?" For a single moment he wavers – even at that stage. So what to say about ordinary human beings? But he saw the point – he was a man of perception, great insight. He relaxed and said, "Thy kingdom come, Thy will be done. Do whatsoever you want to do." He effaced himself utterly.

In that moment Jesus died and Christ was born. To me, in that moment the resurrection happened, not after the crucifixion. In that moment the discontinuity happened: Jesus disappeared the moment he said, "Thy will be done." That is the death of Jesus, the death of any sense of self. Jesus ceased at that moment; he became Christ. This is the real resurrection. The other thing may be just a parable – meaningful, but not historical – a myth, pregnant with great significance but not factual. But this is the real fact. Just a moment before he was wavering, afraid, trembling, and a moment later he settled and relaxed. He surrendered. That moment he was no longer separate from God. When your will is separate from God, you are separate from God. When your will has been surrendered to God's will, you are not separate; then his will is the only will.

These sutras:

Therefore if thou bring thy gift to the altar, and there rememberest that thy brother hath aught against thee;

*Leave there thy gift before the altar, and go thy way; first be
reconciled to thy brother, and then come and offer thy gift.*

Jesus says, "If you come to the temple with flowers, with offer-
ings, to pray, to surrender to God, and you remember that somebody is angry at you – you have done something, you have angered
somebody – then the first necessity is to go back and be reconciled
to your brother. All are brothers here, remember, because the father
is one." The trees are your brothers; that's how St. Francis used to
talk to the trees: "Sisters, brothers." The fish, the seagulls, the rocks,
the mountains – all are your brothers because they all come from
one source.

Jesus is saying that if you are not reconciled with the world, you
cannot come to pray to God. How can you come to the Father if
you are not even reconciled with the brother? And the brother is
concrete, the Father is abstract. The brother exists, and the Father
is hidden. The brother is manifest, and the Father is not manifest.
How can you be reconciled with the unmanifest? You have not even
been capable of being reconciled with the manifest. This is a meaningful sentence. It does not mean only your brother, it does not
mean only human beings; it means the whole existence – wherever
you have been offending. If you have been cruel to anybody…

A great Zen master, Rinzai, was sitting. A man came. He pushed
the door very hard – he must have been angry – he slammed the
door. He was not in a good mood. Then he threw his shoes, and
came in. Rinzai said: "Wait. Don't come in. First go and ask forgiveness from the door and from your shoes."

The man said: "What are you talking about? I have heard that
these Zen people are mad, but it seems true. I was thinking it was
just rumor. What nonsense you are talking! Why should I ask forgiveness from the door? And it looks so embarrassing – those shoes
are mine!"

Then Rinzai said, "Get out! Never come here again. If you can be
angry at the shoes, why can't you ask their forgiveness? When you
were angry, you never thought that it was so foolish to be angry with
the shoes. If you can relate with anger, then why not with love? A relationship is a relationship. Anger is a relationship. When you slammed
the door with such anger, you related to the door; you behaved

wrongly, immorally. And the door has not done anything to you. First go, otherwise don't come in."

Under the impact of Rinzai's silence, and the people sitting there, and that presence, like a flash, the man understood. He understood the logic of it, it was so clear: "If you can be angry, then why can't you be loving? Go!" And he went. Maybe in his whole life that was the first time... He touched the door and tears started flowing from his eyes. He could not hold back those tears. And when he bowed down to his own shoes, a great change happened in him. The moment he turned and came towards Rinzai, Rinzai took him in his arms and embraced him.

This is reconciliation. How can you pray if you are unreconciled? How can you come to a master if you are unreconciled with existence?

Jesus says: *Therefore if thou bring thy gift to the altar, and there rememberest that thy brother hath aught against thee; Leave there thy gift...* The altar is secondary, the prayer is secondary, because right now you are not in the mood to pray. One has to earn prayer. By being reconciled with existence, one earns prayer. Prayer is not just that you go into the temple and you do it. It is not a kind of doing, it is an arousal into consciousness of unknown peaks. But that is possible only if you are reconciled, relaxed with existence.

Now this is something absolutely different from what Christians have been doing down the ages. They are not reconciled. They are not even reconciled with their own bodies – what to say of others? They are not even reconciled with their own existence. They have great condemnation in them. With that condemnation how can they pray? Their prayer will be just so-so, lukewarm; it will not transform them.

Prayer is a magic formula, it is a mantra, it is a spell. But it has to be provoked in the right moment. You cannot pray at any time, in any place. You have to get into the right tuning. That's why all the religions have chosen particular moments – early morning when the sun is just going to rise, and there is more possibility of getting in tune with existence. The whole night you have slept. For eight hours, at least, you have not been in the world. For eight hours, at least, you have not been in business, you have not been cutting each other's throats. For eight hours, at least, you have been in a relaxed state, fast asleep.

When you rise in the morning, your eyes are clear and there are less clouds in your being. There is a kind of innocence – not only in you – it is all around. The trees are innocent, they have also rested. The dewdrops on the leaves are innocent, the sky is innocent, the birds are innocent, and the sun is rising... Again a new day. With great innocence everything is coming back out of the primordial source, refreshed, rejuvenated. That's why religions have decided on *brahmamuhurt* – early morning before the sun rises, – because with the sun, many things start arising in you. The sun is great energy. When it starts pouring into you, it brings all your drives, desires alive, all your quarrels alive. Again you are moving into the world. So the morning has been chosen just as the easiest point from which you can be tuned to existence.

Prayer can be done only when you are tuned. And Jesus is saying a very, very psychologically valid thing. If, while before the altar, you remember that you have angered somebody, and somebody is still carrying a wound because of you – somebody is angry somewhere, then go and help the person to heal, bring things to a reconciliation.

Henry Thoreau was dying and his old aunt came to see him. And she said, "Henry, are you reconciled to God?"

And Henry opened his eyes, and said, "But I don't remember that I ever had any quarrel with him. I have never quarreled with him."

But very few people can say this. Henry Thoreau was very saintly, very holy. You are quarreling every day. Remember, with whomsoever you are quarreling, you are quarreling with God because nothing else exists. Your life is a continuous quarrel. And then those quarrels go on accumulating; they go on poisoning your system, your being. And then one day you want to pray, and the prayer looks so false on your lips. It does not come, it does not fit. It is not possible for you to pray suddenly; you will have to prepare for it.

The first preparation Jesus says is: *...be reconciled to your brother. ...to your brother...* means all human beings, animals, birds. The whole existence is your brother, because we come out of one source, out of one father or one mother. This whole multiplicity comes out of unity.

So, remember, God can be loved only through man. You will never meet God, you will always meet man. Once you have started loving God through man, you can go still deeper – you can love God through animals. And then still deeper – you can love God through trees. And still deeper – you can love God through mountains and rocks. And when you have learned how to love God through all his forms, only then is your love changed into prayer. To me, these three words are very significant: *sex*, *love*, and *prayer*. Sex is a reconciliation of your body with other bodies. Let me repeat: sex is a reconciliation between your body and other bodies. That's why it is so satisfying, that's why it brings such a thrill to you, such excitement, such relaxation, such calm. But it is the lowest reconciliation. If you don't know any higher, then it is okay. But you are living in your house, not knowing that your house has many other rooms. You are living only in a dark cell, and you think this is all – and there are many beautiful rooms in your house. But you will remain a beggar, because you remain only in the body. The body is only your porch, the porch of the palace.

But sex brings joy because it is a reconciliation between two material bodies. Two bodies vibrate to one tune. There is song, a physical song. A poetry arises between the two energies of the bodies – they dance together hand in hand, they embrace each other, they are lost into each other. For a few moments there is ecstasy, then it disappears because bodies cannot melt into each other – they are too solid for that.

Then the second thing is love. Love is reconciliation between two minds, two psychological energies. Love is higher, deeper, greater. If you can love a person, by and by, you will see sex disappearing between you. Western people become very much afraid of that phenomenon.

Every day some couple or other comes to me and they say: "What is happening to us? We have become more loving, but why is sex disappearing?" – because they have been taught that sex and love are synonymous. They are not. And they have been taught if you love the person more, then you will be more sexually involved with the person. Just the reverse is the true case. If you love the person more, sex will start disappearing, because you are getting a higher reconciliation. Who bothers with the lower? This is more satisfying, brings greater contentment, more lasting joy.

And the third state of love energy is prayer. That is reconciliation between one's soul and the soul of existence. That is the highest reconciliation; there is none beyond. So when that happens, the so-called love also starts disappearing – just as when love happens sex starts disappearing. I am not condemning sex – there is nothing wrong in it – it is perfectly beautiful, healthy in its own place. But when the higher energy comes, the lower starts disappearing. There is no need for it; its work is finished.

It is like a child who has grown in the mother's womb for nine months; now he is ready to get out of the womb. Those nine months were beautiful. He will be grateful to his mother for his whole life; he cannot repay the debt. But now he is ready to get out of it. That womb cannot contain it any longer; the child has started to become bigger than the womb.

It happens exactly like that. If you go really deeply into sex, a moment comes when your love is more than the sex can contain. Then you start overflowing, you start moving higher, and soon you are out of sex. One day, again it happens. When love is too much, you start overflowing into prayerfulness, and then love disappears.

There is a very beautiful parable told about Jesus. Meditate over it. This is a very curious episode in which Christ three times asks Peter: "Do you love me?" and Peter affirms with increasing earnestness.

What is the significance of this apparently pointless repetition? Why three times? Once is enough. You ask somebody: "Do you love me?" and he says yes or no and it is finished. Why repeat it three times?

First, three is the symbol of those three layers: sex, love, prayer. Actually the three questions are not identical in the original, but English is a poor language – poor compared to any ancient language – because English is more scientific, more mathematical. And the old languages were not scientific, were not mathematical – that was their beauty – they were poetical. So there were many meanings for a single word, and there were many words with a single meaning too. It was more fluid, there was more possibility. In the original it cannot be said that the three questions are all identical; they are not.

There are two distinct words used for love. Christ's original question uses the verb *agapao,* which means a state of love, not a relationship. When Jesus says: "Are you in love with me?" he is saying: "Are you in prayer with me?" He is asking the highest. The difference has to be understood.

A relationship is a lower state. The highest state of love is not a relationship at all, it is simply a state of your being. Just as trees are green, a lover is loving. They are not green for particular persons; it is not that when you come they become green. The flower goes on spreading its fragrance whether anybody comes or not, whether anybody appreciates it or not. The flower does not start releasing its fragrance when it sees that a great poet is passing by: "Now this man will appreciate, now this man will be able to understand who I am." And it does not close its doors when it sees that a stupid, idiotic person is passing there – insensitive, dull – a politician or something like that. It does not close itself: "What is the point? Why cast pearls before the swine?" No, the flower goes on spreading its fragrance. It is a state, not a relationship.

When Jesus asks for the first time, "Do you love me, Peter?" he uses the word *agapao*. It means: "Are you in a state of love with me?" – *state* of love with me. Jesus means: "Has your love for me become your love for the whole? Have I become the door for the whole, for the divine? Do you love me not only as a person but as a representative of God? Do you see my father in me? Can you see in me God himself?" That is the meaning of *agapao*: it implies prayer, compassion.

Compassion is a beautiful word. It comes from the same root as passion. When does passion become compassion? Passion is a relationship, it is a desire to be related, it is a need; it creates dependence, bondage. And all kinds of misery come in its wake. Compassion is the same energy, but it is no longer a hankering to relate. Not that it does not relate, but that desire has gone. Compassion is a state where you can be alone and perfectly happy, absolutely happy. You can be happy with people, you can be happy alone – then you have attained to the state of compassion. But if you cannot be happy alone and you can only be happy with someone, then it is passion, you are dependent. And, naturally, you will be angry with the person without whom you cannot be happy. You will be angry – that's why lovers are angry at each other, continuously angry – because nobody can like one's bondage.

Freedom is the ultimate value in the human soul, so anything that degrades you from your freedom, that creates a confinement around you, you hate. That's why lovers continuously hate each other. And the psychologists have come to see that the love relationship is not a simple love relationship. Now they call it "love-hate relationship," because the hate is always there. So why call it only love?

Between the friend and the enemy there is not much difference. With the friend your relationship is love-hate, and with the enemy, your relationship is hate-love. That's the only difference – just the difference of emphasis. Love on top and hate hidden behind it – it is friendship. Hate has come on top and love has gone behind it – it is enmity.

Watch it. Observe it. Compassion means you have gone beyond the necessity of depending on anybody else. Now you can share because you don't need. You can share only when you don't need. You can give only when you don't need. Beggars can't be givers. If you are hankering for somebody to give you love, how can you give? You can at most pretend. And the same is the situation from the other side. The other is also pretending that he or she loves you, so that you can love them.

Now both are deceiving each other. That's why honeymoons cannot be very long. How long can you deceive? How long? The more intelligent you are, the shorter will be the honeymoon. If you are really intelligent, the first night will be enough, you will be finished. You will see through and through that you are a beggar and she is a beggar, and both beggars are asking to be fulfilled by each other. And they don't have anything. They are just pretending, promising. This promising is only in order to get. But nobody has it in the first place, so nobody gets it. And sooner or later one starts seeing through the pretensions. Then the wife is angry because she has been deceived, and the husband is angry because he has been deceived. And nobody really has deceived.

Beggars cannot be givers. You can share only when you have. Compassion can be shared because one is overflowing with it – like a cloud full of rainwater, ready to shower.

So in the first question when Jesus asks, "Do you love me?" he uses the word *agapao*. *Agapao* is compassion, *agapao* is conscious love, love through understanding, not love through infatuation; love through awareness, not love through an unconscious liking – because you like the shape of the woman, or you like the nose of the man, or you like the hair color, or the eyes. These are all silly things; how can love happen through these things? Love is not a liking, it is an understanding. It is not emotional. When it has immense intelligence, has compassion in it, then in that intensity of compassion, *agapao* happens.

Peter's reply uses the word *philo*. Peter says, "Yes, my Lord, I love you!" But he uses another word. He does not use *agapao*, he uses *philo* – the word that exists in *philosophy* or the word that exists in *philanthropist*. *Philo*, which has the quality of personal affection, is a relationship, not a state. It is not conscious; it is unconscious. One rises in *agapao*, and one falls in *philo*. That's why we say "falling in love" – you stumble in it, you go down in it, you fall into a dark pit through it. *Philo* is unconscious, it is not out of alertness, awareness, understanding, observation; it is not out of an integrated soul, it is not out of individuation. It is out of some hidden impulses, instincts, infatuation – it is lust.

A second time Christ asks the question, still using the word *agapao*. The master goes on and on hammering. Peter has missed; it was so simple. But you also go on missing the way, remember. He is not aware that Jesus is using one word and he is answering with another word; it is just an unconscious thing. Jesus has to ask again, a second time. Again he uses the word *agapao* so that Peter can hear it – maybe now he hears. But Peter's response is again on the personal level. In fact, he becomes a little angry. He must be thinking, "What does Jesus think of me – stupid or something? I have said 'I love you,' and now he is asking me the same question again." He must have felt a little angry. But he again uses the same word *philo*. In anger you become even more unconscious. Now he cannot hear what Jesus is saying, he cannot see who Jesus is. The question being asked again has disturbed him. He misses again.

The third time, Christ accepts Peter's lack of understanding, and uses the word *philo* himself. Why? Because Jesus sees that he will not understand that state – he has never tasted it; it is beyond him. When the master sees you cannot come to him, he has to come to you. When he goes on shouting, calling and you don't come, then he descends into your darkness to hold your hand and take you from there.

The third time, Jesus uses the word *philo*, and Peter, aggrieved by the insistence, protests his love even more earnestly. He must have become even angrier: "Why is Jesus asking again and again when I have answered it? Is there some kind of suspicion in Jesus' mind? Has he some doubts about my love?" All these questions must have arisen. He goes on missing. Even *philo* – Jesus has come very close to his understanding but there also... Now he is so angry, and Jesus is standing just by his side holding his hand but he cannot see. He goes on declaring, "I love you," but this declaration is his egoistic declaration.

Christ says gently: "Go and feed my sheep." "It is no use," Jesus says, "I will have to wait for another time. Right now it is not going to happen." The master sometimes has to wait for years. The disciple on the one hand wants it to happen, and on the other hand goes on creating all kinds of hindrances, obstructions. But that too is natural, because how can you expect more from an unconscious mind, from a mind which has not known what consciousness really means, which lives in a dark dungeon and has never seen any light? You go on talking about love and light... In compassion, Jesus says, "Okay, Peter, so go and feed my sheep. Forget about it. Right now is not the right time. I should not have asked in the first place. I will have to wait."

Maurice Nicoll, one of the disciples of George Gurdjieff and one of the most significant disciples, says: "As we cease to invent ourselves, so we cease to invent other people. We begin to feel a common existence which is without passion, and is simply what it is, without further definition."

When you stop inventing yourself – your ego is your invention – when you stop creating a false pseudo personality around you, when you just start being whatsoever you are, when you start relaxing into existence: "As we cease to invent ourselves, so we cease to invent other people." Both things go together. If you are inventing yourself, you will be inventing others too. You go on creating a very beautiful image of yourself, and correspondingly you go on creating beautiful images of other people. Neither your image about yourself is true, nor is your image about other people true. So you live in a kind of illusion, and again and again you are frustrated because nothing comes according to your image. It cannot come – your image is just your invention, it is not the truth.

Maurice Nicoll is right. He says: "When we stop inventing ourselves, we stop inventing others, and then suddenly there is a common ground, a common existence. Passion disappears, and when passion disappears, compassion appears." The meaning of the word *compassion* is to have such intense passion that passion itself burns out in that intensity. It is so intense that it burns itself and disappears into fire – the fire of its own intensity. Then there is a totally different kind of love: compassion. It goes on showering from you, goes on in ripples contin-uously, day and night, year in, year out. And whosoever is ready to partake of it can partake of it; whoever is ready to receive and digest, can digest and be fulfilled through it. Then it flows for all, for all things.

In the very fire of passion, compassion is born. Out of passion, compassion is born. Sex cannot contain love, love cannot contain prayer. But love exists in sex like a child exists in a womb, or a bird exists in an egg – the egg protects for a time, then it hinders. Then the egg has to be broken, then the bird has to come out and fly into the sky.

Sex is an egg in which the bird of love grows. Then, the bird itself – love itself – is another egg in which prayerfulness grows. And when prayerfulness has grown to its utmost, only God is, you are not. Then wherever you are, you are in the temple. Then whoever you are, you are utterly blissful. That is the meaning of heaven; that is the meaning of the "kingdom of God."

So Jesus says: "First go and be reconciled with your brother, be reconciled with the creation."

Ye have heard that it was said by them of old time, Thou shalt not commit adultery:

But I say unto you, That whosoever looketh on a woman to lust after her hath committed adultery with her already in his heart.

The question is not of committing something; the question is of thinking. This is the difference between crime and sin. Crime is that which you have committed, sin is that crime about which you have been thinking. Crime is that sin which has become actualized into the world of things: you have done it, you have exposed it to the world. Sin is that crime which you are nursing within yourself.

Jesus says: "If you think in terms of lust, you have already com-mitted adultery."

The law of Moses says: "Don't commit adultery." That is one of the commandments. But it only prevents you from action, it does not say anything about thought. It only says how to relate with people, it does not say anything about what goes on in your dreams.

Jesus says: "That is not going to transform you. You can be absolutely moralistic from the outside and deep inside you may contain all the snakes and all the scorpions and all the poisons of the whole world. The real problem has to be there."

What does he mean? Does he mean, "Don't look at a beautiful woman"? That is not possible. He cannot mean that, because if he says, "Look at the lilies in the field," how can he say, "Don't look at a beautiful woman"? If lilies are beautiful, then why not a beautiful woman or a beautiful man? If lilies represent God and his beauty, then man represents God at a higher point, woman represents the most beautiful phenomenon in the world. Jesus cannot say that. Then what is he saying? Try to understand it.

You see a beautiful woman. If you enjoy the beauty, the form, the way she walks, the grace around her – you are simply thrilled with great awe, you are thrilled by God's beauty in her – there is no lust. Lust enters only when you see a beautiful woman and immediately you start thinking, "How to possess her?" Thought is the culprit, desire is the culprit. When the thought comes, "How to possess her? How to have her? How to snatch her away from others?" then you have become ugly. Violence has come in.

Do you know where this word *violence* comes from? It comes from the same root as *violation*. You have violated a subtle law of God the moment you think of possessing. It is a profanation. The beauty was immense but you have profaned it, you have started thinking how to use it. It is as if you see a flower and you start thinking, "How to take it? How to steal it?" or, "How to take it away and sell it in the market?" This is a violation, this is a profanation – hence, it is violence.

When lust arises – the desire to possess and exploit – the beauty is lost. Then you have already made the woman ugly in your heart. It was so pure, it was so beautiful, it was such a splendor to see. Now you have destroyed everything. And rather than enjoying it, rather than being thrilled by it, rather than rejoicing about it, you have become worried: "What to do? – because she belongs to somebody else, somebody's wife." Now you will be disturbed. Rather than being enhanced and nourished by her beauty, now you will be disturbed. And you will start thinking, "How to take her away? What to do?" You miss the whole point. A door was opening through her beauty. You missed it; otherwise you have corrupted it. That's what adultery is.

Jesus is not saying to become insensitive to beauty. He cannot say it – I can vouch for it, he cannot say it – notwithstanding what Christians have been teaching to the people. He is a man of immense sensitivity, of great love. How can he be insensitive to beauty? He is simply saying: "Don't lust. Enjoy." And there is no need to enjoy anything by possessing it. In fact, how can you enjoy something once you possess it? In the very possession the beauty is destroyed. You have poisoned it, you have corrupted it. That's what adultery is.

And if thy right eye offend thee, pluck it out, and cast it from thee: for it is profitable for thee that one of thy members should perish, and not that thy whole body should be cast into hell.

This has been misinterpreted by neurotic people down the ages. There have been Christian saints who have cut off their genital organs. There have been people who have taken their eyes out according to this. Man seems to be so stupid. But these people have been revered and respected; they have been sanctified, they have become saints. These were simply neurotic people, hysterical people, and utterly stupid. This is not the meaning. This is just a way of saying that the part has to be sacrificed for the whole. The whole cannot be sacrificed for the part – that's all. It is just a way of saying that if you find that any part of your being is creating a disturbance between you and the whole, it has to be sacrificed.

As far as I know, any part that has any pretensions of being whole is the disturbance. And that is only your mind, nothing else. Only your mind pretends: "I am whole, sufficient unto myself." The mind is the only pretender. It gives you the idea of separation, of ego.

Jesus is saying: "Sacrifice the part. If it is your head, sacrifice the head." It does not mean cut your head off. It simply means bow down, surrender your head. If it is your mind, your thinking process, that is creating trouble for you, sacrifice it; it is not of any worth. For the whole, everything has to be sacrificed; only then will you become whole.

Ye have heard that it hath been said, An eye for an eye, and a tooth for a tooth:

But I say unto you, That ye resist not evil: but whosoever shall smite thee on thy right cheek, turn to him the other also.

The greatest saying of Jesus: *...ye resist not evil...* And it has been said of old: an eye for an eye, and a tooth for a tooth. That is the concept of law, justice. Jesus brings love. He says: *...resist not evil...* Why? This looks like a very strange statement: *...resist not evil...* Then evil will grow if nobody resists it. The meaning is very, very different; it is concerned with the inner alchemy. And the same is the meaning in Jesus' prayer in which he asks, "Give us our daily bread."

Hindus and Mohammedans and others have been laughing about the Christian prayer – it looks so childish: "Give us our daily bread." Couldn't Jesus think of anything else than to ask for the daily bread? But these people don't know what he means by the "daily bread."

Jesus says: "As your body exists through air, food, water, every day your soul also gets a certain nourishment from God. That is your daily bread, daily nourishment." Every day you get a certain quantity of spiritual energy. Now, with that energy you can destroy or create. If you destroy you will be misusing it; that will be violence – violation, profanation. If you use it in a creative way it will become your path towards godliness. It will grow in you to higher peaks, altitudes. It will bring a plenitude in you, a *pleroma*.

God's energy that goes on showering on you is what he calls the "daily bread." If this energy is not properly used, but is squandered in useless and destructive activities, then... God goes on giving, and you go on throwing it away, not knowing what you are throwing away.

It happened, a Sufi parable...

A man came to the river early in the morning for a morning walk and stumbled upon a bag. He opened the bag; it was full of stones. Sitting on the bank, just playfully he started throwing those stones into the river. He enjoyed the splash of those stones. By and by, it became lighter and then the sun started coming up. The last stone was left. Then he looked, because now there was light, and he started beating his chest and crying and weeping. And some people gathered and they asked, "What is the matter?"

He said, "This is a diamond, and I have thrown thousands. Continuously, for one hour I have been throwing, not knowing what

I was throwing. I was thinking these are just stones. But only the last is left."

But I say, even he was fortunate – at least he became aware when the last was left. Millions of people are not aware even at that late stage; they simply go on throwing. They live and die, and they don't ever come to know the daily bread, the diamond that descends in you everyday. It is your energy. You can put it into anger – it is the same energy. You can put it into love – it is the same energy. It is your choice. That's why Jesus says ...*resist not evil*... If you start resisting evil your whole energy will go into resistance. There is much evil. It is not a moral teaching; it is an alchemical teaching.

Ye have heard that it hath been said, An eye for an eye, and a tooth for a tooth: But I say unto you, That ye resist not evil: but whosoever shall smite thee on thy right cheek, turn to him the other also. Don't waste your energy. If he wants to hit you, he has already hit you. Give him the other cheek too, and thank him. Say, "Thank you, sir, and if some time you need me again, I will be ready." And go on your way. Don't waste your energy, because that energy is so precious. Don't waste it just in retaliation, reaction, fighting, anger – you will be throwing away diamonds.

We live in a constant inner atmosphere of objecting, complaining, condemning, no-saying. Saying no, we go on missing what is just in front of our noses. This constant objecting inside: "This is not right! That is not good! Things should be like this! Things should be like that!" Much energy gets involved with this objecting. We start putting things right, and life is short and life is fleeting – and nothing is ever being put right. We simply drown ourselves in our activity.

Jesus says: "Be aware. Your energy is precious, and you have only a limited amount of it available." More will become available if you use this amount. Jesus says: "Those who have will be given more" – his statements are the most beautiful ever made – "and those who have not, even that which they have will be taken away from them." Very paradoxical but absolutely true.

If you save this energy you will get more. The more you save, the more you have, the more will be given to you, because you are proving yourself worthy of it. The less you have of it, the less you will be given. And when you don't have anything, even that which you have will be taken away. You will remain just an empty shell, a negative emptiness – not the emptiness Buddha talks about. You will just be an empty shell with no meaning: "A tale told by an idiot, full of sound and fury signifying nothing."

By this constant wrong use of our energy we create a prison around ourselves. Yet the doors of the prison are always open, because no jailer is there except yourself. You are the prison, and the prisoner, and the jailer too. We have but to sacrifice our stupid, habitual attitudes and the same energy that creates the prison becomes our freedom, salvation.

Nicholas of Cusa maintained that right living involved only one thing – what he called "learned ignorance." Learn to be innocent again. "Learn ignorance" he used to say. Become a child. Don't resist, don't fight. Enjoy the energy that is showering on you. Become very, very primal. Learn to be innocent again. Drop your clinging to your dull and dead past, knowledge, mind. "Learned ignorance" means knowing ignorance.

There is a kind of ignorance that knows, and there is also a kind of knowledge that is ignorant. The knowledge of the pundit, the knowledge of the priest is just knowledge for its name's sake; it does not know. And the ignorance of a Jesus or a Buddha... When Bodhidharma was asked by Emperor Wu, "Who are you?" he simply said, "I don't know." This ignorance, this innocence knows.

Stop creating securities for yourself. Stop fighting people. Stop fighting! Jesus says specifically: ...*resist not evil*... Your mind will say, "But when there is evil then one has to resist. Evil cannot be allowed; evil has to be fought and destroyed." Nobody has ever destroyed evil. Evil is eternal. You will be destroyed in fighting it. It can't be destroyed. Beware of that fallacy, that fallacious idea.

Ye have heard that it hath been said, Thou shalt love thy neighbor, and hate thine enemy.

But I say unto you, Love your enemies, bless them that curse you, do good to them that hate you, and pray for them which despitefully use you, and persecute you...

The whole message is very clear and loud. Jesus is saying: "Not a single iota of energy has to be wasted for anything. The whole energy has to be conserved. When the energy comes to a certain degree, the transformation happens automatically. That is the science of alchemy."

You heat water, you go on putting heat energy into it. Then the hundred-degree heat comes and the water evaporates. Ninety-nine – it was hot, but still water. Ninety-nine point nine – and it was very, very hot, but still water. Hundred degrees – and the jump! So it happens in the inner world.

These sayings are not moral maxims. These sayings are concerned with inner transformation. If you go on preserving your energy and you don't go on squandering it anywhere... A dog starts barking and you start barking. You say, "I have to resist evil. This dog has to be taught a lesson." You can teach the dog a lesson. It has never been heard that they have learned any lesson – they go on barking. Many like you have been there, teaching lessons to the dogs. Dogs are very stubborn; they go on barking. You are simply wasted. And barking at dogs, you lose the capacity of praying to God, because the barking and the praying cannot exist together. Fighting, hatred, anger, and love cannot exist together. It is simple inner economics.

That ye may be the children of your Father which is in heaven...

If you want to be the children of God, then this has to be done – you have to preserve energy. And he is giving you energy every day. If a man simply goes on preserving, nothing else is needed. Jesus is giving such a key – a great key. It can unlock the ultimate door.

...for he maketh his sun to rise on the evil and on the good, and sendeth rain on the just and on the unjust.

And Jesus says: "Don't be bothered about the just and the unjust. Look at God! His clouds come and shower on both the just and the unjust. His sun comes and gives light and life to both good and bad. So why are you worried? God goes on giving energy to all."

So, please, don't become a reformer. Remember, if you want to reform yourself, don't become a reformer because you can do either one or the other. If you become a reformer, you start changing other people. Don't become a reformer if you want to be reformed. Preserve your energy. And the miracle is that if you are reformed, if you are transformed, then many will be transformed through you. Your very catalytic presence will be enough: just your being there, and many will be thrilled with the unknown, just your touch, and something will start vibrating in them.

Not that you have to do much: it is just, if your light is burning, people will start coming towards you; groping in the dark, they will start moving towards you. And as they come closer and closer and closer, one day the unlit lamp becomes lit through the one who is already lit. The flame jumps from one place to another. Just close-ness is needed.

Be around a master. Be around somebody who has arrived, and go closer and closer with no resistance, with no fight, with no pro-tection. Be vulnerable, and all else follows of its own accord.

That ye may be the children of your Father which is in heaven: for he maketh his sun to rise on the evil and on the good and sendeth rain on the just and on the unjust. So who are you to be worried about good and bad? Who are you to be worried about how the world should be? That is again just an ego trip.

For if ye love them which love you, what reward have ye? Do not even the publicans the same?

The puritan, the publican, the moralist, the formalist – they also do the same. When people love them, they love them. There is nothing much in it, nothing much that can be said is special. When people love you, you love; when somebody smiles at you, you smile. But that is not the point. When somebody hits you, and you smile, and somebody is full of hatred towards you, and your love goes on flowing – this is the miracle. This is magic, and only this magic can make you the children of God. Nothing else will be of help.

Be ye therefore perfect, even as your Father which is in heaven is perfect.

This too is one of the most fundamental sayings: *Be ye therefore perfect...* Remember, you can be perfect only because intrinsically you are perfect. You come from God, how can you be imperfect? You belong to God, how can you be imperfect? Intrinsically, you are God, because God is in you and you are in God. But you have not given

an opportunity for yourself to see into it. You are so engaged, occupied outside – doing this, doing that, bringing a little good to the
world, justice to the world, making this reform and that. You are so
much concerned with the outside, that's why you have not been
able to look into your innermost shrine. And God is there, God is
abiding in you.

Yes, you can be perfect, because you are perfect. Only the perfect can be perfect. So perfection is not to be created, it has only to
be discovered. It is already there, hidden maybe, hidden behind veils
maybe, but it is there. Remove the veils, and you will find it. You are
not to invent it, you are only to discover it. Or maybe even *discovery*
is not the right word. Let me say, rediscover it.

Enough for today.

man cannot live without meaning

The first question:

Osho,
Life seems to be meaningless. Why?

L ife is, unless you give meaning to it. There is no inbuilt meaning in it; it has to be created. It has to be introduced, it has to be provoked. If you are waiting for some ready-made meaning, you will not get it, and life will seem meaningless. Life is just blank. It is just an opportunity. You can create meaning; you can create meaninglessness too. You can create freedom, you can create an imprisonment too. It all depends on you. Your freedom is total.

Man is very afraid of this freedom because with this freedom comes great responsibilities. You would like somebody to give you meaning so that then you are not responsible. Then meaning is given to you. To create meaning means that if you miss, only you are responsible and nobody else. That creates fear. So, man has always been creating gods who give meaning to life. What exactly is the notion of a god? – someone to look to, somebody to look up to, somebody who will give meaning to you, somebody who will give salvation, bliss, *moksha*. You want to be on the receiving end, that's why people go to churches, to temples, to mosques – just to pray, "Give us meaning."

This prayer is impotent. The right prayer is to do something to create meaning. Existence cooperates, it cooperates with you – whatsoever you are doing, existence is always there to cooperate. Even if you are going against it, it cooperates with you. That's the meaning of Jesus' saying that when the clouds shower, they shower on both the just and the unjust, the good and the bad. When the sunrays fall, they fall on all unconditionally, the sinner and the saint – they don't make any distinction.

If you are simply waiting for some meaning to come into your life, you are waiting like a beggar with a begging bowl. You will never get it, and because you are waiting, you will continuously feel meaninglessness. You have an idea of meaning and you don't create it, and then you go on comparing your life with that idea and life is always falling short – great anxiety…

You are creating both. First, this idea, "I am only to be on the receiving end, I am not to be creative." And second, carrying this great idea, "Life should be like *this*, only then is it life, only then is there significance" – and then comparing it with your life. You will not find anywhere that poetry which gives you significance unless you bring it into existence, unless you create it.

Sannyas means a creative approach towards God. Your prayer should not be impotent. It should show that you really want it to be that way. You should do all that you can do – no stone should be left unturned – only then does God's help arise, come, descend, transform. God certainly comes, but only when you have done all that you could do, never before.

And the problem has become very, very great – particularly for the modern mind. In the past man has always lived with a "giver-God." He was there in heaven and everything was right on the earth. People have lived very lethargically, uncreatively, just dependent on God: praying, praising him, and thinking that they have done all that they can do – prayer and praise. Now, after Friedrich Nietzsche, that is no longer possible. That God is dead.

Let me tell you this small parable from Nietzsche:

Have you not heard of the madman who lit a lantern in the bright morning hours? – ran to the market place and cried incessantly, "I seek God! I seek God!" As many of those who did not believe in God were standing around just then, he provoked much laughter.

"Why, did he get lost?" asked one.

"Is he afraid of us? Is he hiding?" asked another.

"Has he lost his way? Or gone on a voyage? Or emigrated?" asked the third. Thus they yelled and laughed. The madman jumped into their midst and pierced them with his glances.

"Whither is God?" he cried. "I shall tell you. We have killed him – you and I. All of us are his murderers. And now we are plunging continuously into nothingness. Do you not feel the breath of empty space? Has it not become colder? Is not night and more night coming on all the while? Must not lanterns be lit even in the morning? Do we not hear anything of the noise of the grave-diggers who are digging a grave for God and burying him? Do we not smell anything yet of God's decomposition? Gods decompose too. God is dead. God remains dead. And we have killed him."

Here the madman fell silent and looked again at his listeners. And they too were silent and stared at him in astonishment. At last he threw his lantern on the ground, and it broke and went out.

"I come too early," he said to them. "My time has not come yet. The tremendous event is still on its way, still wandering. It has not yet reached the ears of man. Lightning and thunder require time, the light of the stars requires time, deeds require time, even after they are done, before they can be seen and heard. This deed is still more distant from them than the most distant stars – and they have done it themselves."

When Nietzsche's madman said, "I have come a little too early, maybe my right time has not come," people could not understand. That time has come now, after one hundred years. The whole world is full of the smell of the decomposing God. But it always happens. This parable is of infinite significance.

Each age has to create its own God, others' gods won't do. They were created by them for their own purposes, for their own ends. They have become irrelevant. They become irrelevant all the time. And whenever one God becomes irrelevant and dies, decomposes and disappears, in the wake comes great emptiness, great meaninglessness. Because that God was giving a certain meaning to people, that God was their meaning. Now he is no longer there. Suddenly you are left alone – alone on a dark night, alone on a cold night.

God was a kind of warmth; heaven was not far away, it was very close. You could have almost touched his feet any time. God was looking after you all the time. He was always observing you. You were a small child and he was your father or mother. Now that God exists no more. Now it has become very difficult to look at the sky and pray like Jesus did.

Jesus used to call God "my Father." His exact word is *abba,* which is far more loving, affectionate, closer – like *daddy. Father* is a little cold. He used to call God *abba.* You cannot say it – have you tried? Sometimes look at the sky, and just say, "Daddy" – how foolish it looks.

I have heard...

Sherwood Anderson describes his own awakening to this spiritual emptiness. He tells of walking alone late at night along a moonlit road when: "I suddenly had an odd and, to my own seeming, ridiculous desire to abase myself before something not human. And so, stepping into the moonlit road, I knelt in the dust. Having no God – the gods having been taken away from us by the life about us, as a personal God has been taken from all modern men... By a force within, that man himself does not understand, but calls the intellect, I kept smiling at the figure I cut in my own eyes as I knelt on the road."

Visualize a moonlit road, a silent night, a cool breeze, and suddenly Anderson is possessed by a desire to pray. But he says, "...a desire to abase myself..."

When there is no God, how can you pray? When there is no God, it seems to be perfectly logical to say an urge "...to abase myself..." To surrender to the nothing, to surrender to the empty sky, just "humiliate myself." Remember that word *abase.* Nobody who has prayed has said that it is abasing yourself. They have said it is praising God, raising God high. Now that there is no God and you cannot pray to God, then what are you doing kneeling in a dusty road? Maybe it is beautiful, maybe there is moonlight, maybe it is silent. So what? But you are abasing yourself in the dust.

"I kept smiling," he says, "at the figure I cut in my own eyes as I knelt on the road..." There was nobody else, but in his own eyes he was seeing the ridiculousness of it, the absurdity of it. "There was no God in the sky, no God in myself, no conviction in myself that I had the power to believe in a god. And so I merely knelt in the dust in silence and no words came to my lips."

This is the situation. You cannot call out *abba* – the word won't come to your lips. And even if you do bring it, it will be false and you will be laughing at the whole ridiculousness of it. Each age has to create a new God. Not that God dies, but the notions of God die. Now man is left in a vacuum, in an existential vacuum. The old gods have gone, and we have not created new gods. The old temple is a ruin, and we have not built a new temple. Each age has to search again and again, and rediscover God in its own way – that's why life seems to be meaningless. And now the old God cannot be revived, the old God cannot be given breath alone. That's what churches, priests are trying to do: trying to breathe into the dead God. It is not possible; man has become more grown-up. Man needs a more grown-up God. Man needs a God who can fulfill his requirements which are now.

Krishna fulfilled some people's requirement then, five thousand years ago. Jesus fulfilled some people's requirement two thousand years ago. Moses' God was not relevant to Jesus' time. Jesus' God cannot be relevant to yours. Things change, but man cannot live without God.

By "God" I mean – meaning. You can forget the word; the word does not matter. Man cannot live without meaning. He needs to feel that what he is doing has relevance, that whatsoever he is doing contributes something to the total joy, the total beauty of existence. Maybe his effort is small, his hands are tiny, but still he is not irrelevant to existence; he is required. He is fulfilling a certain need that brings meaning to life. When you are fulfilling a need, there is meaning, and with meaning there is joy. When you are not fulfilling any need, you can disappear and there will not be any change in the world; you can be replaced easily, thrown away, and somebody else will do the work. You are only a function – anybody else can fulfill it – then there arises an existential vacuum. You start feeling pain in the heart. Why go on living, for what? What is the point of it all? There seems to be no point, and it drives people crazy.

I understand your question. You ask: "Life seems to be so meaningless. Why?" It seems to be so meaningless because you have not yet taken hold of life. You have not created anything that can give significance to it.

Eliot says that man is hollow. Yes, that is true, man is hollow, but so is a bamboo hollow. But when the bamboo becomes a flute there arises meaning. And so man can become a flute. But you are not flutes, you are simply hollow bamboos.

About modern man Eliot says:

> Shape without form, shade without color.
> Paralyzed force, gesture without motion...

This is his description: "Paralyzed force, gesture without motion..." That's how Anderson must have looked in his own eyes, kneeling on a dusty road. He must have cut a very ridiculous figure.

"Shape without form, shade without color. Paralyzed force, gesture without motion..." Then your life seems to be like a wasteland, a desert where no river flows, no trees grow, no birds sing – nothing happens. It is a nightmare. One goes on and on and nothing happens. And one day one falls down and disappears into the dust – dust to dust...

Leo Tolstoy was very interested in the dreams of his friends. Sitting with Maxim Gorky, they were talking of things, gossiping, and suddenly he asked Gorky, "Can you tell me one of your dreams which you have not forgotten, which has remained special to you in all your life's dreams?"

And Gorky said: "Yes, there has been one dream that I cannot forget. And it has not happened once, it has happened many times in the same way again and again. So it goes on being more and more impressed onto my consciousness."

Tolstoy became very interested. He said, "Tell me, tell me immediately."

And Gorky said: "The dream is that I see a vast desert with no trees, no people, no animals, utterly, utterly empty, sands and sands and sands. And the sun is burning so hot, it is fire. And I see myself walking to nowhere in particular. There is nowhere to go, no destination. Not only that, the strange thing is that I see only my feet and my shoes. I cannot see anything else. I try and I try, and it becomes very, very crazy. I cannot see my face, I cannot see my body, I cannot see my hands – just two feet covered in leather shoes. I can hear the noise that they are making, and those two feet go on and on and on in that desert – to nowhere! And it seems to continue for ages.

"Nothing happens, just those two legs without the body, without the soul, without the face. Where are they going, and why are they going in the first place? And what is the point of going? Why can't they stop? All these questions arise, and great fear grips my soul, and I always awake out of it trembling, shaking, perspiring."

The dream is symbolic. That dream is what modern man has become.

Unless you create your face you will not find a face. You come faceless into the world. Unless you create your soul, you don't have any. You can have only that which you create.

A Buddha has a soul, a Jesus has a soul, you don't. Don't take it for granted. That has been one of the causes of the greatest miseries to humanity: that people think they have souls. How can you have if you have not created it in the first place? You can have only that which you create. You can possess only that which you have created.

Religion should be that creativity – creating a soul, creating a face, creating a being out of nothingness. Then there is joy, there is great exaltation. Then life has zest, juice, flow, thrill. Life pulsates, is adventure, is not a monotony, is not a nightmare. Trees start growing in your desert, birds start singing in your wasteland, flowers come, clouds come, and the emptiness is no longer empty; it is full of life.

Let me repeat, the meaning has to be created.

The second question:

Osho,
Sometimes I have the feeling that you are not quoting the Bible correctly.

That's possible. I am not a scholar, and if sometimes it is correct, it is a miracle. It must be a coincidence. I am not a Christian either. I am not concerned with what exactly is written in the book, I am more concerned with what happened to Jesus in his innermost core. It has happened to me too, so I know what it is. When I am saying anything, I am not saying it according to the Bible, but according to christ consciousness. And if sometimes you find that I am saying something which is not in the Bible, then at least you can add it to your Bible. And it will be absolutely true.

It is possible... I am a drunkard; I speak out of my drunkenness. If you are listening from a scholarly standpoint, you may be worried, puzzled, and you will miss much.

You will have to remember again and again that I may not be true to the letter but I am true to the spirit. But you have been taught what is in the Bible, you have been forced to learn it. It is crammed into your heads, and whenever you see something different, naturally you become puzzled.

Somebody else has also asked: "It seems that Christ is not the type for you. He seems to be too much of a moralist. And the sutras that you have covered," he has said, "were very different to the meaning that you have given to them." That too will be apparent to you many times, but it is only apparent, it is not true. In fact you don't know Jesus as he was. You know the Jesus that Christianity has depicted for you. You know a Jesus through the Christian interpretation, and you have believed that this is so. Those moralistic interpretations are Christian interpretations. Jesus needs better treatment. He needs to be brought to the world again in his originality.

He was one of the most amoral persons. That's why the Jews were so much against him. The Jews of his day were very moralistic people, very law-abiding. Their anger against Jesus was basically that he was not law-abiding, and he was bringing dangerous intuitions to people. He was bringing a kind of lawlessness.

Jews have always been a law-abiding people. That's why all the great revolutionaries of the world have come from the Jews. It is not accidental. When a society is very law-abiding, as a reaction it creates the revolutionary. Jesus is a great revolutionary. Karl Marx is also a Jew, and a great revolutionary. Sigmund Freud is also a Jew, and a great revolutionary. So is Albert Einstein.

These four people have influenced the history of humanity as nobody else has ever done. Why? Jews are so law-abiding, so righteous that sooner or later somebody is born who rebels against it. Only in a law-abiding society can the rebel be born. You will be surprised: here also, more than half the people are Jews, which is strange. It is out of all proportion. Again and again Vivek brings the

news, "This sannyasin is also a Jew. That sannyasin is also a Jew."
And sometimes I start suspecting – maybe I am a Jew, or what? If
everybody is a Jew, then I must be a Jew.

In India, Jews are nonexistent. This may be the only place where
you can find Jews, and there are so many that this is almost a
Jewish place, a Jerusalem. But why? The society is too law-abiding,
too traditional, so anybody who has some intelligence starts
rebelling. He starts escaping, he starts finding new ways of being.
That's why so many Jews are here.

The Jews were angry because he was amoral – not immoral, but
amoral. By amoral I mean his morality was inner, it was not from the
outside. His morality was spontaneous. He lived each moment, he
had no plan, he had no blueprint for how to live. He was a conscious
being, and again and again he would decide each moment. He
would not carry any conclusion from the past. He would simply be
there in the situation and let the situation decide. His response was
always fresh, that's why there are so many contradictions in the
Bible – there are bound to be.

A man who lives moment to moment will have many contradictions. He cannot be very consistent; only dead people can be consistent. A man who is really alive each moment goes on changing,
because life changes, so he changes. He is never out of tune with life,
he is always in tune with life. And life is inconsistent, so he becomes
inconsistent. A truly great man is so vast, he contains contradictions.

Jesus contains great contradictions. One of the logicians of the
French Revolution, Voltaire, has shouted almost madly, "Down with
this scoundrel!" – and by "this scoundrel" he means Jesus. Why?
Why should Voltaire, a man of very rational grounding, logic, philosophy, call Jesus a scoundrel? "Down with this scoundrel!" – because
Jesus is so contradictory. In fact you cannot follow Jesus without
going crazy. You cannot follow me without going crazy. That's why I
say: "Don't follow me. Just understand me."

And so I say about Jesus: "Understand him; there is no need to
follow." If you follow, that will be against Jesus, because he never followed anybody. If you follow Jesus you will be carrying a blueprint in
your head, and you will always be looking from that blueprint: what
to do, what not to do? He never carried any conclusions; he lived an
open life.

When I am responding on Jesus' sayings, many times you will

feel that I am not saying that which has been taught to you.

My situation is like this:

A new priest at his first mass was so scared, he couldn't even speak. After mass he asked the Monsignor how he had got on, and the Monsignor said fine, only next week it might help if he put vodka or gin in his water glass to help relax him.

The next Sunday the priest put vodka in his glass and really talked a storm. After mass he again asked the Monsignor how he had done. The Monsignor said: "Fine, but that there were a few things that should be straightened out. First, there are ten commandments, not twelve. Second, there are twelve disciples, not ten. Third, David slew Goliath with a sling, he didn't knock his head off with the jawbone of an ass. We do not refer to Jesus Christ as 'the late J. C.' And next Sunday there is a taffy-pulling contest at St. Peter's, not a Peter-pulling contest at St. Taffy's. And sixth, the Father, Son and Holy Ghost are not referred to as: 'Big Daddy,' 'Junior,' and 'Spook.'"

I am a drunkard, there is too much vodka in me. So sometimes if I go a little astray, forgive me.

The third question:

Osho,
How can my judgmental, self-opinionated, guilt-inducing, fearful mind be mutated? It is giving me the shits. I'm completely fed-up with it.

First, it need not be mutated, it has only to be dropped – not mutated. You don't mutate a disease, you drop it. You don't mutate something that is wrong inside you, you simply get rid of it. Mind needs no mutation. Just see the point that it is a kind of cancerous growth in you, then drop it. In fact, in understanding that it is a cancerous growth, you will drop it. The very seeing will become the dropping of it.

You still want to mutate it? You still want to keep it – a little more painted, polished, a change here and there, a little whitewash and renovation? Then you are not really fed-up with it. You still have some infatuation with it, you want to keep it. You want to keep it, maybe in a little reformed, modified way, but you want to keep the continuity. And that is the whole point, the very crux of the whole problem.

You should become discontinuous with the mind – that is muta- tion, that is revolution – discontinuous. When you become very intensely aware of all the nonsense and nuisance that the mind has done to you, you don't ask how to transform it, how to reform it, how to make it a little more civilized and tame, how to make it a little more sophisticated, how to make it so one can live with it con- veniently, comfortably, how to rub its corners a little bit and make them smooth. Then it will be the same thing. Maybe the disease will be there in a subtle form, and the subtle form is more dangerous than the gross form, because the subtle goes deeper than the gross.

You say: "How can my judgmental, self-opinionated, guilt induc- ing, fearful mind be mutated?" There is no need to go on having your mind. It is not of any worth. Drop it, and then you will have the universal mind functioning in you. Because of your mind the uni- versal cannot function. You go on interfering, you don't allow the cosmic mind to function in you. You are the barrier, the hindrance, the obstruction. Now, the obstruction is not to be made better, the obstruction has to be removed – utterly removed.

And you say: "It is giving me the shits. I'm completely fed-up with it." Not completely. If you are completely fed-up with it, you will not even ask the question. Who is forcing you to keep this mind? You are not completely fed-up with it. There must be some subtle infatu- ation still lingering. You are still hoping against hope that maybe something better can come out of it: "It is such a beautiful mind, maybe something is wrong that can be put right. Some nuts and bolts are loose, they can be tightened. Something is missing, it can be brought from the outside. Something is nonfunctioning, it can be cleaned, made to function." But this will be just a reformation. You will have a better cultured mind. That does not make any difference. The mind will be there, and the mind creates the barrier between you and God, because *your* mind means the cosmic mind is not allowed to function unhindered. You are standing there, choosing, deciding, concluding – according to your notions, ideologies, ideas, scriptures, experiences. God comes to you, but your mind colors the whole thing so much that you cannot know what is coming to you.

Open the window, let there be no hindrance, no curtain. Look directly into existence without your mind coming in. If it happens even for a single moment, you will have such a great insight. It can happen. It has happened to me, it has happened to Jesus, it has happened to Buddha. It can happen to you because you all carry the seed; the essential seed of it is in you. So don't be in a hurry. If you are not totally fed-up with it, get a little more fed-up with it. But it needs a let-go.

A mountain climber was halfway up a steep precipice when suddenly he slipped and began plummeting towards the valley below. After falling several hundred feet, he was luckily able to grab on to a small tree growing out of a crack in the sheer vertical face of the mountain.

As he was clinging on for dear life, he looked up into the sky and said, "Lord, please save me."

A booming voice answered back and said, "Let go and have faith!"

The man, still hanging on, thought for a moment and then looked up again and said, "Is there anyone else up there?"

That is the situation. I am telling you: "Let go of it. In its very dropping is the benediction." But you are afraid of dropping it. You are so much identified with it – you think it is you! That is the problem. And when you say, "I am fed-up with it," who is this "I am"? It is again part of the same mind. The mind is very cunning in playing games. It divides itself and goes on playing games. This one who says, "I am fed-up," is but a part of the mind and this is the game of the mind: it divides and then goes on playing the game of hide-and-seek. The one that you are fed-up with and the one which is fed-up are both the same. The object and subject are both the same. See it! Look into it, and you will be able to see because it is so. I am just stating a fact. Seeing it, you will start laughing. If you listen to this mind which says, "I am fed-up with the mind," you will again strengthen the mind from another side. They are complementary to each other. They are not enemies, they supplement each other.

Just be choiceless. Don't choose. Choice brings the mind in. Choice is mind. That's why all the ancient scriptures and all the ancient masters have been talking about only one thing: "Be a witness. Just watch what is happening."

Ask, "Who is fed-up with the mind?" And you will see that it is the mind creating a new game – deceiving you again on a subtler and deeper level. And it can go on and on. Just watch. Don't decide. Don't take sides. Go on watching. Watching is a little arduous, because the mind says: "Do something. Either be for this side or that, but do something. Don't just go on sitting there silently and watching" – because mind becomes very afraid when you simply watch.

My suggestion for you is, for three months simply watch without deciding that you have to do anything about the mind. Go on watching. On each subtler level, go on watching. And in those three months some day you will have the first glimpse of no-mind. It may only be for a moment, but that will become the turning-point in your life. From that moment, more and more moments will be coming to you. And soon you will see that without doing anything about the mind, the mind has started receding backwards. It is going far away. It still makes a noise, but it is very distant, you remain unperturbed by it. One day, suddenly it has gone; you are left alone. And when you are left alone, you are in godliness.

You have always been in godliness, but because of the interference of the mind, it was not possible for you to look into your own self.

The fourth question:

Osho,
This question has been hovering in me for years. A few times you have talked around it, but this has mystified me more, so please enlighten. When and where did enlightenment happen to Jesus? Was he born enlightened? – as it is said some three wise men from the East traveled to have darshan with the baby Jesus. Or did enlightenment happen to Jesus when he was secretly and anonymously traveling in Tibet and India, visiting Buddhist monasteries? Or did enlightenment happen to Jesus when he was initiated by John the Baptist in the river Jordan? Or did enlightenment happen to Jesus when he was on the cross saying, "Lord, thy kingdom come, thy will be done"?

There are three stages of enlightenment.
The first is when the first glimpse happens. I call it mini-satori:

when, for the first time, for a single moment the mind is not functioning, there is a gap – no thought between you and existence.
You and existence, you and existence... For a moment... And the
meeting, and the merging, and the communion, and the orgasm...
But for a moment. From that moment the seed will be in your heart
and growing.

The second I call satori: that is when you have become capable
of retaining this gap as long as you want. For hours together, for
days together you can remain in this interval, in this utter aloneness,
in godliness, with godliness, as godliness. But a little effort is still
needed on your part. If you drop the effort the satori disappears. The
first satori, the mini-satori, happened almost by accident – you were
not even expecting it. How can you expect? You had not known it
before, you had never tasted it. How can you expect it? It came just
out of the blue. Yes, you were doing many things – praying, meditating, dancing, singing – but they were all like groping in the dark.
You were groping.

It will not happen if you are not groping at all. It happens only to
"gropers," real gropers – they go on groping, they never feel tired
and exhausted, and they never feel hopeless. Millions of times they
are defeated in their effort, and nothing happens, but they go on and
on. Their passion for godliness is so tremendous. They can accept
all kinds of defeats and frustrations, but their search continues.
Unwavering, they go on groping. The darkness is great, it seems to
be almost endless, but their hope is greater than the darkness. That
is the meaning of faith; they grope through faith.

Faith means hoping for that which seems almost impossible.
Faith means hoping against all hope. Faith means trying to see that
which you have not seen, and you cannot even be certain whether it
exists or not. A great passion is needed to have that much faith.

So to a groper who lives in faith and goes on and on, nothing
ever prevents him. No failure ever settles in him; his journey continues. He is the pilgrim. Then one day it comes just out of the blue.
You were not expecting it. Unawares, it comes close to you and surrounds you. For a moment you cannot even believe it. How can you
believe it? – for millions of lives a person has been groping, and it
has not happened. The first time it looks almost like imagination,
dream. But it is there, and it is so real that all that you have known
as real before pales before it, becomes very faint. It is so real that it

carries its certainty intrinsically. It is self-evident. You cannot suspect it. That is the criterion of whether the mini-satori has happened or not: you cannot doubt it. You can try, but you cannot doubt it. It is so certain that no doubt arises in that moment. It is simply there. It is like the sun has risen – how can you doubt?

Then the second becomes a more conscious groping. Now you know it is, now you know it has happened. Now you know it has even happened to you! Now there is a great certainty. Now faith is not needed, now experience is enough. Now belief is not needed. Now its certainty permeates your whole being, you are full of it. Now you grope more consciously, you make an effort in the right direction. Now you know how it happened, when it happened, in what space it became possible. You were dancing? – then what was happening when it happened? In what way did the contact become possible? By and by, it happens again and again, and you can make out, figure out, reckon out how it happens, in what mood. In what mood do you fall in tune with it and it happens? Now things become clearer, now it is not just waiting in the darkness. You can start moving, you can have a direction.

Still you falter, still sometimes you fall, still sometimes it disappears for months. But never again can doubt arise in you. The doubt has been killed by the first satori. Then, more and more, it will come. And sooner or later you will become capable of bringing it on order. Whenever you want you can create that milieu in you which brings it. You can relax, if it comes in relaxation; you can dance, if it comes in dance. You can go under the sky if it comes there. You can watch a roseflower if it happens there. You can go and float in a river if it happens there.

That's how all the methods have been discovered. They have been discovered by people when they found out that in a certain situation – when they make certain arrangements – it happens. Those became methods. By and by you become very, very certain that if you desire it, any moment you will be able, because you can move your focus towards it. You can move your whole consciousness, you can direct your being.

Now you become able to see that it is always there; just your contact is needed. It is almost like your radio or like your TV, it is always there, sounds are always passing; you just have to tune the radio to a certain station, and the song, and the news... This is the second stage.

But still, effort is needed to tune. You are not continuously tuned on your own, you have to work it out. Some days it is easy, some days it is hard. If you are in a negative mood it is hard, if you are angry it is hard. If you are loving it is easier. In the early morning it is easier, in the evening it is more difficult. Alone on a mountain it is easier, in the marketplace it is more difficult. So you start coming closer and closer, but still effort is needed.

Then the third thing happens. When you become so capable of finding it that any moment, whenever you want it – not a single moment is lost – you immediately can pinpoint it, then the third thing happens. It becomes a natural quality. That I call *samadhi*.

Satori one, satori two, satori three... The first satori must have happened somewhere in the East – in Tibet or in India. Jesus was with Buddhist masters. The first satori must have happened somewhere here, because to the Jews, *samadhi* had never been a concern.

Jesus brings something very foreign to the Jewish world: he introduces Buddha into the Jewish world. It must have happened somewhere in Nalanda, where he stayed for many years. But he was traveling – he was in Egypt, he was in India, in Tibet – so nobody can be certain of where it happened. But the greater possibility is India: it remains for centuries the country where satori has been more available than anywhere else, because so many people have been meditating here. Their meditation has created very potential spots, very available spots. It must have happened somewhere here, but there is no record, so I'm not saying anything historical.

But about the second: it is certain it happened in the River Jordan with John the Baptist when he initiated Jesus into his path – the path of the Essenes. John the Baptist was a great master, a very revolutionary prophet. The second satori must have happened there. It is depicted as a white dove descending on Jesus. The white dove has always been the symbol of peace, silence. That is the symbol for satori: the unknown descending. The second satori must have happened there, and John the Baptist said, "My work is finished. The man has come who will take it over from me. Now I can renounce and go into the mountains. I was waiting for this man."

And the third happened just on the cross – the last effort of the ego – very tiny, but still... Jesus must have desired how things should be in some way. Deep down, in some unconscious nook or corner of his being, he must have been hoping that God would save him. And

God never moves according to you. Man proposes and God disposes – that's how he teaches you to disappear, that's how he teaches you not to will on your own, not to have a private will. And the last lesson happened on the cross, at the last moment. Jesus shouted, almost in agony: "Why have you forsaken me? Why have you deserted me? What wrong have I done?"

But he was a man of great insight – the man of second satori. Immediately he must have become aware that this was wrong: "That means I still have a desire of my own, a will of my own. That means I still am not totally in God. My surrender is still only ninety-nine percent." And a surrender that is ninety-nine percent is a no-surrender, because surrender is one hundred percent. A circle is a circle only when it is complete. You can't call half of a circle a half-circle, because *circle* means complete. There are no half-circles. There is no approximate truth. The approximate truth is still a lie; either it is true or it is not true. There is nothing like approximate truth, and there is nothing like approximate surrender.

In that moment he realized. He relaxed, he surrendered. He said: "Let thy kingdom come. Who am I to interfere? Let thy will be done..." and the third satori: *samadhi*. That moment, Jesus disappeared. And I call that moment his resurrection. That is the moment Buddha says, "*Gate, gate, paragate, parasamgate, bodhi svaha* – gone, gone, gone beyond, gone altogether beyond." What ecstasy! Alleluia! That is the moment of absolute benediction. Jesus became God. The Son became Father in that moment; all distinction disappeared. The last barrier dissolved, Jesus had come home.

The fifth question:

Osho,
What happens in, and with the relationship between two partners if their egos drop?

Then relationship happens. Before that it is just an empty name. Relationship cannot happen before the egos are gone.

You only believe that it is a relationship. It is a conflict, it is enmity, it is jealousy, it is aggression, it is domination, it is possession, and many things – but not a relationship. How can you relate with two egos there? When there are two egos, then there are four persons.

In every bed you will find four persons sleeping together. It is very rare to find a double bed, because then there are four persons overcrowding it. The wife is there and the ego, and the husband is there and the ego – the husband is hidden behind his ego, the wife is hidden behind her ego, and those two egos go on making love. The real contact never happens.

The word *relationship* is beautiful. The original meaning of the root from which the word *to relate* comes, is exactly the same as *to respond*. Relationship comes from that word *respond*. If you have any image of your wife or husband, you cannot respond, and hence relate, to the truth of the person. And we all go on carrying images.

First, we have the image that is our ego: who I am. And then we have the image of the other: who she is, or he is. The husband relates not to the woman that is there, he relates to the woman he thinks is there. So now there are not four, there are six, and it goes on become more crowded. Now *you* are there – that is one thing, and your ego is there – that is another thing. And now you don't relate to the woman who is there, you relate to the idea of your woman: "My wife is such and such, or should be such and such," and she is also having these things – so six persons. It is really a miracle how people go on managing. It is very complicated. A relationship is not possible, there are too many people in between. You go on reacting to the image, not to the person, and hence there is no relationship. When there is no image, then there is a relationship.

See it! And see it immediately, without the interference of thought. Don't have any image of the person you love. If you love me, don't have any image of me. There is no need. Just look into me as I am. The image will not allow you to see who I am. Don't have any image of the person you love; the person is enough. The truth of the person is enough, whatsoever it is. And don't have any image of yourself; just be true, authentic, as you are. There will be a relationship. Then there will be a response. Then two realities will respond to each other. And when realities respond there is great harmony, melody, joy. There is great beauty.

Don't have any image of me, don't have any image of your husband, don't have any image of your son, don't have any image of Jesus, and don't have any image of God. If you can drop all your images, you will enter into a totally different dimension: the separate reality, the other shore. Approach truth imageless, thoughtless, nude, empty, uncovered, and the response will come out of your being of its own accord.

You ask me: "What happens in and with the relationship between two partners if their egos drop?" Then love happens, then ecstasy happens. Then that very relationship becomes sacred, it becomes a shrine. And through that door you can reach to God. You have to grow more and more towards the state where the "I" is not present at all. This is the goal of all love, and this is the misery of all lovers. They want this to happen and it doesn't happen, then there is great misery, then they feel cheated, then they feel frustrated. Then they start thinking of changing the partner.

Every day some couple comes to me and says, "We would like to change partners. Enough is enough. We are tired." But what will you do? You will do the same with another person. It is not going to make much difference. Maybe for a few days, the fantasy, the romance, the honeymoon, and again... And they know it – because they have done it before too. They nod their heads in agreement. And they say, "Yes, that's true. I have been doing this to many women. But what to do? I am stuck again."

Rather than changing the partner, rather than dropping your woman or man, drop your ego. Dropping that ego, a different quality starts taking shape in your life, a different light, a different vision. And things settle in that vision. With that light coming in, all old miseries and conflicts and anguishes disappear. The same energy that was becoming conflict starts becoming your joy. That's what Jesus means when he says: "Don't go on squandering your energies in fighting, anger, objecting."

Veetmoha's mother has come here, a beautiful old woman. She has heard me – I think only once, yesterday. And she was puzzled about one thing. She said to Veetmoha: "What is the matter? I like what Osho says, but nobody objects. Whatsoever he goes on saying, people listen. Nobody is objecting, what is the matter?" Her question is very natural. She must have seen lectures where somebody speaks, somebody objects – raises a question – and there is a quarrel, and discussion and argument. She must have been hoping for something like that. Here she sees people just sitting silently, utterly in silence, listening. This is the whole approach here. Objecting has to be dropped. Listening has to be evolved. Argument has to be dropped. A no-arguing communion has to be developed.

That is the difference between an ordinary meeting and a meeting of the master and the disciples.

The disciples are not there with their egos to object or to argue. They are there to dissolve themselves; they are there to fall in tune with the master. What he is saying is not relevant, it is not a question of agreeing or not agreeing. That is irrelevant. What I go on saying to you is just an excuse to allow you to be here with me. It will be difficult for you to be with me if I go on sitting in silence. Your mind has to be kept engaged. Your mind remains engaged, your heart opens. And the real thing is going to happen there in the heart, not in the mind. If the mind starts objecting, the heart closes. Then you become too hung-up in the head.

Yes, I go on giving you toys for the head. These are all toys. Your head goes on playing with the toys, and the real work is happening somewhere else. It is happening in the heart. If you are arguing, it will be difficult. Then your heart cannot open. And remember, let me repeat, it is not a question of agreeing with me or not agreeing, that is irrelevant. There is no need to agree and no need to disagree. You can just be here without agreeing, without disagreeing, and something will start growing in you. And that is the real thing.

What I say is just an excuse. What I am is the real thing.

The last question:

Osho,
Why did Jesus' parents name him Jesus?

I don't know. I don't even know why my parents named me Rajneesh. I have never asked them. But I have heard a story. Maybe that will help you a little bit.

I have heard…

It was in Bethlehem. The child had just been born and the three wise men were paying their respects. Each of them took it in turn to bow and present their gift.

The first said, "Truly a savior," and went out.

The second: "He will influence the whole world."

The third, overcome with emotion and awe, silently placed his gift at the babe's feet and left. As he passed out of the stable door he bashed his head on the low beam and cried out "Jesus!"

Mary smiled and said, "That's nice! – we were going to call him Fred."

Enough for today.

CHAPTER 5

a journey between two infinities

Matthew 6

Jesus said unto his disciples:

And when thou prayest, thou shalt not be as the hypocrites are: for they love to pray standing in the synagogues and in the corners of the streets, that they may be seen of men. Verily I say unto you, they have their reward.

But thou, when thou prayest, enter into thy closet, and when thou hast shut thy door, pray to thy Father in secret.

But when ye pray, use not vain repetitions, as the heathen do: for they think that they shall be heard for their much speaking.

Be not ye therefore like unto them: for your Father knoweth what things ye have need of, before ye ask him.

After this manner therefore pray ye: Our Father which art in heaven, Hallowed be thy name.

Thy kingdom come. Thy will be done in earth, as it is in heaven.

Give us this day our daily bread.

And forgive us our debts, as we forgive our debtors.

And lead us not into temptation, but deliver us from evil: For thine is the kingdom, and the power, and the glory, for ever.

Amen.

Matthew 7

Give not that which is holy unto the dogs, neither cast ye your pearls before swine, lest they trample them under their feet, and turn again and rend you.

Ask, and it shall be given you; seek, and ye shall find; knock, and it shall be opened unto you:

For every one that asketh receiveth; and he that seeketh findeth; and to him that knocketh it shall be opened.

Therefore all things whatsoever ye would that men should do to you, do ye even so to them: for this is the law and the prophets.

Enter ye in at the strait gate: for wide is the gate, and broad is the way, that leadeth to destruction, and many there be which go in thereat:

Because strait is the gate, and narrow is the way, which leadeth unto life, and few there be that find it.

Man is mind. The word *man* itself comes from the Sanskrit root *man*, which means mind. If you understand the workings of the mind, you will understand the reality of man and the possibility too. If you understand the inner mechanism of the mind, you will understand the past of man, the present and the future too.

Man in himself is not a being but a passage. In himself man is not a being, because man is continuously a becoming. There is no rest in being a man. Rest is below man or above man. Below is nature, above is godliness. Man is just in between: a link, a ladder. You cannot rest on a ladder; you cannot stop on the ladder. The ladder cannot become your abode. Man has to be surpassed, man has to be transcended.

Man is a journey between your two infinities. One infinity is your nature; the other infinity is your hidden godliness. And man is just between the two, a ferry boat. Use it, but don't be confined by it. Use it, but don't be defined by it. Always remember that you have to go beyond. The whole message of Jesus is how to go beyond man. That's why he says again and again: "I am the Son of man and the Son of God." He goes on insisting on this contradiction, because he wants it to be completely clear that man is both: on the one hand part of nature, on the other hand part of God. That is the meaning of the word *son*; son means a part of the father.

And because man belongs to these two realities – two separate realities – there is anxiety in man, there is tension in man, there is constant conflict in man, because these two natures go on fighting. Hence, as man, there is no possibility of peace. Either you have to become absolutely unconscious, like a drunkard when he has taken so much alcohol that he has lost all his consciousness – then there is peace. Or you will have to become so conscious that all the nooks and corners of your being are full of light – you become a buddha or a christ – then there is peace. Either fall below man, or go beyond man. Don't go on clinging to being a man, because then you are clinging to a disease.

That's exactly what man is: a disease, a constant tension – to be or not to be, to be this or to be that – a constant fight between the soul and the body, the lower and the higher, unconsciousness and consciousness. To understand man as a conflict, to understand man as a constant tension will help immensely, because then you stop clinging to man as such. Rather, on the contrary, you start thinking: "How to go beyond, how to transcend, how to surpass?"

Friedrich Nietzsche is right when he says that man is the only animal who tries to surpass himself, the only animal who can surpass himself. It is the greatest miracle in the world: to surpass oneself. But it has happened. It has happened in a christ, in a buddha, in a krishna. It can happen in you. You are a great promise, a project, an adventure. But don't start thinking about yourself as if you have arrived. Then you cling somewhere in between, and a part of you will be pulled to one side and the other part to another side – you will be torn apart. You will remain in anguish, and your existence will be nothing but a long, long ongoing nightmare.

Before we enter the sutras, a few things about the mind – because man is mind. The first state of mind we can call "pre-mind." It exists in a very small child – very primitive, animal-like. Hence the beauty of children, and the innocence, and the grace, because that anxiety which we call man has not yet evolved. The child is at ease. The child is not yet a traveler, he has not yet left his home in search for some other home. The pilgrimage has not started yet. The child is at rest – perfectly at ease and happy to be whatsoever he is. That's why his eyes have no anxiety, and the child has a certain grace around him. But this grace is going to be lost.

This grace cannot stay forever, because it is unconscious, because it has not been earned, because it is a natural gift, and the child is completely oblivious to it. He cannot hold onto it. How can you hold onto something when you are unconscious of it? It has to be lost. The only way to gain it is to lose it. The child will have to go into corruption, into perversion. The child will have to go into the cunningness of the mind, and then the child will understand that he has lost something – something immensely valuable.

One can know it only when it is lost. There is no other way to know it. Then the search starts. Religion is nothing but the search for the lost childhood. Everybody carries the memory of it, the very alive memory of it, somewhere deep down. Maybe not very consciously, but it functions like an unconscious substratum that something has been lost, something has been forgotten, something was there which is no longer there; something is being missed, and one starts searching for it.

The first stage is pre-mind. There is no responsibility, because a child knows nothing of duty, the child knows nothing of values, virtues. The child knows nothing of sainthood, so he is not aware of sin either. He exists before the diversion, he exists before those two paths of sin and sainthood diverge, separate and go apart. He is in a kind of primitive unity. This cannot last for long, it is going to go, but it has not gone yet. This is the state of the child nearabout three years of age.

Between three and four the child loses his innocence, loses his virginity, loses nature and becomes part of the civilized world – really becomes man.

This pre-mind is instinctive. It is very intelligent, but the intelligence is not intellectual, the intelligence is purely instinctive. The child functions very intelligently but not intellectually. The intelligence that a child shows is natural, he has not learned it. It is part of the wisdom of his body, it is inherited. The child has no idea of good and bad, so there is never any conflict. His desires are pure. Whatsoever he desires, he desires passionately, totally. No problem arises in his mind whether this desire is right or wrong. Whenever he is in a certain mood, he is totally in it – but his moods are momentary. He has no identity, he is unpredictable: one moment he is loving, another moment he is angry. And you cannot say to him, "You are contradictory." He is very inconsistent because he is always true to the moment – not that he does anything consciously, it is just natural.

So the innocence is there, but it is not very deep. The innocence is there, but it has no meditativeness in it. It is shallow, momentary, temporary, tentative. The child is more like an animal than like a man. The child is the link between the man and the animal. The child passes through all the stages that man has passed through down the ages. The scientists say that during the nine months in the mother's womb the child passes through millions of years of evolution. He starts like a fish – as life started on the earth – and then by and by, he goes on growing. Within days he is passing through thousands, millions of years; in nine months he has passed through the whole of evolution. But even when the child is born, he is still not yet man – at least not civilized – he is primitive, the cave-man.

The child lives in an inner chaos. He has no idea what he is going to do. He has no future, he carries no past; he lives utterly in the present. But because he lives utterly in the present and unconsciously, his life cannot have a discipline, an order. It is chaotic, it is anarchic. This is the first stage of man, the first stage of mind. And remember that although sooner or later you lose it, it remains like a substratum in you. You can lose it totally only when meditation has gone deep, when meditation has transformed your being. Otherwise it remains there, and you can fall into it at any moment; in any stress, in any strain, you can again become childish.

For example, your house is on fire, and you can start crying like a child. And you are not a man who cries ordinarily – nobody may have ever seen you crying – but your house is on fire and suddenly you forget that you are a grown-up man. You become like a small child, you start crying, tears come to your eyes, you are completely lost, helpless. What has happened? That pre-mind has reclaimed you. It was always there. You had grown a second layer upon it, on top of it, but it was there deep down. When the second layer cannot function, in a deep helplessness you fall to the first layer. This happens every day.

In anger you become more childish, in love also you become more childish. Listen to the dialogue of two lovers, and you will find it very childish. Remember your own memories when you first fell in love: how you behaved, what you said to your beloved or your lover, and you will find childishness. Or remember when somebody provoked you and you became angry – you started doing things which were very illogical, unintelligent, undisciplined, chaotic. You repent for them later on, because later on, when the second layer comes back, the second layer repents for the first layer. When the civilized mind comes back, takes hold again, it repents. It says, "It was not good of me. It was not good to do."

The first layer never completely goes unless you become a christ or a buddha. It remains there. Watch it. The first layer is very, very chaotic. The second layer is collective. The second mind I call the "collective mind." Now the group, the family, the society, and the nation become more important than yourself. A child is very, very self-oriented, he thinks only of himself. He does not care for anything else; he is utterly selfish. The second mind starts thinking of others, starts sacrificing its own interests, becomes more collective, becomes more part of society, a clan, a tribe – starts becoming civilized. Civilization means to become part of a society, to become part of many people: to become responsible, not to go on living a selfish existence. Civilization means sacrificing oneself for others.

This second mind is very prevalent. Except in very rare cases, the first mind sooner or later disappears. In some imbeciles, idiots, the first layer never disappears; it remains predominant. They never learn how to be social; they remain primitive. Otherwise, normally the second layer evolves: the schooling, the family training, the teachers, the society, the experiences, the observation. And the child starts learning that he is not an island, but a member of an organism: the society, the church, the nation.

This second, collective mind has a certain identity. The first mind knows no identity. If you ask a child, "Who are you?" he can't answer it. He does not know the answer: who he is. But a grown-up person can say, "Yes, I am a Catholic, I am a communist, I am a Hindu, I am an Indian, I am a German, I am an Italian." What is he saying? He is saying, "I belong to this group called Hindu, or Christian, or Mohammedan. I belong to this nation, to this geography: India, Germany, Italy." Or, "I belong to this ideology: communism, Catholicism, fascism." He is saying, "I am to whom I belong."

Now he has an identity. He can say, "I am a doctor, or an engineer, or a businessman," then too he is saying, "This is what I do. This is my function in society." When you ask somebody, "Who are you?" he answers by showing you where he belongs, to whom he belongs, what his function is in society. Now this is not much self-knowledge. If this is self-knowledge then everybody knows who he is. But for utilitarian purposes it is enough, and many people stop there.

If you stop there you will never know who you are. Then you have taken just a false identity. Just a few labels, and you think, "This is me." It is not you. You exist on a far higher plane, or in a deeper depth. These labels that you have collected about yourself are good for functioning in the society as a member, but they don't show anything about your reality. The inward reality remains untouched by them. But this is the second layer where almost everybody stops. The society does not want you to go beyond it. Their effort of the school, the college, the university is that you should not remain childish, you should become civilized, and then their effort ends. Then society's work is finished.

The society has made you a member of the mass, has made you a kind of slave, has given you a certain imprisonment, has taken all that was dangerous in you: the chaos, the freedom, the irresponsibility; has made you dutiful, responsible, given you values – what is good and what is not good – has pigeonholed you, categorized you. Now the society is finished. Now live silently, go to the office, come home, take care of your children, your parents, and so on and so forth. One day, die; your existence is complete. This is a very false completion, a routine existence.

Friedrich Nietzsche has called this state "the camel": the beast of burden. This is the "camel" state. People go on carrying great loads and burdens for no reason at all. And they go on moving in a desert, like the camel moves in a desert. You can see these camels all around: dry, dull, dead, still carrying, carrying great loads. The loads are crushing them, killing them, but they are carrying – maybe just out of habit, because yesterday they were carrying and the day before yesterday they were also carrying. It has become part of their habit, it has become part of their definition. Their load, their anxiety, their sadness, their misery has become part of their definition, their identity. These camels you will find everywhere, and this desert is all over the earth.

The child has to come from the first to the second, but nobody should stop there. To be a camel is not the goal. Something more is needed, something more existential is needed. Yes, you will have respectability if you are a good camel and carry great loads. People will respect you, they will all show honor towards you. That's a kind of mutual understanding. When a person is carrying so much of a load, he has to be given some awards – that's what respect is.

The word *respect* is beautiful, it means to look again, *re-spect*. When a person is carrying a great load of responsibility, duty, family, society, people look at him and say, "Look, what a great man!" *Re-spect*. They look again and again and they say, "Look how much of a burden he is carrying. What sacrifice!" He has sacrificed his whole being.

Naturally if you sacrifice yourself for the religion, the religion will sanctify you, will call you a saint. If you sacrifice for the country, the country will give you respect. If you sacrifice for something else, they will give you respect. One can go on collecting this respect, and one can go on dying without living at all. Beware of this situation.

In this state, there is a collective responsibility; the collective mind functions, you don't yet have a personal responsibility. The child has no responsibility. The second stage has a responsibility, but it is collective. You don't feel personally responsible for anything, you feel responsible only because you are part of a certain collectivity.

In an Indian village you can find this camel state very, very pronounced. A brahmin has no responsibility of his own. His whole responsibility is that he is a brahmin, he has to behave like a brahmin. In Indian villages you will not find individualities; you will find only collectivities. The brahmin, the sudra, the kshatriya all function according to their community, according to the rules. Nobody has any responsibility to think, there is no question of thinking. The rules have been given down the ages, they are written in the scriptures. Everything is clear-cut – there is no need to speculate, to philosophize, to ponder, to meditate. All problems have been solved – Manu, the Indian Moses, has solved them.

That's where Jesus found the Jews – at the second stage. Moses had done the first work; he had brought the primitive mind to a civilized state. Now Jesus was needed to bring another revolution, another transformation. People were existing just as cogs in a wheel, parts of a great mechanism. The only question was how to function efficiently.

That is not enough to live a joyous life. To be efficient is not enough because the efficiency makes you a good mechanism but does not give you a soul. It does not give you a celebration, it can't be ecstatic. But there are a few beautiful things about the second mind you have to remember; they will help you to understand the third.

The second mind is non-tense, there is no anxiety in it. The Indian villager, or the people of the East are more calm, quiet. They move with a certain ease, dignity. Even if they are starving, hungry, ill, they have patience, deep acceptance. They don't rebel. Rebellion has no appeal for them; they live in acceptance. They don't have enough individuality to rebel. Indians feel very good about it, they think America is going mad; they think, "We are fortunate." But this is not my observation.

America is in a difficulty. America is in great anguish, but that anguish is higher than the so-called Indian peace. That anguish can be more creative, that anguish can bring a higher stage of mind and consciousness into the world than this cow-like peace. This peace is not very creative. Yes, it is good in a way – one lives one's life without much anguish – but nothing comes out of that life. It is just peaceful and peaceful, and that peace is never creative: creative of something out, or creative of something in. That peace seems to be very impotent. But in this second stage the peace is there, obedience is there, patience is there, and there is a feeling of belonging to the community, to the church. Nobody feels alone.

In America people are very alone. Even in a crowd they are alone. In India, even if people are alone, they are not alone. They know they belong, they know they have a certain function somewhere; they know they are needed. They know that they need not choose, everything has been chosen beforehand. A brahmin is born a brahmin. He will be respected by the society; he will become the priest. He has not to work for it; it is already decided by fate, by existence.

When you don't have to decide, naturally you don't feel any anxiety. Decision brings anxiety. If you have to decide, then there is a problem: to go this way or that way? And there are a thousand ways, and so many alternatives – and then one is disturbed and whatsoever you choose you will choose trembling, because who knows whether you are choosing the right or the wrong way? The only way to know is to choose it. But then it will be too late. After ten years, if you come to know that it was a wrong choice, it will be too difficult to go back and choose again, because then those ten years will have gone – gone down the drain.

There is a kind of belonging in the second state of mind. You need not choose, everything has been chosen, decided already; there is a kind of fatalism. All that happens has to be accepted because it cannot be otherwise. If it cannot be otherwise then why be worried? That's why there are fewer psychological breakdowns in India than in America. But remember, it is not a good state. And I am not saying that a psychological breakdown is a great thing, and I am not saying that to be tense and to be anxious is something valuable, but I am saying that just not to be anxious and not to be tense, is not some achievement either. This state, the second state, is a kind of patriarchy. The father remains very important. The father-figures are very important. God is thought to be a father.

There is a difference between the mother and the father. The father is very demanding; the mother is non-demanding. The mother's love is unconditional, the father's love is conditional. The father says, "Do this, then I will love you, if you don't do this you will not get my love." And the father can get very angry.

This state is a state of patriarchy: the father remains important, the mother is not important. Unconditional love is not known. Society appreciates you, respects you if you follow the society. If you go a little bit astray, all respect is taken away and the society is ready to destroy you. The Jewish God says, "I am a very jealous God. If you go against me I will destroy you!" And that's what the state says, the government says, the priest says, the pope says. They are all very jealous. They are very dominating. This state is very repressive; it does not allow anybody to have his own say, it does not allow anybody to have his own being. It is repressive; it does not allow one's own impulses. It is dictatorial, it teaches you to say yes; no is not accepted, yes is enforced violently, aggressively.

Of course this yes cannot be of much value, because if you cannot say no, your yes is going to be impotent. But this is the yes that exists all around. People believe in God because they have been told to believe in God. People go to the church because they have been told to go to the church. People go on doing things formally, ritualistically. Jesus called these people hypocrites.

Before we enter into the sutras, these things will be good to understand, then the sutras will be very clear. This state of mind has only a painted exterior, the interior remains untouched, unevolved. A kind of theism – people believe in God, people believe in hell and heaven, and people believe in punishment and reward, but people *believe*, people don't know. *Yes* is there, but it has been forced. It has not been given a chance to evolve and unfold within you. There is a communal solidarity because you are never alone, you are always together with people, and the crowd is all around you and it feels good. The moment you are alone, trembling arises. When the great crowd is all around you, you can trust. So many people can't be wrong, so you must be right, because so many people are going in the same way, in the same direction, and you are also going with them.

The third mind I call "the individual mind"; Nietzsche calls it "the lion." It is independence, it is assertion, it is rebellion. The ego has evolved. The ego has become very, very crystallized. The man is no longer just a part of a church, country, tribe, clan, family; he is himself. The real culture can only start when you have become an individual. The sense of the self is a must, and this is the third stage of the mind. The identity is no longer of belonging, the identity is no longer that you are a Hindu, or a Mohammedan, or a Christian. The identity is more personal: that you are a painter, that you are a poet. The identity is more creative; it is not of belonging but of contribution – what you have contributed to the world.

In the nebulous mind a center arises by and by. In the child's mind there was no center. In the collective mind there was a false center imposed from the outside. In the individual mind an inner center arises. The first was a kind of chaos – no order. The second was a kind

of patriarchy – an imposed order by the father, by the demanding society and the father-figures. The third is a kind of fraternity
– a brotherhood arises. You don't belong to any crowd; nobody can
impose anything upon you, nor do you want to impose anything upon
anybody. You respect others' freedom as much as you respect your
own freedom. All are brothers.

In the first, the basic question was: "Who is the father-figure?" In
the second, the question is not, "Who is the father figure" – there is
none, God is dead. That is the situation in which Nietzsche declares
that God is dead: God, as father, is dead. That is the situation where
Buddha says there is no God, and Mahavira says there is no God.
And Patanjali says that God is just a hypothesis – needed in certain
stages, and then is needed no longer.

Responsibility arises, and a very personal responsibility. You start
feeling responsible for each of your acts, because now you know what
is right and what is wrong. It is not that somebody says, "This is
right," but because you feel, "This is right," because you feel, "This
is good." A greater understanding, a greater consciousness will be
needed. There will be more joy because you will be more crystallized,
but there will be more anxiety too, because now if something goes
wrong, you go wrong.

And you alone are responsible for each step. You cannot look to a
father figure, and you cannot throw your responsibility onto somebody else – no fate, no father exists – you are left alone on the road,
with thousands of alternatives. You have to choose, and each choice
is going to be decisive, because you cannot go back in time. Great
anxiety arises. This is the place where people start having psychological breakdowns. This is a higher stage than the second, and the West
exists at a higher stage than your so-called East. But of course there
are problems. Those problems can be solved, and those problems
should be solved rather than slipping back to a lower stage of mind.

There is freedom, so there is tension. There is thinking, there is
concentration – abstract philosophy is born, science grows, and "no"
becomes very important. Doubt becomes very significant. In the
collective mind faith was the rule; in the individual mind doubt
becomes the rule. No becomes very basic, because rebellion cannot
exist without no, and the ego cannot grow and ripen without no. You
have to say no to a thousand and one things, so that you can say
yes to the one thing you would like to say yes to. Now the yes is

significant, because man is capable of saying no. Now the yes has potency, power. The yes of a man who always says yes is not of much worth. But the man who says no ninety-nine times and says yes one time, means it. It has an authenticity.

It is a very creative crisis because if you go above it, it will be creative. If you fall from it, you will not fall to the second, you will fall to the first. This has to be understood. If you fall from the third, the individual mind, you will go immediately into madness, because the second is no longer possible. You have learned no-saying, you have learned being rebellious, you have tasted freedom, now you cannot fall back to the second. That door no longer exists for you. If you fall from the third you will fall to the first: you will go mad. That's exactly what happened to Friedrich Nietzsche himself. He was a lion, but the lion went mad, roaring and roaring and roaring, and could not find a way beyond the third.

When a man falls from the third, he falls to the first. This has to be remembered. Then you cannot go to the second – that is finished forever. Once your no has become conscious you cannot go back to faith. A man who has doubted, and who has learned to doubt, cannot go to faith again – that is impossible. Now the faith will be simply cunningness and deception, and you cannot deceive yourself. Once a man has become an atheist then ordinary theism won't do. Then he will have to find a man like me. Then ordinary theism won't do – he has gone beyond it.

Nietzsche needed a man like Buddha. And because Buddha was not available, and because the Western mind has not yet been able to make it possible for people to go beyond the third, he had to go mad. In the West it is almost a certainty that whenever a person becomes really evolved at the third stage, he starts slipping into madness, because the fourth is not available there yet. If the fourth is available, then the third is very creative. If there is a possibility to surrender the ego, then the ego is of immense value. But the value is in its surrender. If you cannot surrender it, then it will become a load – a great load on you. It will be unbearable. Then the lion will go on roaring and roaring and there will be no other way than to go mad.

This is a very critical stage: the third, it is just in the middle. Two minds are below it and two minds are above it. It is exactly the mid-link. If you fall, you go into the abyss of madness; if you rise, you go into the beatitude of being a christ or a buddha.

The fourth mind is the "universal" mind. Remember, it looks collective but it is not collective. *Collective* means belonging to a society, a certain time, a certain period, a certain country. *Universal* means belonging to the whole existence, to existence as such. The ego, when ripe, can be dropped, in fact, it drops itself if the fourth door is available. And that is the function of religion: to make the fourth door available. That is the problem in the West now: the third mind has developed to its uttermost, and the fourth door is not available. The West urgently needs the fourth door.

Carl Gustav Jung has said in his memoirs that through observing thousands of people in his whole life, he has come to a few conclusions. One conclusion is that people who are near about forty to forty-five are always facing a religious crisis. Their problem is not psychological, their problem is religious. Near the age of forty-two, forty-five, a man starts looking for the fourth mind. If he cannot find it, then he goes berserk. Then the hunger is there and the nourishment is not available. If he can find it, great beatitude, great benediction arises.

It is almost like at the age of fourteen you become sexually mature. Then you start looking for a partner – for a woman, for a man. Near the age of fourteen, you want a love object. Exactly near the age of forty-two, another thing in you matures and you start looking for *samadhi*, for meditation, for something that goes higher than love, something that goes higher than sex, something that can lead to a more eternal orgasm, more total orgasm. If you can find it, then life remains smooth. If you cannot find the door – hunger has arisen and the nourishment is not available – what will you do? You start breaking down; your whole structure is shaken. And when a man breaks down, he always breaks down to the first; he falls to the lowest.

This fourth I call the universal mind – the ego can be dissolved because the ego has matured. Remember, let me repeat: the ego can be dissolved only when it has become mature. I am not against the ego, I am all for it, but I don't confine myself to it. One has to go beyond it.

Just the other day I was reading Frankl's book. He says: "We must be willing to discard personality." Why should we be willing to discard personality? And how can you discard personality if you have not grown it? Only the perfectly ripe can be discarded.

What is personality? Personality is a persona, a mask. It is needed. The child has no mask, that's why he looks so animal-like.

The collective mind has a mask, but imposed from the outside; it has no interior definition of its being. The egoist, the individual mind, has an interior definition; he knows who he is, he has a kind of integration. Of course, the integration is not ultimate and will have to be dropped, but it can be dropped only when it has been attained.

"We must be willing to discard personality. God is no respecter of persons." That's true. God loves individuals, but not persons. And the difference is great. A person is one who has an ego definition. An individual is one who has dropped his ego, and knows who he is. A person is a circle with a center; and the individual is a circle without the center – just pure space. "The personality is only a mask, it is a theatrical creation, a mere stage-prop." The longing for freedom, salvation or nirvana, simply means the wish to be relieved of your so-called personality and the prison that it creates.

"The trouble with the self is that it is derived from others." Your ego is also derived from others. You depend for your ego on others. If you go to the Himalayas and sit in a cave, what ego will you have? By and by the ego will start disappearing. It needs support. Somebody needs to appreciate it. Somebody needs to say to you that you are a beautiful person. Somebody needs to go on feeding it. The ego can exist only in society. Although it tries to get rid of society, in a subtle, unconscious way it remains dependent on society.

"The trouble with the self is that it is derived from others. It is constructed in an attempt to live up to the expectation of others. The others have become installed in our hearts, and we call them our-selves." The self is not you. It belongs to others who surround you. It exists in you, but it is possessed by others. That's why it is so easy to manipulate an egoistic person. That's what flattery is, flattery is a trick to manipulate the egoistic person. You go and say to him that he is the greatest man in the world, and he is ready to fall at your feet; you are manipulating. He knows, you know and everybody else knows that this is just false. He also knows that he is not the greatest man in the world, but he will believe it. He would like to believe it. And he would like to do anything that you want him to do. At least one person in the world believes that he is the greatest person. He cannot afford to lose you.

The ego exists in you but is possessed by others. It is the sub-tlest slavery yet invented by the priests and the politicians. It is like a Delgado electrode inserted in your head and manipulated by remote control. The society is very clever. First, it tries to keep you at the second level. If you go beyond that, then it starts manipulating you through flattery.

You will be surprised that in India there has never been a revolution. And the reason? The reason is that the brahmin, the intellectual, was so flattered down the ages that he was never angry enough to revolt against the society. And only intellectuals revolt – only intellectuals, because they are the most egoistic people. They are the most independent people, the intelligentsia. In India the brahmin was the highest; there was no one higher than him, even the king was lower than the brahmin. A beggar brahmin was higher than the emperor, and the emperor used to touch his feet. Now there was no possibility of revolution because who would revolt? These are the people, these intellectuals, who create trouble. Now they are highly respected, they are highly flattered. The revolution could not exist; it was not possible.

It has been the same in the Soviet Union. For these fifty years in Soviet society, the intellectual has been praised as much as anything. The academician, the writer, the poet, the professor are the most highly respected persons. Now who is going to revolt? Revolution is not possible, because the revolutionary has so much investment in the conventional mode of the society, in the traditional society. In India revolution didn't happen, and in the Soviet Union it cannot happen. Revolution is possible only through the egoist, and the egoist can be manipulated very easily. Give him the Nobel Prize, give him a doctorate, and he is ready to do anything.

This third state of mind is now prevalent all over the world. If it is satisfied, then you are stuck in it. If it is not satisfied, then you fall back and become mad. Both are not healthy situations.

One has to go beyond it, and the fourth state, the universal mind, has to be created. The separation with the cosmos has to disappear. You have to become one with the whole. In fact you are one, you just think that you are not. That barrier of the thought has to be dissolved; then there is relaxation, peace, non-violence. In India we say *satyam, shivam, sunderam*: there is truth, there is good, and there is beauty. With the universal mind these three things flower: *satyam*: truth, *shivam*: good, *sunderam*: beauty. With the universal mind these three flowers come into bloom, and there is great joy. You have disappeared, and all the energy that was involved in the ego is freed. That energy becomes beauty, good, truth.

This is the state of matriarchy. The collective mind is patriarchy; the individual mind is fraternity, and the universal mind is matriarchy. Mother love is non-demanding, so is the love of the universe towards you. It demands nothing, it is unconditional, it is simply showering on you. It is for you to take or not to take, but it is showering on you. If you have an ego then your doors are closed and you don't take it. If the ego has disappeared, then it goes on and on showering on you, goes on nourishing you, goes on fulfilling you.

The first stage was chaotic, the second was intellectual, the third was intelligent. The fourth is emotional: it is of love, of the heart. With the third, intellect comes to its peak; with the fourth, love starts flowing. This state can be called "God as mother." When God as father has died, God as mother has to arise. This is a higher stage of religion. When the father is important, the religion is more institutional, formal, because the father himself is formal, institutional. The mother is more natural, more biological, more intrinsic. The father is external; the mother is internal. The universal mind brings the matriarchy. The mother becomes more important. God is no longer a he, but becomes a she. Life is thought about not according to logic, but according to love.

The poet Schiller has called it "the universal kiss." If you are available, the universal mother can kiss you, can embrace you, can take you again into her womb. *Yes* comes again into existence, but it is no longer imposed from the outside, it comes from your innermost core. This is trust. The collective mind lives in faith. The individual mind lives in doubt, the universal mind lives in trust: *shraddha*. It is not belief, it is not that somebody has forced you to believe; it is your own vision, it is your own experience.

This is true religion: when you can become a witness of godliness, of *samadhi*, of prayer; when you are the witness. When you have not taken it as borrowed – it is no longer knowledge, no longer belief – it has become your own existential experience. Solidarity again enters, but it is solidarity with existence itself, not with society. Creativity again comes, but it is no longer the egoistic creativity. It is not you as doer; you become instrumental – existence is the doer. Then existence flows through you. You may create great poetry. In fact, you cannot create great poetry before it. The ego will create a shadow, the ego can never be transparent. The real creativity is possible only with the universal.

You must have read Gopi Krishna's books on kundalini. He says that when kundalini arises, great creativity arises. That's true. But whatsoever he gives as examples are not true. He says, "Sri Aurobindo became creative when his kundalini arose." But Sri Aurobindo has written poetry which is simply mediocre. It is not creative, but at least it is mediocre. Gopi Krishna has written poetry which cannot even be called mediocre – just rubbish, junk.

Yes, when you come to the universal, great creativity is born. Your very touch becomes creative.

There is an ancient story in Buddhist scriptures...

A very rich man accumulated much wealth, accumulated so much gold that there was no place to hoard it any longer. But suddenly something happened. One morning he woke up and saw that all his gold had turned into dust. You can think he must have gone mad.

Somebody helped him towards Buddha – Buddha was staying in the town – and the man went there. And Buddha said, "Do one thing. Take all your gold into the marketplace, and if somebody recognizes it as gold, bring that man to me."

But he said, "How is it going to help me?"

Buddha said, "It is going to help you. Go."

So he took all his gold – thousands of bullock-carts of dust, because now it was all dust. The whole market was full of his bullock-carts. And people were coming and asking, "What nonsense is this? Why are you carrying so much dust to the marketplace? For what?"

But the man kept quiet.

Then a woman came. Her name was Kisagautami. And she said to this man, "So much gold? From where could you get so much gold?"

He asked the woman, "Can you see the gold here?"

She said, "Oh yes. These thousand bullock carts are full of gold."

He took hold of the woman and asked her what secret she had. "How can she see? Because nobody, not even I can see that there is any gold; it is all dust."

He took the woman to Buddha, and Buddha said: "You have found the right woman – she will teach you the art. It is only a question of seeing. The world is as you see it. It can be hell; it can be heaven. Gold can be dust, and dust can be gold. It is a question of how you look at it. This is the right woman. Become a disciple of Kisagautami. She will teach you. And the day you know how to see rightly, the whole world turns into gold. That is the secret of alchemy."

That Kisagautami was a rare woman of those days. And the man learned through her, the art of turning the whole world into gold.

When you enter the universal mind you are capable of creativity – not as you, but as existence. You become a hollow bamboo and its song starts descending through you. It turns you into a flute.

If from the third, the fourth is not available you will fall into madness. Nietzsche talks only of three minds: the camel, the lion and the child. From the lion he falls back into the child: becomes mad.

There is another door too, and that is the universal mind – which is really childhood again, but a second childhood. It is no longer like the first; it is not chaotic, it has self-discipline. It has an inner cosmos, an inner order – not irresponsible like the first, not responsible like the second. A new responsibility, not towards any values, not towards any society, but a second kind of valuation arises because you can see what is right – how can you do otherwise? You see the right and the right has to be done. Knowledge here becomes virtue. You act according to your awareness; your life is transformed. There is innocence, there is intelligence, there is love, but all is coming from your innermost core; your inner fountain is flowing.

And then the fifth, the last: when you go beyond even the universal. Even to think that it is the universal mind is to think that you have some ideas of the individual and the universe still left lingering somewhere. You are still conscious that you are one with the whole, but you *are*, and you are one with the whole. The unity is not yet total, is not utter, is not ultimate. When the unity is really ultimate, there is no individual, no universal. This is the fifth mind: christ-mind, buddha-mind.

Now three other characteristics appear: *sat-chit-anand. Sat* means being, *chit* means consciousness, *anand* means bliss. Now these three qualities appear, now these new flowers bloom in your being. You are for the first time a being, there is no more becoming. Man has surpassed himself, there is no longer a bridge. You have come home, you are a being: *sat.* And you are utterly conscious because there is no darkness left: *chit.* And you are *anand*, because there is no anxiety, no tension, no misery. All that has gone; the nightmare is over. You are fully awake. In that wakefulness is buddhahood, or christhood.

These are the five stages, and remember, the third is the central. Two are below it, two are above it. If you don't go above you will fall below. And you cannot go above without passing through the third, remember. These are the complexities. If you try to avoid the third you will remain stuck in the second, and you can think that it is universal. It is not; it is simply collective. If you try to avoid the third, you may even remain in the first, which is idiotic. And sometimes the idiotic looks saintly.

In Hindi we have two words from one root for both the stages, that root is *budh*. The fifth we call buddha, the ultimate stage, and the first we call *buddhu*, the idiotic stage. Sometimes the idiot looks like the saint – he has some similarities, and sometimes the saint looks like the idiot. But they are far away – the farthest points in existence. Jesus sometimes looks idiotic. And there have been many idiots who looked like Jesus. The similarity is that both are without mind. The idiot is below mind and Christ is above mind, but both are beyond mind. That is the similarity, but that is where it ends too. Beyond that nothing is similar.

Remember, the first is not the goal; it is the beginning. The second is very comfortable, but comfort is not the question – creativity... The third is creative but very uncomfortable, very anxious, tense. And how long can you remain creative? There is so much tension. The tension has to be lost; hence, the fourth. In the fourth all is silent. Just the last lingering of the ego has remained, that one feels, "I am one with the whole."

A disciple of Rinzai came to the master and said, "I have become one with the whole! Now, what next?"

The master turned him out and told him, "Now you get rid of this idea that you have become one with the whole. Get rid of this idea – this is the last barrier."

Another disciple said to Rinzai, "I have attained to nothing."

And Rinzai said, "Drop it! Drop that too!"

With the fourth just a very thin wall remains – almost transparent, you cannot see it. That also has to be dropped. Then arises the fifth.

These sutras of Jesus are for the fifth:

And when thou prayest, thou shalt not be as the hypocrites are: for

they love to pray standing in the synagogues and in the corners of
the streets, that they may be seen of men. Verily I say unto you,
They have their reward.

And Jesus says: "Don't be a hypocrite. Don't pray just to show
others that you are praying." That creates the collective mind. You
are always looking at others – what they think about you. You are
asking for respectability.

The hypocrite is one who lives for respectability. Whatsoever
gives respect to him, he goes on doing; whether he wants to do it or
not is not the point. He may even be against it. He may want to do
just the opposite, but he goes on fulfilling the desire of the people
because he needs their respect.

Jesus says: *And when thou prayest, thou shalt not be as the*
hypocrites are... At least when you pray, forget the society, the collective mind. At least when you pray, forget formalities. Pray only for
God, not for anybody else.

Verily I say unto you, they have their reward. And if you pray
only to show others that you are great in praying, then that is your
reward – the respect that you will get will be all that you get. That is
not of any worth.

But thou, when thou prayest, enter into thy closet, and when thou
hast shut thy door, pray to thy Father in secret.

Jesus says, "Pray in secret, pray in privacy. Pray outside the collective mind. Forget the society and the church and the people –
forget all." When you forget all, only then can you remember God,
not otherwise. In secret, in privacy, let your prayer be.

But when ye pray, use not vain repetitions, as the heathen do: for
they think that they shall be heard for their much speaking.

And Jesus says, "It is not a question of repeating any formal
prayer, the real question is of the heart – not what you say, but what
you mean." It should not be formal; a formal thing becomes dead. It
should be alive, authentic, pulsating. It should show your heart, and
it should represent this moment where you are. It should be true
and real. "And don't be worried," Jesus says, "that you have to say

much to God." The only way to talk with him is in silence.

Be not ye therefore like unto them: for your Father knoweth what things ye have need of, before ye ask him.

There is no need to say anything. Just bowing down in silence will do. Just becoming utterly quiet will do. Silence is the language for prayer. But it may be difficult to go into silence directly, because all that we know is language.

So Jesus says, then:

After this manner therefore pray ye...

If it is very difficult to be silent, to be utterly silent, then start in this manner. Remember, Jesus says: *After this manner...* not "exactly like this." Find your own way; create your own prayer. At least create your own prayer if you cannot create anything else.

...therefore pray ye: Our Father which art in heaven, Hallowed be thy name.

Thy kingdom come. Thy will be done in earth, as it is in heaven.

Give us this day our daily bread.

And forgive us our debts, as we forgive our debtors.

And lead us not into temptation, but deliver us from evil: For thine is the kingdom, and the power, and the glory, for ever.

Amen.

Jesus says: *After this manner...* He is just giving you an example, he is not giving you a prayer, remember, he is simply saying: "In this way..." just to show you a way. Then you create your own prayer.

The whole point is that you should be surrendered, that you should be full of gratitude, praise, that you should be ready to receive, open, listening, that you should be silent: *...in secret...* in privacy. Your love has to be poured out at his feet. *After this manner...* Find your own prayer, create your own prayer. Let it be your own. A borrowed prayer is a false prayer.

> *Give not that which is holy unto the dogs, neither cast ye your pearls before swine, lest they trample them under their feet, and turn again and rend you.*

Jesus says, "You need not pray in the marketplace, you need not pray just to show others that you are praying." That will be wrong, that will be like giving *...that which is holy unto the dogs...* If you pray where there are people who don't understand prayer, you will be misunderstood. *...neither cast ye your pearls before swine...* These pearls of your heart should not be thrown before the swine. *...lest they trample them under their feet, and turn again and rend you.*

> *Ask, and it shall be given you...*

Just ask your God, just let your prayer be for him, absolutely for him.

> *Ask, and it shall be given you; seek, and ye shall find; knock, and it shall be opened unto you.*

God is always ready. It is not that only you are searching for him, he is also searching for you *...knock, and it shall be opened unto you...* He has been waiting there a long time for you. Man's search is not one-sided. From the other side there is as much longing to meet – that is the meaning of this message:

> *Ask, and it shall be given...seek, and ye shall find; knock, and it shall be opened unto you:*
>
> *For every one that asketh receiveth; and he that seeketh findeth; and to him that knocketh it shall be opened.*
>
> *Therefore all things whatsoever ye would that men should do to you, do ye even so to them: for this is the law and the prophets.*

Pray in secret. Prayer should be just an address between you and your God, a dialogue. And then your behavior... Jesus has completed the whole sketch of the religious life: with people, do only that which you would like them to do to you. That is all! In short, the whole message of the law and the prophets: "Do unto others what you would like them to do to you." That should be your behavior, and that is enough preparation for prayer. And then, close your doors, go in secret and pray to your God.

If you have not done anything wrong to people, then there is nothing blocking your path. If nobody is angry, if nobody is against you, if you have not been hurting anybody, you are ready. Your prayer is going to be heard. Then let your prayer be your own, authentic, informal.

Enter ye in at the strait gate: for wide is the gate, and broad is the way, that leadeth to destruction, and many there be which go in thereat:

Because strait is the gate, and narrow is the way, which leadeth unto life, and few there be that find it.

Jesus says: "There are two gates. One is that of the crowd, the collective mind, and another is of the universal mind. They are in one way similar – they are both strait gates." The difference is: ...*for wide is the gate, and broad is the way, that leadeth to destruction*... Where crowds move, naturally, the gate is wide, and the way is broad. Multitudes move there. But the real gate is narrow, only you alone can move there. They are both gates – the collective and the universal look alike, but in the collective you are just part of the mass, in the universal you are not part of the mass. Before the universal you have attained to a certain freedom, ego, individuality, self definition – you move alone.

Because strait is the gate, and narrow is the way, which leadeth unto life, and few there be that find it. This thing has to be remembered: you can enter into godliness only in your absolute aloneness. You cannot take even your friend with you, not even your beloved. One has to go alone. The gate is very narrow. You cannot go as a Hindu, you cannot take Hindus with you. You cannot go as a Christian, you cannot go as part of the Christian mob. You will have to go as an individual. And to have individuality you will have to develop the third mind. Only from the third can you enter the fourth. And from the fourth, slowly, slowly, the fifth comes on its own. It grows, it opens like a lotus.

These are the five stages of the mind. Watch, observe. The first exists in everybody, the second also in ninety-nine percent of people, the third in very few – three, four, five percent at the most, the fourth not even in one percent, and the fifth is very rare.

Only once is a christ or a buddha born. But the fifth is the goal. Keep the goal in your vision, and go on moving, slowly, slowly, from the first to the second, from the second to the third, from the third to the fourth.

Man is a becoming. With the fifth mind arising, buddha mind, christ mind, man becomes a being. Then man is no longer man, because man is no longer mind. Then man is godliness. And only that can be fulfilling, nothing else. Never be satisfied by anything less.

Enough for today.

silence belongs to the universal

The first question:

Osho,
I could not follow the relationship between the five minds you
talked about and the sayings of Jesus. Will you please enlighten?

M y God, so I have to go into it again? I was thinking I was finished with those five minds. But it is not a surprise; I was
expecting something like that because I had not made it
clear. I had only given you a few hints, and those too, very indirectly.
If you had meditated over it you would have found the relationship,
but you don't want to work at all. You don't want to do any home-
work. Let us try to go into it again.

The five minds were: first, the pre-mind – let us call it the primal;
second, the collective mind – let us call it the social; third, the individual mind – the ego mind; fourth, the cosmic mind – the universal
mind; and the fifth, the no-mind, christ-mind, buddha-mind – let us
call it the transcendental.

The first thing to be understood is that Jesus' sayings are
addressed to the third mind, the individual, because they can be

addressed only to the third mind. All the scriptures are addressed to the third mind, because only at the point of the third is understanding possible – difficult, but possible.

Up to the second mind, the social, you don't have any understanding. You are imitative, you are just a member of a great mechanism called society. You don't have any identity. You cannot be addressed, you cannot be provoked. Nobody exists in you. You are just an echo – an echo of the society, the church, the state, the country; an echo of many things, but just the echo. You are not yet real. How can you understand before that? That's why a Jesus or a Buddha is born into a highly evolved society. They are not born into primitive societies.

Buddha was born in Bihar, not in Bastar. Bihar was the highest peak of the Indian mind in those days. Never again has the Indian consciousness touched that climax. Jesus was born at the pinnacle of Jewish consciousness – he is the fruit and the flower of the whole of Jewish history; he could not have been born anywhere else. For Jesus to exist a certain milieu is needed, certain people are needed who can understand him. Certain people are needed who can not only understand him, but can be transformed by him.

So the first thing is that the sutras of Jesus are addressed to the third mind, the individual mind, the ego mind. The ego has a certain function to fulfill; it is not just useless. It becomes a hindrance if you go higher than the third, but you cannot go higher than that if it is not there. It is a must, it is a necessary step; only the ego can understand the misery of being in an ego. The social mind cannot understand it; the problem has not yet arisen, so the solution is meaningless.

If you are suffering from a disease, then the medicine, the remedy becomes significant. If you are not suffering from a disease, the remedy is not a remedy for you. The social mind has not yet suffered from the ego. Hence anything that helps to go beyond the ego is utterly meaningless; it has no point of reference, it has no context. Jesus talks to the third mind, remember. If you are still in the second mind Jesus will remain an enigma to you. If you are just a Christian or a Jew or a Hindu then you will not be able to understand Jesus.

Just think, in those days the people who gathered around Jesus must have been very, very individualistic people. Otherwise how was it possible for them to listen to somebody who was so rebellious, who was so radical, who was turning the whole society upside down, who was continuously saying: "It has been told to you in the old days, but I say unto you..."? And was denying all that had been said, was continuously dismantling, destroying – of course, to create something new. But an ordinary Jew would not have been able to come into close quarters with Jesus. It would have been too much. Only a few individuals, rebellious people, must have gathered around him.

The social mind gave him crucifixion. The society, the formalist, the Pharisee, the rabbi, the moralist, the puritan, all gathered together to kill him, because he was bringing something of the individual consciousness, he was creating individuality in people. This is the first thing to understand in how the sutras are related to the five minds.

First: they are addressed to the third, and they can only be addressed to the third. The first, the primal, will not even be able to listen. The second, the social, can listen, but will not be able to understand. The third, the individual, can understand but will not be able to follow. But once understanding has arisen – intellectual understanding, at least – then the door opens. Only the fourth mind, the universal, can follow when ego has been dropped. When ego has been used and dropped, when the ego's function is fulfilled – it's no longer necessary, one has gone beyond it – the boat can be left behind.

So remember, the first cannot even listen; the second can listen, but cannot understand; the third can understand, but cannot follow. The fourth can follow, but only follow; the fifth can become the transcendental mind. This is how they are related.

The second thing to remember: Jesus says...

Enter ye in at the strait gate: for wide is the gate, and broad is the way, that leadeth to destruction, and many there be which go in thereat:

Because strait is the gate, and narrow is the way, which leadeth unto life, and few there be that find it.

Visualize the third mind; it is just in the middle, half-way. Two minds are below it, two minds are above it. The social mind is below it and the universal mind is above it. Both look alike. And these are the only two ways open for the individual mind to go, otherwise you will feel stuck.

In life, one has to continuously move. It is movement, it is a process. If you feel stuck you will become miserable; one has to go on and on till the goal is reached. Standing in the third mind, the individual ego faces two possibilities: either it can go up and become the universal mind, or it can fall back and can become the social mind.

Both look alike, that's why Jesus says: *Enter ye in at the strait gate...* Both are gates and they look very alike. What is their similarity? The universal mind has dropped the ego, it is in tune with the whole. The social mind has not created the ego yet, it is in tune with the social. But both have a kind of attunement.

The social mind is at ease with the society, it flows rhythmically, smoothly. It has no struggle, conflict. It fits together; it is adjusted – adjusted with the society. But society is a big thing; it almost looks as if you are adjusted with existence. The social mind is very normal. That's what psychoanalysts go on doing. Whenever somebody becomes too much of an individual, they say he is maladjusted. Then what do they do? They bring you to a gate – the social; they help you to adjust with society. They call that normal health. They call that psychological health. It reduces tensions, it reduces inconveniences; it makes you more comfortable and secure but at a great cost.

Religion also helps you to go beyond tensions, but not through the second door. Religion helps you to go through the third door. That is the difference between psychoanalysis and religion. Religion also makes you adjusted, but not with the society; it makes you adjusted with the whole, with the universe, with existence. That is real adjustment, and great joy arises out of it.

To be adjusted with society is a very tiny arrangement. You will be less tense but not more joyous, remember it. The fourth mind will give you joy, celebration; the second mind will simply help you to remain more calm and quiet and collected, but there will be no ecstasy.

Let ecstasy always be the criterion. Whenever you go high, ecstasy grows. If you go low, your ecstasy is diminished. But they look alike because both are adjustments. In one you drop being the individual, you become a sheep. You start imitating people, you become part of the mob. The mob itself may be wrong – that's not the question – but you adjust to it. The mob may be neurotic, and in fact is so: mobs are more neurotic than individuals.

Friedrich Nietzsche has said – and rightly – that as far as individuals are concerned, neurosis is a rare accident. But as far as mobs are concerned, that is the rule not the exception. Mobs have always been neurotic. Adjust to the mob and you will feel good, because now you are part of the social neurosis, you don't have a private neurosis. You will never feel it – everybody is just like you – things feel perfectly good. That's why Jesus says the gates are alike: both are gates. But there is a great difference.

The difference is: *Enter ye in at the strait gate: for wide is the gate...* If you go backwards, the gate is wide: *...and broad is the way...* If you go upward *...narrow is the way...* very narrow. In fact, you have to go alone. You cannot take anybody with you. If you go to the fourth you will have to go alone. You will have to go in absolute aloneness. That's why solitude, meditation, prayer, all have to be done in aloneness. You cannot get into the fourth with all your friends, family, acquaintances, etcetera. You will have to leave everybody behind, you will have to move on a very narrow path. It is so narrow that it cannot even contain two at once. You cannot even take your wife, your husband, your son, your mother – there is no way. You have to go alone. It is solitary. You can help others also to go to it, but they will go in their own solitariness. Remember, the higher you go, the more alone you are. The lower you go, the more you are with people.

It is like a pyramid. The lowest part of the pyramid has the biggest base: the base is the biggest. Then, as you go higher, the pyramid becomes smaller and smaller and smaller, and at the apex, it is just a point. You can visualize these minds in this way. The primal is the base of the pyramid; the social is very close to the base – a little smaller than the base. The individual is very close to the apex, to the peak – far away from the base; and the universal is just a point, the apex. When you have jumped beyond even that, the pyramid disappears. The fifth, the transcendental, it is not part of the pyramid at all.

The third mind is addressed by Jesus, and is told that these are the two possibilities. If you enter with the collectivity you will be destroying yourself; it will be destructive, it will not be creative. You will not be born out of it, it will be simple suicide. There will be no resurrection in it.

Enter ye in at the strait gate: for wide is the gate, and broad is the way, that leadeth to destruction, and many there be which go in thereat... The majority follow this. That is why you don't see flowering, you don't see eyes full of splendor, you don't see people in a

---

dance, you don't see hearts singing, you don't see pulsating life energies, you don't see streaming vitalities. You simply see dull, stale, stagnant, dirty pools – no more flow. And when the flow disappears, the glow also disappears. Then you are slowly, slowly dying and doing nothing. This is destruction.

If you follow the higher, the universal mind: ...*because strait is the gate, and narrow is the way*... That "narrow" has to be remembered always. With the social you can be with the mob, with the individual you cannot be with the mob.

You can only be with a small group of people. You will always find whenever there are egoistic people that they will create small groups, their own societies, clubs, lodges. They will not move with the mass, they will have their own chosen few, select few; they will move with them. Authors will move with authors. Poets will move with poets. Painters will have their own clubs, their own restaurants where they will meet. They will have their own superior, small groups, and they will be very choosy about who is to be allowed in.

With the fourth, you are alone – not even a club of the chosen people; you are alone. With the fifth you are not even alone, even you have disappeared. This is how it goes. Slowly, slowly things go on disappearing. First the mass, then the small societies, groups, clubs; then you, and one day there is only emptiness in your hands. That emptiness is what Jesus calls the kingdom of God, and Buddha calls nirvana.

Third: Jesus talks about prayer. Prayer is the way – Jesus' way – to be alone. Buddha's way is meditation, Jesus' way is prayer. But the intrinsic quality has to be the same. Jesus says, "Be silent, language is not needed."

Language is helpful in the social. In the universal, language is not needed. Language is a social phenomenon. Animals don't have language because they don't have societies. Man has language because man has society; man is a social animal. When you start moving beyond society, language becomes irrelevant. Language is to relate with the other, and God is not the other, God is your innermost core. There is no need for any language.

So Jesus says:

And when thou prayest, thou shalt not be as the hypocrites are: for they love to pray standing in the synagogues and in the corners of

the streets, that they may be seen of men. Verily I say unto you,
they have their reward.

Don't pray for people to see that you are praying, that you are
religious. Don't pray as a show, don't make it a performance. It is
sacrilegious. Prayer should be in solitude, nobody should know
about it. There is no need. It is nobody else's concern.

But thou, when thou prayest, enter into thy closet... What does
he mean by *closet?* He means drop all language from your mind, all
verbalization from your mind. The moment you drop verbalization
from your mind, you have moved into such a private world that
nobody else can go there. Language dropped, you have dropped the
whole world. Just think of it. If for a moment there is no language
inside you, then where are you? You are no longer here, no longer in
this world. You are in a world totally different from this. When there
is no language in you, you are utterly private. Language makes you
public. "No language" makes you private.

This is what Jesus means when he says: *But thou, when thou*
prayest, enter into thy closet... – drop all language and verbalization.
All communication has to be dropped. You just have to be there
silent, present – but utterly non-verbal, not saying a single thing.

...and when thou hast shut thy door... When the door on the
language, on the verbal, on the linguistic mind has been closed
...pray to thy Father in secret. Then just be in deep gratefulness,
gratitude. Then bow down to the unknown. Then surrender before
the mysterious, just be in awe, in wonder. This is what prayerfulness
is. This is the entry from the ego to the universal, from the third to
the fourth.

Language is the medium to relate with others, and silence is the
medium to relate with God – because God is not the other. Only in
silence do you commune with your own inner being.

Logic is the way in the world, love is the way in God. Prayer is
a loving silence – nothing else. If you ask me what prayer is, I will
say a loving silence. Silence, but utterly full of love, overflowing
with love. If silence is there and love is not there, then it is meditation. If silence is there, and suffused with love, fragrant with love,
then it is prayer – that is the only difference. If you can shower your
silence with love, it becomes prayer. If you cannot, then it remains
meditation. Both lead there, so there is no problem of higher and

lower: meditation is not higher, nor is prayer higher.

There are two types of people in the world: the man and the woman – the people of intelligence and the people of love. Jesus belongs to the second type; his path is the path of love. Buddha's path is the path of intelligence. Buddha says: "Just be silent and you will jump from the third to the fourth." Jesus says: "Be silent and full of love, and you will jump from the third to the fourth." Both are bridges.

If it appeals to you, if you feel that it strikes in your heart – that the idea simply clicks in your being – then prayer is your way. But try both. If you are confused, try both. Whichever feels good is good, because each is as potent as the other.

All words belong to the social; silence belongs to the universal. And in the transcendental even silence disappears. First language disappears, then silence too. Then there is absolute silence – when silence has also disappeared. This is the meaning when Jesus says: *Thy kingdom come. Thy will be done in earth, as it is in heaven.* He surrenders in deep love, in silence.

And remember, these are not words to be repeated. Christians have misunderstood Jesus. These are not words to be repeated, these are the emotions to be lived. Not words to be repeated, but emotions to be lived.

Thy kingdom come... Now this can be just a word in you, you can repeat it; or this can be a feeling in you: *Thy kingdom come...* Not a single word is uttered inside but this is your feeling. Your hands are raised to receive the kingdom, you are surrendered, your heart is open. You are ready for godliness to descend in you.

Do you see the difference? Don't repeat the words. Let it be a feeling and then it will go deeper, and then it will really become a prayer.

And the fourth thing about the transcendental:

Ask, and it shall be given you; seek, and ye shall find; knock, and it shall be opened unto you...

For every one that asketh receiveth, and he that seeketh findeth; and to him that knocketh it shall be opened.

What does Jesus mean by saying: *Ask, and it shall be given you...?* He means that really it is already given to you. You have not been able to see it because you have not asked for it. The door is already open! But because you have not knocked at it, it has remained open and yet closed for you. Is it just for the sake of asking that you will get it? It is possible only if you have already got it, otherwise how can you get anything just by asking?

Try. You want to have a big palace – are you going to get it just by asking? You are not going to get it just by asking, otherwise all beggars would be emperors. You don't have it, and you will have to work hard, and then too there is no certainty that you will have it. You may succeed, you may not succeed. There are a thousand and one competitors too. You will have to go through being aggressive, and you will have to put all that you have at stake. And then too, the possibility is greater that you will be a loser. You want money? – you cannot get it just by asking. You want prestige, power, respectability, fame? – you will not get it just by asking.

But Jesus says: "You can have God just for the asking." What does he mean? It is an incredibly simple statement. He simply means what Buddha means when he says that you have it already there. You are not to achieve it; it is your intrinsic nature. This is Jesus' way of saying the same thing: you can get only by asking because you are already there. The asking will make you alert, that's all. If you ask consciously, if you knock consciously, if you start groping consciously, you will become alert to that which has already been there – that which has always been there, which has been the case from the very beginning. God is given to you. You are carrying God within you. But you have not asked. Your desire has not become conscious.

So God is there, you are there, but there is no bridge. By asking you will create the bridge. If the asking is immense, tremendous, total, then in a single instant the bridge will be projected. The kingdom of God is within you. That's why: *Ask, and it shall be given you; seek, and ye shall find; knock, and it shall be opened unto you...* This is how these sutras are related with the five minds. But they are basically addressed to the third mind.

To those who seek identity, Norman Brown advocates: "Get lost!" and Timothy Leary says: "Drop out!" But I say to you that to get lost, one must have found oneself first, and to drop out one must have been *in* first. You can drop out if you *are,* you can get lost if the ego is ready and ripe. That is the difference between a sannyasin and a hippie.

A hippie is one who has been trying to drop something which he does not yet have, who is trying to drop something which he has not yet earned, who is trying to renounce something which is not there. A sannyasin is one who has come to feel the ripe ego and, feeling the misery and anguish of it, drops it. They look alike. They look alike, but the hippie is not going from the third to the fourth. The hippie has not been in the third yet, he will fall to the second. That's why hippies start creating their own clan, their own tribe, their own society. It has almost the same structure as the old society that they have left.

If in the old society you cannot have long hair, in a hippie society you cannot have short hair. The structure is the same. If in the old society you cannot go on without taking a bath for months, in the hippie society you are not allowed to take a bath every day. That is too conventional. You will look a little anti-social if you take a bath every day. But it is the same society repeated, the same structure. Even though it is against, it is the same structure. The hippie is not going beyond society; he is going against one society and creating another.

The sannyasin is going beyond society. He is moving away from the very need to be part of a society.

The sutras are addressed to the egoist. But remember, the egoist can understand them, but cannot follow. To follow them you will have to start dropping your ego. Then you can follow, then the universal mind will arise in you.

Prayer or meditation is the way. And when the universal has arrived, don't stop there. One more step... This very consciousness that you have arrived, this very consciousness that you have realized God, this very consciousness that you have become one with God has to be drowned too. This is the last barrier to be dropped. Once it has gone, you and the whole are one – so much one, that there is nobody even to say, "I am one with the whole." That is the transcendental. That's what Jesus calls the kingdom of God.

The second question:

Osho,
Where is the meeting between Christ's love and Buddha's intelligence?

In me!

The third question:

Osho,
Do you teach then that one should not plan for the future at all?

Psychologically one should not plan for the future at all, but that does not mean that practically you should not plan. The difference is great, and has to be understood.

If you are going to travel, if you are going to the Himalayas, you will have to go to the railway station and book your ticket a few days ahead. That's simply practical. You cannot say, "When the idea arises to go to the Himalayas I will simply go." It will be difficult: you may not get a ticket on the train or on the plane. Don't be foolish. But psychologically, yes, don't plan for the future.

What is the meaning of "psychologically"? You are here, and in your mind's eye you start trekking in the Himalayas, and you start enjoying – just in fantasy. You are already there where you are not. This is psychological. This has to be dropped. But practical things are perfectly okay.

Don't live psychologically in the past or in the future. But practically, sometimes you will have to remember past things. You will have to remember your name, and you will have to remember your wife. You cannot come home every day and ask, "Who are you? Let us introduce ourselves." You will have to remember the past for practical purposes. But don't live there; the past has gone. The memory is there, use it whenever it is needed, but don't start living in those memories. Don't waste time, because if you live in your memories who is going to live in the present? Then the present is wasted. And living in the memory is just a dream, it is not real life; it is pseudo, it is false.

And don't live in the future. People live in the future: they are always planning to go to Kashmir or to Switzerland. And they are living there already! They dream, they think, they fantasize what they are going to do there, how they will enjoy the life there. And remember, when they reach Switzerland they will not be there because by that time they will start planning how to come back home. And the business, and the family, and everything...

They are never where they are; they go on missing. They are always rushing and never arriving. Don't live in the future, don't live in the past. But that doesn't mean don't think of practical things.

A man was on a holiday in Ireland. One day he was driving along a little-used road when he came across a pretty young girl trying to hitch a lift. So he offered her a lift.

After a few minutes he asked if he could hold her hand.

"To be sure," came the reply.

A little further on, he asked if he could kiss her.

"To be sure," she replied.

A few miles later, they passed through a village. The girl asked him to stop at the chemist's shop.

"Why?" asked the man.

"To be sure," replied the girl.

This much practicality is allowed. More than that is not needed.

The fourth question:

Osho,
You said that sometimes it is dangerous to push. And you are pushing me very hard. Well, I guess you know what you are doing, but what are you doing?

That is none of your business.

The fifth question:

Osho,
Why do I cry whenever something real happens in meditation?
Sometimes, even during lecture, when you say something that strikes me as my own truth, tears come to my eyes and I tremble with silent sobs. What is the connection between truth and tears?

The question is from Michael Gottlieb.

First, it may be that only tears are true in you, everything else has become false. Your smile, your face, your gestures, your words may all have become false. It may be that only your tears are still true. That's why whenever you hear something of truth, they start surfacing. They are in tune with truth. And this is not only so with you, it is so with many people.

Tears have not been corrupted too much, particularly in men. About women it is not so true. Their tears may he just a facade, their tears may be their diplomacies, their tears may be their tricks, strategies. But about men... Men have not been allowed tears at all. People have been told from their very childhood that if you are a man, tears are not available for you. You should never cry. So tears have remained there, uncorrupted by the society, unpolluted by the society – at least it is so with men. So whenever you hear something of truth – something that simply becomes a song in your heart, something that simply penetrates like a ray of light into your darkness – tears come, because the true calls forth the true in you.

Michael Gottlieb's name is beautiful: Gottlieb means God-love. Maybe there is a great desire for God, a great love for God which is getting ready every day, which is going to possess you. Allow those tears, because there is a danger you may be repressing them.

Gottlieb is a psychologist – that is the danger. You may start rationalizing, you may start finding explanations. You may stop those tears which are innocent – as innocent as dewdrops – which are uncorrupted by your mind; they come from the beyond. Those tears are coming from your heart. Don't start explaining them. Psychologists have become very clever at explaining away everything. Live with the mystery of the tears. When they come, allow them. Go into those sobs, those sobs are the beginning of prayer in you. Flow in those tears, totally unashamed. Don't feel embarrassed. Go wholeheartedly into them, and through them you will be cleansed and purified. Those tears will become your very alchemy. Their very touch will turn you into gold.

I have been watching Gottlieb. He has been here for only a few days, and deep down he is afraid of sannyas. First he was only going to stay for ten days, then he extended it for a few days. Now he has extended a little longer, and by and by he is getting trapped. Now the tears have started to come. Now it is dangerous, Gottlieb.

But still you are not allowing the tears a total flow. Be swayed by them. Let that throb go to your very cells and the fibers of your being. Let those tears dance in and around you, and through those tears you will be initiated. Through those tears you are coming close to me and I am coming close to you. If you allow it, something is going to happen, something immensely valuable. But it depends on you whether you allow it or whether you escape before it becomes too much.

To be here needs courage. To be with me means risk. If you decide to be with me, you are risking finding yourself. The risk is there. And to find oneself, one has to die to one's whole past, because the new can come only when the old has disappeared. Let those tears take away your past, let them wash you. They are preparing you for me. And you have a heart which can grow in prayer, but only if you allow. Nothing can be done against you. And up to now you have been fighting, you have been protecting, safeguarding yourself. You are keeping a little bit aloof, distant. You are doing it at your own risk. You may miss the opportunity.

The sixth question:

Osho,
In today's lecture you said there are three stages – sex, love and prayer. But if one keeps on changing partners how can one go into depth? How can one reach the highest stage at all?

The question is from Mukta.

This question arises in many people, and because she is an Indian it has more relevance to her conditioning. People think that if you are in love with one person, only then can love go deep. That is utter nonsense!

The depth of love has nothing to do with one person or two persons. The depth of love has certainly something to do with your remaining always in love – that brings depth. Now, for example, you love a man or a woman. For a few days things are really fantastic. Things are going beautifully. And then, naturally, things start becoming dull. There is nothing wrong in it, it is just the very course of nature. You become acquainted with the woman, her ways; she becomes acquainted with you, your ways, your lifestyle, and when everything is known, interest starts dimming. When everything is known and there is nothing surprising any longer, how can the relationship remain fantastic? The wonder starts disappearing, things settle, become mundane, day-to-day, ordinary. This is what ordinarily happens.

Now, you can go on living with the man or with the woman with the idea that if you change the man or the woman, love will never go deep. But the love is not going deeply at all; the love is becoming shallower every day. Sooner or later, you will start taking the other for granted. There will be no joy in the other's presence, you will not be thrilled by the other's presence. You can go on clinging...

Mukta has asked this question because she was trying to cling to a certain sannyasin, trying hard to cling. And because she tried hard, the sannyasin escaped. My people are very intelligent! If you cling too hard, then nobody is going to be with you, because nobody wants an imprisonment, nobody wants you to become a fetter. The more you cling, the more the relationship becomes ugly. First it loses joy, loses all charm, loses all magnetism, and then it starts becoming ill, pathological.

I call a relationship pathological when you are clinging only for clinging's sake, there is nothing else to cling for. You are simply clinging because you are afraid to lose, afraid to change, afraid to move in a new relationship. Because who knows how the new is going to turn out, where it will lead? The new is dangerous because the new is not yet familiar. The old is familiar, settled, there is certain security, comfort, convenience. When you start clinging for clinging's sake, then it is pathological, it is ugly; it is not going to bring any depth to your relationship. All depth will disappear. You can go and see millions of husbands and wives... What depth, what intimacy is there?

Now I am not saying that if you are with a certain person – with a man or a woman, and things are still growing – to change. I am not saying that. Don't misunderstand me. There are a few people who are so sensitive that they can go on finding something new in the other every day. There are people who are so aesthetic that they never feel that things are ever finished. Their sensitivity, their intensity, their passion goes on bringing new depths. Then it is perfectly good.

My criterion is if a relationship is growing towards depth it is perfectly good. Go on! Exhaust it if you can. But if it is not growing, if it is not deepening, if the intimacy is not flowering anymore; all has stopped, and you are simply stuck because you don't know how to leave and how to say good-bye, then you are destroying your capacity for love. It is better to move, change the partner, than to destroy love – because love is the goal, not the partner. You love a person not for the person's sake; you love the person for love's sake.

Love is the goal, so if it is not happening with this person, let it happen with somebody else, but let it happen! Allow it continuity. That continuity, that flow of love constantly happening, will take you deeper into it, will bring depth, will bring new dimensions, will bring new realizations.

So remember, if it is going well with one person... And by well, I don't mean what is ordinarily meant when somebody says that they are a good couple or very nice. I don't mean that; those words just hide facts. A "nice family" means no conflict, no problem, things are going smoothly, the wheels of the mechanism are moving smoothly, that's all. But a really beautiful relationship is not just nice; it is far out! Never settle for less. Only a far-out relationship can bring depth. If it is not happening, be courageous enough to say good-bye – with no complaint, with no grudge, with no anger. What can you do? If it is not happening, it is not happening.

You cannot make the other feel guilty. What can he do? Whatsoever he can do he is doing, whatsoever you can do you are doing. But if somehow it is not happening, you are not fitting with each other, you are not meant for each other, don't go on forcing it. It is like putting a square plug in a round hole. Go on – it won't happen. And if you succeed, there is every possibility that you may have destroyed the plug completely. Then it will not be of any worth.

But mind functions through conditionings. Now, Mukta's mind is basically Indian. The Indian conditioning is very long. For thousands of years in India it has been thought that you should be true to one person. I am teaching you a totally different thing. I am teaching you to be true to love, not to persons. Be true to love. Never betray love, that's all. If sometimes persons have to be changed, they have to be changed, but never betray love. The old Indian tradition is: betray love but never betray the person, go on clinging to one person. And when things have been there for thousands of years, they become part of your blood and bones, part of your marrow, and you start functioning unconsciously.

Become a little more conscious. Meditate over this anecdote:

The day for the execution arrived and the three prisoners – a Frenchman, an Englishman and a German – were led out of their cells to the guillotine. The Frenchman was the first to be led up the steps and was asked if he preferred to face upwards or downwards on the guillotine block.

He replied: "I have led a full and good life enjoying all the delights of good wine from the finest French vineyards, excellent cheeses, the best cuisine and the wonderful charms of the loveliest mademoiselles of France. I have nothing more to wish for and nothing to fear. Therefore, I will face upwards."

He was then positioned on his back looking up so he could watch the blade as it descended. The blade was released and it began falling with full speed until it was only half an inch from his neck, at which point the blade suddenly stopped.

Unable to explain this, the authorities who were standing by interpreted it as a sign from God, and proceeded to release the prisoner to become a free man.

The Englishman was next to be led to the guillotine and was asked the same question. He replied: "I have served my Queen loyally throughout the empire. In the true tradition of the refined Englishman, I have helped to spread our great English civilization around the world and I have never flinched at danger. Therefore, I am ready to face death and will face upwards."

He was positioned on his back and the blade was released and began falling. Again, at the last instant, the blade came to an abrupt stop just half an inch above his throat. This was again interpreted as a sign from God, so the man was freed.

Next the German was led to the guillotine and as he was being asked the same question, he immediately interrupted and said: "Before I answer your question, I want you to know that I refuse to be under that machine until you get it fixed!"

A German is a German. His conditioning is there: the machine should be fixed first!

And that's how the Indian mind also functions. Down the ages you have been taught to remain true to persons, which is not a very high value. The higher value is to remain true to love. If it is happening with one person, perfectly good, I am not saying to change – what is the point of changing? If it is not happening with this person, then let it happen somewhere else.

But let it happen because if you miss love, you will miss all that is beautiful in life. If you miss love, you will miss the possibility of prayer too because only love, when it becomes deep, brings you closer to prayer.

The seventh question:

Osho,
I do not believe in anything, but I do believe in God. Why are you so much against beliefs?

Because a belief is a belief, and is not an experience. Belief is a barrier. If you believe in God you will never know God. That's why I am against belief – because I am for God. Your very belief will never allow you to know that which is, because the belief means that before knowing it you have decided already what it is. Your decisive mind will not relax. Your mind with a conclusion is a prejudiced mind, and to know God an empty mind is needed: unprejudiced, pure, uncontaminated by any belief, by any ideology. I am against all beliefs because I am for God.

And you say: "I do not believe in anything..." But if you believe in God, then what more is needed? That is enough. You have made the greatest mistake! Now every other mistake is very small. And if the great mistake has been done, then other mistakes will follow in its wake. If you can believe in God without knowing God – without understanding what it means, without ever experiencing even a little bit of it, without ever seeing a single ray of light; if you can believe in God, if you can be so deceptive, if you can be so cunning – then you can believe in anything. And what else is needed? You think this belief is not a big mistake? It is the biggest mistake.

A husband walked into his house unexpectedly one evening, and noticed some men's clothing at the foot of the bed. He asked his wife, who was in the bed at the time, where the clothes came from. His wife told him that the clothes belonged to him, and she was taking them to the cleaner's. Going to the closet to hang up his coat, he eyed a man bare as the day he came into the world.
The husband: "What are you doing here?"
The man: "Did you believe what your wife told you?"
The husband: "Yes!"

The man: "Well, I'm waiting for a bus."

If you can believe that, then you can believe anything. The naked man standing in the closet, waiting for the bus...

If you can believe in God, then you can believe in Adolf Hitler, in Josef Stalin, in Mao Zedong, then you can believe in any nonsense because you have accepted the basic nonsense. Never believe in God. God has to be known, not to be believed. God has to be lived, not to be believed. God has to be experienced, not to be believed.

And why do you believe in God? If you have not known, then it must be out of fear, then there can be no other reason. Remember, God can be known only out of love, and beliefs come out of fear. And love and fear never meet; they never cross each other's path. Love knows no fear. Fear knows no love. If you are afraid of somebody you cannot love that person. That's why it is very difficult for children to love their parents because parents make them afraid. It is very difficult for husbands to love their wives because their wives make them afraid. It is very difficult for wives to love their husbands because their husbands make them afraid.

Wherever fear comes, fear comes from this door, and love escapes from the other. They never live together, they can't live together. Have you not observed? When you love a person all fear disappears. In that very love there is no fear.

God has to be known through love. And belief is based in fear. Belief stinks!

A salesman couldn't make the lady understand the power brakes on the car he was selling her, so he took her for a ride. When he was almost five hundred feet from a brick building, he speeded up and at the last minute he hit the brake.

Lady: "What is that smell?"

Salesman: "Rubber burning, madam."

She brought the car home to show her husband and took him for a ride. Coming to the same brick wall she slammed on the brakes, missing it by about three inches. Looking at her husband, she said, "Do you smell that, honey?"

Husband: "I should. I'm sitting in it."

All beliefs stink. Drop beliefs! Have the courage to know.

God is an invitation for the ultimate journey. Let God be a quest, not a belief. Let it be a question mark on your heart, at the deepest core of your being. Let the question trouble you, let the question become a turmoil. Let the question create a chaos in you because only through chaos are stars born. Only when the quest has destroyed all your belief systems, and you are freed of all conclusions given by others, will you be able to open your eyes to the naked truth. And it is facing you. It is always facing you. It is just in front of your nose, but there is a Great Wall of China of beliefs, and you cannot see that which surrounds you from everywhere.

The last question:

Osho,
I and my wife both love you, but we often quarrel about you and your thoughts because we cannot agree in our interpretation of your ideas. What should we do?

There is no need to agree. And how can you agree? When you listen to me, you listen through your preoccupation. When your wife listens, she listens through her preoccupation. When you listen, you listen through your own beliefs, ideas, conditioning. When she listens, she has her own mind. Interpretations are going to be different.

Just because you are both listening to me does not mean that you will agree. You will interpret, you will give colors, you will give turns to ideas according to your mind. See the fact that with the mind there can be no agreement. There is no need to argue. Rather, try to do what I am saying. Don't waste your time. I am not here to make you more argumentative. I am not here to make you more logical. I am not here to make you more capable of discussing, analyzing, interpreting things. I am here to help you to see. And seeing comes when you are without the mind.

Now this simple fact that you go on quarreling with your wife... And you both love me; it should become a great experience. You are here with a thousand people. I am saying the same thing to you all, but there are going to be a thousand interpretations. You can't agree with the other. The other has looked from a totally different angle because the other is hooked from a totally different angle. That is

the only way he or she can see it. And this is so if you are not
related with the person. If you are related with the person, then there
are more difficulties – particularly in the relationship of a wife and
husband. Their quarrel is eternal. It does not matter about what, but
they quarrel. There seems to be only one agreement: to disagree.
That is their only agreement; about that they have agreed. That they
will disagree is a tacit agreement in every marriage.

Mulla Nasruddin goes on fighting with his wife and the wife goes
on arguing. One day I told Mulla: "You have been arguing for thirty
years, and there seems to be no possible solution. Why don't you
drop it?"

He said, "How to drop it?"

I said: "Simply agree with your wife! Next time it happens,
simply agree and see what happens."

He said, "Okay."

So next time it happened, first, in the heat of it, he forgot. He
argued for half an hour. And then he suddenly remembered, so
he went out in the garden to cool down. Then he cooled himself, collected himself, decided that he would agree.

He went in and he said to his wife, "Okay, you are right. I agree
with you."

His wife looked at him with great surprise, and said, "What? But
I have changed my mind!"

And the argument starts again. They have changed sides, but
the argument is the same. When you are related with somebody,
relationship brings many complexities. There is a constant struggle
to dominate. It is not really argument that you are interested in
or your wife is interested in; it is really a question of who dominates whom. Each point becomes a power struggle: who dominates
whom? See it, and don't waste your time.

You ask me, "What should we do?" Let her have her opinions,
you have your opinions. Rather than wasting time in opinions, start
doing something according to your mind and let her do something
according to her mind. But do something.

If I say meditate – whatsoever you understand by it – start doing
something. In the beginning it is always a groping in the dark. But
by and by, the gropers reach.

Jesus says:

Ask, and it shall be given you; seek, and ye shall find; knock, and it shall be opened unto you...

Start groping, and don't be worried that you may commit some error or some mistake. Errors have to be committed, mistakes are going to happen. Nobody can reach directly; everybody has to stumble. Many times one goes astray, but if one goes on working sincerely, authentically, then sooner or later the door opens.

Open your door, let her open her door. Don't make me an excuse for your power struggle. And remember, always have compassion on other people. They have their minds, they are hooked there just as you are hooked in your own mind. See! If you cannot see without your mind, how can you expect the other to see it? Watch life, and sooner or later you will see an insight arising in you. In that very insight you will become capable of understanding the other's standpoint. I am not saying that you have to agree with the other, but you can understand. There is no need to agree, but you can see why the other is looking at this point in this way, and you can have compassion for the other.

If you have compassion, you will be surprised – the other has started feeling compassion for you. If you argue, the other argues. Argument creates argument. It goes on becoming bitter and bitterer; it poisons relationship. If you can understand the other's standpoint you will find the other is also more compassionate towards your standpoint. And people have their own standpoints because people are not enlightened.

Standpoints are bound to be there up to the third mind, the individual mind. With the fourth mind there is no argument; compassion arises. One can see the other – where the other is hooked – and feel sorry for the other because it is an imprisonment. Only with the fourth comes understanding, compassion. And with the fifth, one forgets about others or about oneself; then there is no division.

Listen to a few anecdotes. First:

A housewife complains to the psychologist, "Something is wrong with my husband. At night when he comes back from work, he always first kisses our dog and then me."

The psychologist thinks about it for a while, then he suggests thoughtfully, "Would you mind bringing a photograph of your dog the next time you come?"

You would not expect it, but this too is a possibility. There are millions of possibilities as to what the response is going to be. Now this psychologist must have been a very logical person – hooked on logic. If the husband kisses the dog first, then the dog must be more beautiful than the wife, so bring a photograph. That is his standpoint. And everybody is closed in his own world.

Two Frenchmen are standing on the platform from where the train is pulling out of Paris. One of them waves to a friend at the station, and calls, "Thanks loads! Had a marvelous time! Your wife was a wonderful lay!" Then he turns to the man standing next to him and says, "It's not true, she's no good at all. I just wanted the husband to feel good."

There are different visions. Now, whether the husband is going to feel good or bad... But this man has simply appreciated – maybe in France it is possible!

In a certain Western city where drivers too often have a way of using only one hand on the steering wheel, devoting the other to the inevitable girl at the side, an ordinance was recently passed requiring two hands on the wheel of a moving car. As a result of this law, a member of the police force stopped an approaching Ford coupe and severely reprimanded the spooning couple in this manner: "Young man, do you know the laws of this city? Why not use both hands?"

The derelict at the wheel frankly retorted, "Why, I have to use one hand to drive with!"

Different visions, different understanding...
The last:

Olga was returning to Czechoslovakia after working for a year in Britain. On the plane she began to writhe and moan, clutching her belly at the same time. The stewardess was quickly at her side to find out what was the matter. "Have you had a check-up recently?" she asked Olga.

"No, no" wailed Olga, "it wasn't a Czech, it was a Scotsman."

Enough for today.

CHAPTER 7

life is open opportunity

Matthew 7

Jesus said unto his disciples:

Not every one that saith unto me,
Lord, Lord, shall enter into the kingdom of heaven;
but he that doeth the will of my Father
which is in heaven.

Many will say to me in that day,
Lord, Lord, have we not prophesied in thy name?
and in thy name have cast out devils?
and in thy name done many wonderful works?

And then will I profess unto them, I never knew you:
depart from me, ye that work iniquity.

Therefore whosoever heareth these sayings of mine,
and doeth them,
I will liken him unto a wise man,

which built his house upon a rock:

And the rain descended, and the floods came,
and the winds blew, and beat upon that house;
and it fell not: for it was founded upon a rock.

And every one that heareth these sayings of mine,
and doeth them not,
shall be likened unto a foolish man,
which built his house upon the sand:

And the rain descended, and the floods came,
and the winds blew, and beat upon that house;
and it fell:
and great was the fall of it.

M an is not a meaning but an opportunity. The meaning is possible, but is not given. The meaning can be created, but it is not already there. It is a task not a gift. Life is a gift, but life is open opportunity. Meaning is not a gift; meaning is a search. Those who seek will certainly find it. But those who simply wait will go on missing. The meaning, the logos, has to be created by man. Man has to transform himself into that meaning. It cannot be something exterior to man; it can only be something interior.

Man's inner being has to become illumined.

Before we enter into these sutras, a few things will be helpful to understand about man, because only then is the work possible. The first thing to be understood is that man is a four-dimensional space-time continuum, just as the whole existence is. Three dimensions are of space; one dimension is of time. They are not separate: the dimension of time is but the fourth dimension of space. The three dimensions of space are static; the fourth dimension of time brings movement, makes life a process. Then existence is not a thing, but becomes an event.

And so is man. Man is a miniature universe. If you could understand man in his totality, you would have understood the whole existence. Man contains all – in seed. Man is a condensed universe. And these are the four dimensions of man.

The first dimension is what Patanjali calls *sushupti*, deep sleep, where not even a dream exists. One is utterly silent, not even a thought stirring, no wind blowing. All is absent. That absence, in deep sleep, is the first dimension. It is from that, that we start. We have to understand our sleep, only then can we go through a transformation. Only then can we build our house on a rock, otherwise not. But there are very few people who understand their sleep.

You sleep every day, you live one-third of your life in deep sleep, but you don't understand what it is. You go into it every night, and you also gain much out of it. But it is all unconscious: you don't know exactly where it leads you. It leads you to the simplest dimension of your life – the first dimension. It is very simple because there is no duality. It is very simple because there is no complexity. It is very simple because there is only oneness. You have not yet arisen as an ego, you have not yet become divided – but the unity is unconscious.

If this unity becomes conscious you will have *samadhi* instead of *sushupti.* If this unity becomes conscious, illumined, then you will have attained godliness. That's why Patanjali says, "Deep sleep and *samadhi,* the ultimate state of consciousness, are very much alike – alike because they are simple, alike because in both there is no duality, alike because in neither does the ego exist."

In the first, the ego has not yet arisen; in the second, the ego has been dissolved – but there is a great difference too. The difference is that in *samadhi* you know what sleep is. Even while asleep your consciousness is there, your awareness is there. Your awareness goes on burning like a small light inside you.

A Zen master was asked... It is a very famous saying in Zen. Thus we are told that before we study Zen the mountains are mountains and the rivers are rivers. While we are studying Zen, however, the mountains are no longer mountains and the rivers are no longer rivers. But then when our study of Zen is completed, the mountains are once again mountains and the rivers are once again rivers.

"What is meant by this?" a disciple asked a great master.

The master explained this: "It simply means that the first and the last states are alike. Only just in the middle is the disturbance. First the mountains are mountains, and again in the end the mountains are again mountains. But in the middle the mountains are no longer mountains and rivers are no longer rivers – everything is disturbed and confused and clouded. That clouding, that confusion, that chaos, exists only in the middle. In *sushupti* everything is as it should be; in *samadhi* again everything is as it should be. Between the two is the problem, is the world, is the mind, is the ego, is the whole complex of misery, hell."

When the master explained this, the disciple exclaimed: "Well, if that's true, then there is no difference between the ordinary man and the enlightened man."

"That's true," replied the master. "There is no difference really. The only thing is – the enlightened man is six inches off the ground."

But those six inches make all the difference. Why is the master six inches off the ground? He lives in the world and is yet not in it – those are the six inches, the difference. He eats, and yet he is not the eater; he remains a witness – those six inches. He is ill, he knows the pain of illness but still he is not in pain – that difference is those six inches. He dies, he knows death is happening, and yet he is not dying – that difference is those six inches. He is asleep and yet he is not asleep, he is alert too.

The first state is of *sushupti*. We will call it the first dimension. It is dreamless undividedness, it is unconscious unity, it is ignorance, but very blissful. The bliss too is unconscious. Only in the morning, when you are again awake, do you start feeling that there has been a good sleep in the night, that you have been in some faraway land, that you are feeling rejuvenated, that you are feeling very fresh, young and alive again – but only in the morning, not exactly at the time when you are in the sleep, only later on. Just some fragrance remains lingering in the memory. It reminds you that you have been to some inner depth, but where? What? You cannot figure it out. You cannot give any account of it – just a vague memory, a faint remembrance that somewhere you have been in a good space. There is no ego yet, so there is no misery possible, because misery is not possible without the ego.

This is the state in which the rocks and the mountains and the rivers and the trees exist. That's why trees look so beautiful; an unconscious bliss surrounds them. That's why mountains look so silent: they are in *sushupti*, they are in deep sleep, continuously in deep sleep. That's why when you go to the Himalayas an eternal silence is felt – virgin silence. Nobody has ever been able to disturb it. Just think of a mountain and suddenly you start feeling silent. Think of trees and you feel life flowing in. The whole of nature exists in the first state, that's why nature is so simple.

The second dimension is that of dream – what Patanjali calls *swabha*. The first disturbance in the sleep is dream. Now you are not one anymore; the second dimension has arisen. Images have started floating in you: the beginning of the world. Now you are two: the dreamer and the dreamed. Now you are seeing the dream and you are the dream too. Now you are divided. That silence of the deep sleep is no longer there, disturbance has entered because division has entered.

Division, duality, disturbance – that is the meaning of the dream. Although the duality is still unconscious it is there, but not very consciously, not that you know about it. The turmoil is there, the world is born, but things are still undefined. They are just coming out of the smoke; things are taking shape. The form is not yet clear, the form has not yet become concrete, but because of the dualism – even though it is unconscious – misery has entered. The nightmare is not very far away. The dream will turn into a nightmare.

This is where animals and birds exist. They also have a beauty, because they are very close to *sushupti*. Birds sitting on a tree are just dreams sitting in sleep. Birds making their nests on a tree are just dreams making their nests in sleep. There is a kind of affinity between the birds and the trees. If trees disappear, birds will disappear; and if birds disappear, trees will not be so beautiful any longer. There is a deep relationship; it is one family. When you see parrots screeching and flying around a tree, it almost looks as if the leaves of the tree have got wings. They are not separate, they are very close. Birds and animals are more silent than man, happier than man. Birds don't go mad. They don't need psychiatrists; they don't need any Freud, any Jung, any Adler. They are utterly healthy.

If you go into the forest and see the animals you will be surprised – they are all alike! And all healthy. You will not find a single fat animal in the natural state. I am not talking about the zoo. In the zoo things go wrong, because the zoo is no longer natural. Zoo animals start following man, they even start going mad and committing suicide. Zoo animals even turn into homosexuals. The state of the zoo is not natural; it is man-created. In nature they are very silent, happy, healthy, but that health too is unconscious – they don't know what is happening.

This is the second state: when you are in a dream. This is the second dimension. First: dreamless sleep, *sushupti* – simple one-dimensional; there is no "other." Second: dream, *swabha* – there are two dimensions, the dreamer and the dreamed, the content and the consciousness. The division has arisen: the looker and the looked at, the observer and the observed. Duality has entered. This is the second dimension.

In the first dimension there is only the present tense. Sleep knows no past, no future. Of course because it knows no past, no future, it cannot know the present either, because the present exists only in the middle. You have to be aware of the past and the future, only then can you be aware of the present. Because there is no past and no future, sleep exists only in the present. It is pure present, but unconscious.

The division enters with dreams. With dreams the past becomes very important. Dreams are past-oriented; all dreams come from the past. They are fragments of the past floating in the mind, dust from the past, which has not settled yet.

"It's her old man I feel sorry for. He was in bed the other night fast asleep. Suddenly she noticed he had a smile on his face. She thought 'Hello, he's having one of those dreams again.' So she put down her crisps and her bottle of stout and woke him up."

He said, "Blimey, you would, wouldn't you. I was having a lovely dream then. I was at this auction where they were selling mouths. They had small rosebud ones for a quid. Pert little pursed ones for two quid, and little smiling ones for a fiver."

She said, "Ooh! Did they have a mouth my size?"

"Yes. They were holding the auction in it."

Whatsoever you dream has something to say about your past. It may be that you see an auction – little smiling rosebud mouths are being sold – but the auction is being held in your wife's mouth. Maybe you have never said to your wife, "Shut up, and keep your big mouth closed!" Maybe you have not said it so clearly, but you have been thinking it so many times. It is lingering in the mind. It is there. Maybe you have never been as true in your waking state as you are when you are asleep. And you can be, you can afford to be true. All dreams float from the past. With the dream, the past becomes existential. So the present is there, and the past.

With the third, the third dimension, the waking state – what Patanjali calls *jagrut* – multiplicity enters. The first is unity, the second is duality, the third is multiplicity. Great complexity arises. The whole world is born. In sleep you are deep inside yourself; in dream you are no longer that deep inside yourself and yet you are not out either. You are just in the middle, on the threshold. With waking consciousness you are outside yourself, you have gone into the world.

You can understand the biblical story of Adam's expulsion in these three dimensions. When Adam is there in the Garden of Eden and has not yet eaten the fruit of the Tree of Knowledge it is deep sleep, unconscious – it is unconscious bliss. There is no disturbance; everything is simply beautiful. He has not known any misery. Then he eats the fruit of the Tree of Knowledge. Knowledge arises, images start floating, dreams have started functioning. He is no longer the same. He is still in the Garden of Eden but no longer part of it – alien, a stranger, an outsider. He has not yet been expelled, but in a subtle way he is no longer centered there. He is uprooted. This is the state of the dream – the first taste of knowledge because of the first taste of duality: the distinction of observer and the observed. And then he is being expelled from the Garden of Eden, thrown out – that is the third state, the waking state. Now he cannot go back; there is no way back. He has forgotten that he has an inside too.

In deep sleep you are inside. In wakefulness you are outside. In dream you are just in the middle, hanging, not settled yet where to go, still indecisive, in doubt, uncertain. With the waking state, the ego enters. In the dream state there are just rudimentary fragments of the ego arising, but they settle in the third. The ego becomes the most concrete, most solid, most decisive phenomenon; then whatsoever you do, you do because of the ego.

The third state brings a little consciousness: just one percent, not much of it, just a flickering consciousness, momentary consciousness. The first was absolutely unconscious, the second was unconsciousness disturbed, the third is the first glimpse of consciousness. And because of this – the momentary glimpse of consciousness – that one percent of consciousness coming in, creates the ego. Now the future also enters.

First there is only the present unconscious, then there is the past unconscious, now there is the future. Past, present, future, and the whole complexity of time revolves around you. This is the state where people are stuck, where you are stuck, where everybody is stuck. And if you go on building your house with these three dimensions you will be building it on sand, because your whole effort will be unconscious.

To do something in unconsciousness is futile; it is shooting arrows in the dark, not knowing where the target is. It is not going to bring much of a result. First, light is needed. The target has to be looked for, searched for. And enough light is needed so you can move towards the target consciously. That is possible only when the fourth dimension starts functioning. It rarely happens; but whenever it happens, then meaning is really born, logos is born.

You will live a meaningless life if you live only with these three. You will live a meaningless life because you will not be able to create yourself. How can you create in such unawareness?

The fourth dimension is of awareness, witnessing – what Patanjali calls *turiya*. And in the Gospels Jesus goes on saying again and again to his disciples: "Awake! Beware! Watch!" All these words indicate *turiya*. And it is one of the misfortunes of history that Christianity has not been able to bring this message clearly to the world. It has failed utterly.

Rarely has a religion failed so utterly as Christianity. Jesus was not very fortunate because the disciples that he found turned out to be very ordinary, and the religion became almost a political organization. The church became not a follower of Jesus but deep down really antagonistic to Jesus. The church has been doing things, in the name of Jesus, against Jesus.

Buddha was more fortunate. The followers never became a church, they never became so organized politically and they never became so worldly. They carried little bits of Buddha's message down the ages.

This fourth dimension has to be understood as deeply as possible, because this is the goal. It is again pure consciousness, simplicity. The first was simple but unconscious; the fourth is simple but conscious. Unity again, bliss again – with only one difference: now everything is conscious, the inner light is burning bright. You are fully alert. It is not a dark night inside you but a full-moon night, moonlit. That is the meaning of enlightenment: the inner illumination.

Again there is only one time left: the present, but now it is a conscious present. The past is no longer hanging around. A man who is aware cannot move in the past, because it is no more. A man who is aware cannot move in the future, because it is not yet. A man who is aware lives in the present, herenow. Here is his only space and now is his only time. And because he is only herenow, time as such disappears. Eternity is born, timelessness is born. And when one is totally alert, ego cannot exist.

Ego is a shadow cast in unawareness. When all is light, the ego cannot exist. You will be able to see the falsity of it, the pseudo-ness of it. And in that very seeing is its disappearance.

These are the four dimensions of human consciousness. People live only in the first three. The fourth carries the meaning; hence, the people who live only in three live a meaningless life. They know it. You know it! If you look into your life you will not find any meaning there, just a haphazard, accidental progression of things. One thing is followed by another, but with no particular consistency, with no particular relevance. One thing is followed by another, just accidentally.

That's what Jean-Paul Sartre means when he says, "Man is a useless passion, man is accidental." Yes, he is right if he is talking about the three dimensions: first, second and third, but it is not true about the fourth. And he cannot say anything about the fourth because he has not experienced anything of it. Only a christ or a buddha can say something about the fourth.

Christ consciousness is of the fourth, so is buddha consciousness. To remain confined in the three is to be in the world. To enter into the fourth is to enter into nirvana, or call it the kingdom of God. They are only different expressions for the same thing.

A few more things: the second dimension is a shadow of the first: sleep and dream. Dreams cannot exist without sleep; sleep is a must. Sleep can exist without dreams. So sleep is primary, dreams are secondary – just a shadow. And so is the case with the third and the fourth. The third is the shadow of the fourth, because the third can exist only if there is some consciousness. A little bit of consciousness has to be there, only then can the third exist. The third cannot exist without a little bit of consciousness in it, a ray of light. It is not much of a light, but a ray of light is needed. The fourth can exist without the third, but the third cannot exist without the fourth. The fourth is awareness, absolute awareness; and the third is just a small ray of light in the dark night. But it exists because of that small ray of light. If that ray of light disappears it will become the second; it will not be the third any longer. Your life looks like a shadow life because you are living with the third. And the third is the shadow of the fourth. Only with the fourth do you come home. Only with the fourth are you grounded in existence.

The first is absolute darkness; the fourth is absolute light. Between these two are their two shadows. Those two shadows have become so important to us that we think that is our whole life. Hindus have been calling the world *maya*, illusion, because of these two dimensions which have become predominant: the second and the third. We have lost track of the first, and we have not yet searched for the fourth.

And one more thing: if you find the fourth you will find the first. Only one who has found the fourth will be able to know about the first, because once you have come to the fourth you can be asleep and remain alert. In the Gita, Krishna defines the yogi as one who is awake while asleep. That's his definition for the yogi. A strange definition: one who is awake while asleep.

Just the reverse is the situation with you. You are asleep while awake. That is the definition of a non-yogi: asleep while awake. You look awake, and you are not. It is just an idea, this awake state. Ninety-nine percent consists of sleep – only one percent of wakefulness. And that one percent also goes on changing. Sometimes it is there and sometimes it is not there at all. It was there; somebody insults you and it is not there. You have become angry, and you have lost even that small awareness. Somebody treads on your foot and it has gone. It is very delicate. Anybody can take it and destroy it, and very easily. You were perfectly okay; a letter comes and something is written in the letter, and suddenly you are no longer okay. All is disturbed. A single word can create such a disturbance! Your awareness is not very much.

And you are awake only in rare moments; you are awake in danger, because in danger you *have* to be awake. But when there is no danger, you start snoring. You can hear people snoring – walking down the road, they are snoring. They are caged in their own unconsciousness.

A drunk bumped into a stop sign. Dazed and disoriented, he stepped back and then advanced in the same direction. Once more he hit the sign. He retreated a few steps, waited awhile, and then marched forward.

Colliding with the post again, he embraced it in defeat and said, "It is no use. I am fenced in. I am stopped in every direction."

And yet he has not moved in any other direction. He has been moving to the post again and again. And being hit, naturally he concludes that he has been fenced in from every direction. This is the situation of the ordinary human consciousness. You go on moving in the same unconscious way, in the same unconscious direction. Again and again you are hit and you think, "Why is there so much misery? Why? Why did God create such a miserable world in the first place? Is God a kind of sadist? Does he want to torture people? Why has he created a life which is almost like a prison, in which there is no freedom?"

Life is absolutely free, but to see that freedom first you will have to free your consciousness. Remember it as a criterion: the more conscious you are, the freer; the less conscious you are, the less free. The more conscious you are, the more blissful; the less conscious you are, the less blissful. It depends on how conscious you are.

There are people who will go on looking into the scriptures to find out ways to become freer, to become more blissful, to attain to truth. That is not going to help because it is not a question of the scriptures. If you are unconscious and you go on reading the Bible and the Koran and the Vedas and the Gita, it is not going to help, because your unconsciousness cannot be changed by your studies. In fact the scripture cannot change your consciousness, but your unconsciousness will change the scripture – the meaning of the scriptures. You will find your own meanings there. You will interpret in such a way that the Bible, the Veda, the Koran, will start functioning as imprisonments. That's how Christians and Hindus and Mohammedans are – all imprisoned.

I have heard...

After booking into a large hotel, a self-styled evangelist read in his room for an hour or two – and he was reading the Bible – then went down to the bar, and after a couple of drinks, he struck up a conversation with the redheaded barmaid. He stayed up until closing time, and after the girl had cleared up they both went up to the evangelist's room.

When he started to interfere with her clothing, the barmaid

seemed to have second thoughts. "Are you sure this is all right?" she said. "After all you are a holy man."

"My dear," he replied, "it's written in the Bible."

She took him at his word, and they spent a very pleasant night together. The next morning, however, as the girl was preparing to leave, she said, "You know, I don't remember the part of the Bible you spoke about last night."

The evangelist picked up the Gideon's Bible from the bedside table, opened the cover, and showed her the flyleaf, on which was inscribed "The redheaded barmaid screws."

Reading the whole Bible for one hour and this was his finding. Somebody had inscribed on the flyleaf...

If you read the Bible, *you* read it, remember. And the meaning that you give it will be yours; the interpretation will be yours. It cannot help you because it cannot even protect itself from you. How can it help you? The only way to have any change in life is to change consciousness. And to change consciousness you do not have to go into the Bible and the Vedas. You have to go inwards, you have to go into meditation. Scholarship won't help.

A blind man was invited to a festivity and there he ate some delicious pudding. He was so enchanted by its taste that he asked someone sitting next him to tell him what it looked like.

"White," the man said.

"What is white?" the blind man asked.

"White? – like a duck," came the answer.

"How does a duck look?" persisted the blind man.

Puzzled for a moment, the man finally said. "Here, feel this," and took the blind man's hand in his hand and guided it along his other hand and arm, which he bent at the elbow and wrist to resemble the shape of a duck.

At this, the blind man exclaimed, "Oh, the pudding is crooked!"

That's what is going to happen. You cannot help the blind man to know what white is, or what color is, or what light is. All your help is going to give him something wrong. There is no way to help the blind man by definitions, by explanations, by theories, by dogmas, by scriptures. The only way to help him is to heal his eyes.

Buddha has said: "I am a physician. I don't give you definitions of light, I simply heal your eyes." And that's what Jesus is. All the miracles that are reported in the Bible are not miracles but parables – that a blind man came to him and he touched his eyes, and the blind man was healed and he could see immediately. If it is just about the physical eye, this is not much. Then Jesus is already out of date, because medical science can do it. Sooner or later, Jesus will have to be completely forgotten. If he was simply curing physical eyes, then it is not going to mean much in the future. This can be done by science. And that which can be done by science should be done by science; religion should not enter into it – there is no need. Religion has far higher things to do. So again and again I insist that these stories are not miracles but parables. People are blind, and the Jesus touch is a magic touch. He helps them to see, he helps them to become aware, he helps them to become more conscious. He brings the fourth.

To go into the fourth, work is needed. *Work* in the sense that Gurdjieff used to use that word. Work means a great effort to transform your being, a great effort to center your being, a great effort to drop all that which creates darkness, and to bring all that which can help a little light come in. If a door has to be opened, then open the door and let the light come in. If a wall has to be broken, then break the wall and let the light come in. Work means a conscious effort to search, to inquire, to explore into the dimension of the fourth – into light, into awareness – and a conscious effort to drop all that which helps you remain unconscious, to drop all that which keeps you mechanical.

A man bought a farm and a sow. He asked his wife to watch the sow, explaining that if she saw it eating grass it was ready for mating and could be taken to the next farm. A couple of days later his wife told him that the sow had started to eat grass. So the farmer put it on a barrow and took it to the next farm to be mated. When he came back, he told his wife to watch the sow again. "If the sow eats grass again, it has not taken," he explained.

A few days later, his wife reported that the sow was eating grass again. So it was put on the barrow and taken for mating again. The farmer brought it back and again asked his wife to watch it closely. Two days later he asked his wife if it had been eating grass again.

"No," she said, "but it's sitting in the barrow."

The mechanical mind, the instinctive mind, the repetitive mind has to be broken and dropped. Work means an alchemical change. Great effort is needed. Hard and arduous is the path. It is an uphill task.

Now the sutras:

Not every one that saith unto me,
Lord, Lord, shall enter into the kingdom of heaven;
but he that doeth the will of my Father
which is in heaven.

Jesus says: prayer is necessary but not enough. It has to be supported by work. *Not every one that saith unto me, Lord, Lord, shall enter into the kingdom of heaven...* Just by praising me, Jesus says, you will not enter into the kingdom of heaven – not just by praising God. Flattery won't help, and people go on flattering God in the hope that flattery will work there too. Only work, only conscious effort, hard effort will help – nothing else can help. Prayer is good, prayer prepares the way, but then you have to walk on it!

And a very strange statement it is: *...but he that doeth the will of my Father which is in heaven.* Two things to be understood: this sentence is strange because it says: *...but he that doeth the will of my Father which is in heaven.* Heaven means the unknown. Heaven means that which you have not entered yet, heaven means that which you have not experienced yet. You can take it on faith, you can trust Jesus. If you love him, you will trust him. But Jesus' God is not available for you to inspect. You cannot see Jesus' God. He sees him; it is his experience. But for you it is only a trust. And Jesus says: *...but he that doeth the will of my Father which is in heaven.*

First, God is not known to you, not even his whereabouts are known. Heaven means the unknown, the mysterious, the unexplainable. His whereabouts are unknown. You have never encountered God, and the demand is that if you surrender your will to his will, only then...

Now in this amazing statement, there are two things: you have to surrender your will and you have to follow God's will. First, surrender is possible only if you have a will. Ordinarily people think that a man who has a will, will not be able to surrender. People think that weaklings, those whose wills are not very strong, can surrender. That is not right. Only very, very willed people, who have a strong willpower, can surrender – because surrender is the ultimate in willpower. It is the last and there is nothing higher than that. To surrender you will need great will. You will have to put all your willpower into it, only then will the surrender happen. That's why I say it is an amazing statement. It is very contradictory, but life is like that – paradoxical. And this is one of the fundamental paradoxes: the paradox of will and surrender.

Surrender happens only when there is great will. But when surrender happens, the will disappears and not even a trace is left. Surrender is the will committing suicide. And only when your will has committed suicide can God's will flow into you. These two opposites can meet: your surrender and God's will.

Surrender means receptivity. When you are receptive, utterly receptive, God can descend into you. You cannot say: "First I have to encounter God, only then will I surrender," because there is no way for you to encounter him. The only way to encounter him is to surrender because when you are surrendered he comes. You can know him only after surrender, not before surrender.

Now this is asking the impossible. But religion asks the impossible, and there have been a few people who have been able to do the impossible. Those who have done the impossible have achieved the impossible. That is how it is, and it cannot be otherwise. You cannot have a sample of God's experience and then decide whether to purchase or not. You cannot have a look at God's being: he is not available for window-shopping. First you have to surrender, and you have to surrender in darkness and you have to surrender in absolute ignorance. You have no proof, and no argument can help you. Great courage is needed – daredevil courage is needed. That's why I say the religious man is the most courageous man in the world. Those who walk on the moon are nothing. Yes, they take great risk, but that is nothing compared to religion, because the demand, the very demand is impossible.

First you surrender, and then you come to know – but how to first surrender? How to know what is God's will? The only way to know God's will is to surrender *your* will. You efface yourself; you don't stand in between, you simply disappear. In your disappearance God appears. Your absence becomes his presence. When you are empty as far as your self is concerned, you become full with his presence. He comes only when you are not, then the great transformation happens: the meeting of the drop with the ocean, the meeting of the part with the whole. And then there is great jubilation.

Again and again, Jesus says to his disciples, "Rejoice!" What is he talking about? Why does he go on saying, "Rejoice! Celebrate! Be glad!"? He is taking them closer and closer to that ultimate revolution where they will surrender, and God will take over. Each step is a rejoicing, is a celebration, because each step taken towards God is taken towards your fulfillment. You can be fulfilled only when God has become a resident in you, otherwise you are empty, hollow, stuffed with straw and nothing else. Only when he comes will your temple have a deity in it. He can fulfill you by becoming a host in your being.

> Not every one that saith unto me,
> Lord, Lord, shall enter into the kingdom of heaven;
> but he that doeth the will of my Father
> which is in heaven.
>
> Many will say to me in that day,
> Lord, Lord, have we not prophesied in thy name?
> and in thy name have cast out devils?
> and in thy name done many wonderful works?
>
> And then will I profess unto them, I never knew you:
> depart from me, ye that work iniquity.

Jesus says, "In that moment, in that space, many would like to tell me, 'I have been doing miracles in your name.'" There are many who are healing in the world in the name of Christ, who are serving people in the name of Christ, who are converting people in the name of Christ, and doing a thousand and one good things in the name of Christ. But deep down, if you look, the name of the Christ is just a label; deep down is the ego.

A woman came to Jesus and touched his garment and was healed. And the woman was very thankful; she fell at his feet and thanked him from her very heart.

Jesus said: "Don't thank me. I have not done anything. It is your faith that has healed you. And if you want to be grateful, be grateful to God. I am nobody, I am just a passage, I am instrumental. Forget about me. It is your faith and God's presence that has healed you. If I was there, I was just like a link, a bridge."

When you cross a river you don't thank the bridge. You don't even remember, you don't look at the bridge. Jesus says: "I am just a bridge, a vehicle."

Jesus says: *Many will say to me in that day. Lord, Lord, have we not prophesied in thy name? and in thy name have cast out devils? and in thy name done many wonderful works?* And behind all their works is the ego. They are claiming. The claim comes from the ego – the claimant is always the ego. If you are not there, if there is no ego, you cannot claim; you will be silent in that moment. You will not start bragging that I have done this, and I have done that.

Jesus says: *And then will I profess unto them, I never knew you...* Jesus knows only those who are absolutely silent, who have no claims. Jesus knows only those who have utterly disappeared, who have become just vehicles of God – who cannot claim because they are not. *And then will I profess unto them, I never knew you: depart from me, ye that work iniquity.* Jesus uses the word *iniquity.* It means unrighteousness, wickedness, gross injustice. It is always God who works through you; whenever you claim, it is gross injustice.

Just watch, observe, meditate over it. You saw a man drowning in the river; you rushed and you jumped into the river, and saved the man. By the time you are back on the bank you start bragging "I saved this man." But is this true? When the man was drowning and you were on the bank, had you thought about it? Had you thought in this way – "This man is drowning, I have to save him. If I don't save him, who will? Saving is good, and righteous and virtuous" ...and all that? No, in that moment, God possessed you. There was no thinking about it. You simply jumped into the water. It was not that you did it; God did it through you. But later on, back on the bank, you start bragging "I saved this man."

This is injustice. This is gross injustice. Jesus says that this is unrighteous. It is something that God has done through you, and you are claiming it as your ego glory, claiming it as an ornament for your ego?

Remember, whenever something good happens, it happens through God. Good is that which happens through God. And bad is that which happens through you. This is religious understanding. A religious person cannot claim any virtue. Yes, he can repent for all the sins, but he cannot claim any virtue. He will cry and weep, and he will say, "I have done this wrong and that wrong!" But not for a single moment will the idea arise in him: "Look: this good I have also done." That is not possible for the religious mind. The religious mind knows that whenever something goes wrong: "I must have come in between me and God. If something goes wrong, I must have misinterpreted it, I must have deviated the energy, I must have distorted it. If something goes right – who am I? That simply shows that I have not distorted, that's all."

When you are standing before a mirror and the mirror mirrors perfectly, it is not anything special; it is how it should be. But if your face is distorted, then the mirror is at fault, then things are not as they should be. Good is that which happens through God, and bad is that which happens through the ego. So if the ego claims the good, the good also becomes bad. And the claim is wrong.

Buddha came back to his home after twelve years, when he became enlightened. His father was very angry, naturally – understandable. He was the only son, the father was old, and the son had become a dropout. His father was really ill, old, and he had to carry the whole load and responsibility of the kingdom. When he was thinking that his son would take charge, he escaped. He escaped without saying anything. One night he simply disappeared. The father was angry.

The first meeting of the son and the father was at the great gates of the town, and the father said, "Son, although I am angry I will forgive you. Come back home and forget all this nonsense."

And Buddha said, "Sir, will you look at me unprejudiced? I am not the same man who escaped from your palace. I am not your son!"

The father started laughing, and he said, "Who are you kidding? You are not my son? Can't I recognize you? Can't I see my own blood? I have given birth to you. And what are you saying – that you are not the same person?"

Buddha said, "Sir, don't feel offended. I came through you, but you have not given birth to me."

That's what Jesus is saying. He is saying that whenever something comes through you, you are not the originator of it. If good comes through you, God is the originator.

Never claim the life of your child; life belongs to God. You cannot produce life; you were just instrumental. While making love to your woman, what exactly were you doing? You were just instrumental. In fact, love has also happened. It was not any doing on your part. Love has happened; you were making love to your woman and something happened. And you don't know what exactly – the mystery remains mystery. The woman becomes pregnant, and a child is born. And you start claiming, "This is my child."

I lived in Raipur for a year. One day I saw the neighbor beating his small child, so I rushed into his house and said to him, "What are you doing? I will call the police!"

He said, "What are you talking about? This is my kid! I can do anything that I want to my kid! And who are you?"

I said: "This is not your kid. This is God's kid. And I can claim as much as you can claim."

He could not believe what nonsense I was saying. He said, "This is my kid. Don't you know? – you have been living here for a year."

He could not understand because of the claim: "This is my kid, and I can do anything that I want to do."

For centuries parents were allowed to kill their child if they wanted to. They were allowed because the thought that they had given birth was accepted. How can you give birth? You have just been instrumental. Don't claim; no child belongs to you. All children belong to God, they come from God. You are at most a caretaker. And all good comes from God. If something goes wrong, then certainly you must have distorted it. If evil is born, it is through you.

That's what Jesus means when he says: *And then will I profess unto them, I never knew you: depart from me, ye that work iniquity.* You are claiming that you did miracles, that you did this and that? This very claim makes you irreligious. And Jesus says, "I will have to say to them that I don't know you at all."

Therefore whosoever heareth these sayings of mine,
and doeth them,

I will liken him unto a wise man,
which built his house upon a rock...

By doing, not just by praying. Prayer is cheap. One can do it because nothing is at stake. That's why people have become church-goers, worshippers. They go to the mosque and the *gurudwara* and the temple. It is very cheap and easy – the Sunday religion. You go to church for one hour: it is a kind of social formality which you fulfill. And you think you have fulfilled your life, you have fulfilled your med-itation, you have fulfilled your innermost passion for God?

...whosoever heareth these sayings of mine, and doeth them, I will liken him unto a wise man, which built his house upon a rock... Only if you *do*, if you work hard, if you try to transform your-self. A thousand and one times you may fail, but if you go on and on, then success comes. Certainly it comes because it has come to Jesus, it has come to Buddha; it can come to everybody. It is every-body's birthright. You can have it, but you cannot have it cheaply. You will have to pay for it and you will have to pay with your whole life. Less than that and you will not attain it.

That's what Gurdjieff means when he says "work."

And the rain descended, and the floods came,
and the winds blew, and beat upon that house;
and it fell not: for it was founded upon a rock.

And every one that heareth these sayings of mine,
and doeth them not,
shall be likened unto a foolish man,
which built his house upon the sand:

And the rain descended, and the floods came,
and the winds blew, and beat upon that house;
and it fell:
and great was the fall of it.

I talked about four dimensions. If you make your house uncon-sciously you will be making it on sand. If you make your house in time, then you will be making it on the sands. Time is the sand. If you make your house in eternity, in timelessness, in the fourth dimension of *turiya*, of awareness, of witnessing, then you will be making it on a rock. And if you have made it on a rock, nothing can destroy it; it is immortal, it is deathless. If you have made it on the sand, then anything – any wind, any rain – is going to destroy it. And you will be utterly crushed under it, because you live in that house.

People are making sand castles – with money, with power, with prestige. Unconscious, asleep, snoring, they go on making their houses, not knowing what they are doing. They will be crushed under those houses. *...and it fell: and great was the fall of it.* Make your house on a rock. And there is no other rock than consciousness. Jesus called one of his disciples "Peter." The word *Peter* means "the rock." He called that certain disciple Peter because he was the most conscious of them all. He told his disciples that Peter would function as the rock for his church.

These are symbolic things. Peter was the most conscious of them all. He called him Peter because he was conscious, because he was like a rock. And he said: "My church will be built on Peter. He will function as the cornerstone, the very foundation of it." But that church was never made. The church never used Peter as the foundation. The church used Paul as the foundation, and Paul is not christlike at all. Paul is a dangerous fellow.

At first he was against Jesus and he was against the message of Jesus. He was going towards Jerusalem to persecute Christians, and then, on the road, something happened.

This conversion happens sometimes — it is very psychological. He was so obsessed by Jesus and how to destroy his message that he was continuously thinking about Jesus, dreaming about Jesus. Jesus was his obsession twenty-four hours a day. Moving on the road towards Jerusalem alone one night, he heard a voice as if Jesus had shouted and said, "Why are you persecuting me? Why?" It may have been just his own unconscious: it may have been just his whole obsession that his whole unconscious started feeling. His conscious was against Jesus, and the unconscious always goes against the conscious – it is just the polar opposite. When the conscious was too much against Jesus, the unconscious must have become by and by interested in Jesus. This voice must have come from his innermost core, "Why? Why are you persecuting me?"

Hearing this voice, he fell on the ground in the dust. He was very shocked, and it proved to him that Jesus was powerful. He became converted. His name was Saul; his name now became Paul – he became converted. First he was persecuting Jesus' disciples... He was not a contemporary of Jesus; Jesus had gone. And now he changed his whole energy. First he was persecuting Christians, now he started converting people to Christianity. This Paul became the foundation of the Vatican church. This Paul had never known Jesus. He had never walked with the master; he was not a contemporary. And this Paul was a dangerous man – obsessed, angry, violent, aggressive. But he converted the world to Christianity, he became the foundation.

Peter was lost, and Peter was the rock chosen by Jesus. And why had he chosen Peter, why had he called him "rock"? – because he was the most conscious. Jesus' whole message is the message of consciousness. But great work is needed, only then can you make your life on a rock; otherwise you will be building on sand.

Therefore whosoever heareth these sayings of mine, and doeth them... Doing is the question, because only by doing will you attain to being; not by saying, not by thinking. Doing means to be committed to whatsoever you feel is right.

Just the other night a young woman was here and she was saying, "I am already a sannyasin and you are in my heart, but I cannot take sannyas yet." If I am in your heart, if you think you are already a sannyasin, then why not be committed? Then why not be involved? It is easy to say that you are in my heart – it is very easy. It is very easy to say, "I am already a sannyasin in my heart." But to become committed, to declare to the world "I am a sannyasin," is more difficult, takes more courage, needs more guts.

Jesus says, "Unless you do what you think is right, nothing is going to happen." You can go on thinking and thinking. Thinking never transforms anybody; thoughts are impotent. Only acts are potent, only doings ultimately become your being.

...I will liken him unto a wise man... who doeth what I am saying: *...which built his house upon a rock: And the rain descen-ded, and the floods came, and the winds blew, and beat upon that house; and it fell not: for it was founded upon a rock.* And there are many winds that will come; there are many rains and floods that will descend. They will all try to shatter your house because life is a challenge, and anything that you attain has to be tested against challenges. The higher you grow, the greater the challenges that will be coming.

...And the rain descended, and the floods came, and the winds

blew, and beat upon that house; and it fell not: for it was founded upon a rock. If you don't have anything, there will be no challenge. This has to be understood. If you don't love, there will be no challenge; if you love, there will be great challenge in your life. If you don't meditate, there will be no challenge; if you meditate, the whole mind will strike against you, will become antagonistic, will try to destroy your meditation. It is a basic law in life that if you try to attain something higher, it has to be tested, it has to pass through many tests and many criteria. Those tests look like winds and floods, and they will strike hard on you. But they are good, because only they will make you strong and crystallized. And only they will show you whether you have built on rock or on the sands.

Remember, only if you do what you feel, think is right, is there going to be any change, mutation – otherwise not. Be a wise man, don't be a fool. Make something in timelessness. Make something out of your consciousness, so death cannot destroy it. There is something which is deathless, and unless you attain it you will live in agony, suffering and fear. Once it is attained all agony, all misery, all hell disappears. And then there is beauty, and then there is benediction.

Enough for today.

live in eternity

The first question:

Osho,
Since I have been with you I have come to know Jesus in a new
light. As a Jew I could never accept his teachings. Never before did
I think of him as an enlightened being, as I think about the
Buddha. When I first came in contact with Buddhist teaching in
Nepal, I felt an immediate affinity towards it. Here now in Pune,
Jesus' sayings are becoming comprehensible and acceptable. Yet
still doubts persist. Why did he say it all in such a roundabout way,
especially considering that he was talking to the common people?
And look at all the confusion that has now been caused by the
manner in which he spoke. It doesn't make any sense to me, and I
won't feel completely at ease with Jesus as I do with Buddha until
this question is resolved. I have the feeling that if I need to read
the New Testament I would still reject it.

First, it is very easy to accept something that is absolutely strange
to you. To a Jew, Jesus is not a stranger, Buddha is a stranger. It
is very easy to accept Buddha, it is very difficult to accept Jesus.

First, with Jesus you are acquainted, and acquainted through a certain conditioning: the Jewish conditioning. Jesus is a rebel for the Jew. The same is the case with Buddha for a Hindu: the Hindu finds it very difficult to accept Buddha. It is easier to accept Jesus, because for the Hindu and the Hindu mind nothing is involved with Jesus, no attitudes are involved; the relationship is a new one. But with the Buddha much is involved. Buddha was a rebel who spoke against Hindu orthodoxy, who tried to destroy the Hindu organization. Although he was the highest flowering of Hindu consciousness, still he was against the Hindu past. He was the future, but he was against the past. The future *has* to be against the past.

So was the case with Jesus: he was the crescendo of Jewish consciousness, he was the ultimate flower of the whole Jewish history. But because he was the ultimate flower, he had to reject many things. He had to rebel against Jewish lethargy, the Jewish past, Jewish prophets. And the Jew feels very hurt.

It is like... I was born in a Jaina family. Now, the most difficult thing for the Jaina is to accept me. It is not so difficult for a Christian, for a Jew, for a Hindu. The most difficult thing is for the Jaina to accept me because he has involvements with me. He was hoping that I would confirm his past. He was expecting that I would go to the world and spread the message of Mahavira. Then he would have been happy. But now I have my own message, his expectations are destroyed. And not only my own message; I have a thousand and one things to say against the Jaina tradition – that hurts.

So here it is very rare to find a Jaina. You can see it. You will not find many Indians here, because to them too I am close, and it hurts. But for the non-Indian it is not a problem. In the first place the Jew has no expectations of me, so there is no involvement. He is not expecting anything from me. He comes to me with an open heart, without any prejudice. He wants to understand me, he does not want to manipulate me. The Jaina wants to manipulate me and because of the expectation, the frustration, there is difficulty.

The Jews were waiting for the Messiah for thousands of years. They were hoping the Messiah would come and would fulfill all their desires. The Messiah would come and would prove that they were the chosen people of God. "The Messiah will come, and that will bring a Jewish era in the world."

And then comes Jesus and all the hopes are destroyed forever.

After Jesus, the possibility of the world turning into a Jewish world has become impossible. After Jesus, the chosen people are no longer chosen. After Jesus, Christians have become the chosen people of God. The Jews were hoping that Jesus would give them more consolidation, and he started to uproot them. He had to uproot – that is the only way to bring the future in. The past has to be destroyed, the old has to be destroyed to give birth to the new. The known has to be thrown out – that is the only way to invite the unknown.

Naturally, Jews were very offended. They were very offended by Jesus. And then, because of Jesus, Jews have been in misery for these two thousand years: Christians have been torturing them, killing them, murdering them. All that the Christians have done in these two thousand years provokes again and again a great enmity towards Jesus.

So the first thing to be understood is that is very easy to accept a stranger. Jesus says two things again and again. One: "Love your neighbor," and another: "Love your enemy." And my feeling is that both are the same – the neighbor is the enemy. It is the most difficult thing in life to love your neighbor. It is very easy to love a stranger. You meet a certain man or a woman on the train. You don't know anything about him, he does not know anything about you. And how open you become! Within minutes of being introduced, you are saying things to each other that you have not even said to your beloved. Nothing is involved; the next station will come and he will get down and disappear forever, you will never see him again. You can be open with him, you can be true with him. Have you not observed this? With strangers you start confessing things that you dare not confess to anybody you are related with, because then there is danger. There is no danger with a stranger.

So when a Jew comes across Buddha, it is very easy to understand, because there is no prejudice, no presupposition. Your being a Jew does not become a hindrance with Buddha. He is so far away, so unrelated. He was not against Moses, he was not against Abraham, he was not against David; he is not related to Jewish history at all – alien, a foreigner. You can accept him as a guest.

But Jesus... Jesus is not alien to you. He was born into your family, and then he started destroying the very house. Then he started to destroy the very temple that you and your ancients had always worshipped in, although he says, "I have come not to destroy, but to fulfill." But to fulfill, he has to destroy. The old has to be dismantled, the old has to be completely effaced from the earth; only then can the new temple be built.

So the name of Jesus hurts. You cannot forgive Jesus yet; it is impossible to forgive unless you drop your Jewish conditioning. Then there will be no problem; then Jesus will be as comprehensible as Buddha or Krishna. The problem is coming from your Jewish conditioning, the problem is not coming from Jesus. The problem is in you, not in the New Testament.

You say, "Since I have been with you I have come to know Jesus in a new light." Yes, through me it will be easier because I am not a Jew. Through me, Jesus becomes non-Jewish. The way I interpret him is the way I would like to interpret Buddha, Patanjali, Shankara. The way I interpret Jesus has nothing to do with the Jewish mind. Then you can start looking at Jesus in a new light because I am throwing a new light on him. In my light he starts changing; he is no longer Jewish. I don't put him in the context of the Jewish mind – I cannot because I am not a Jew. You will find it easier, far easier, to approach Jesus through me, because through me Jesus is no longer a Jew.

"Since I have been with you I have come to know Jesus in a new light. As a Jew I could never accept his teachings." It is not that *you* could not accept his teaching, it is the *Jew* within you. The Jew has to be dropped. And when I say the Jew has to be dropped, I am saying the Hindu has to be dropped, the Buddhist has to be dropped, the Mohammedan has to be dropped. Then your eyes will be open, then you will have a clarity, a transparency to your vision. You will be able to see through and through, and things will come into a totally new context. And then Jesus will look beautiful. He was one of the most beautiful persons to have walked on the earth.

But, it is unfortunate: Jews missed him just the way Buddha was missed by the Hindus. It has always been the tragedy. It is very difficult for a Hindu to understand Buddha. The very name and antagonism arises because he said things which are against the Vedas. He said things which are against the brahmins, he said things which are against the code of Manu. He said things – not only said, but he started creating a new society; he created a non-Hindu world. He created a world where there would be no distinction between the sudra, the untouchable, and the brahmin, the high priest. He created a world which would be classless, with nobody inferior, nobody superior. He started putting down foundations for an utterly new society. The Hindus were angry; they destroyed Buddhism.

Do you know that Buddhism no longer exists in India? Buddha is almost a foreigner. He is loved in China, in Tibet, in Japan, in Sri Lanka, in Thailand. The whole of Asia is Buddhist except for India; he was born in India and he is no longer here. What happened? The Hindus took revenge: they destroyed... And remember, their destruction was far cleverer than the Jewish destruction of Jesus – because the Jews killed Jesus, and that is where they committed a great mistake. The Hindus didn't kill Buddha, they are a far cleverer people. They didn't kill Buddha, but they killed Buddhism.

The Jews killed Jesus, but because they killed Jesus, they made Jesus so important, so significant – the very center of human history – because of the crucifixion. If they had neglected Jesus there would have been no Christianity. You cannot conceive of Christianity without the crucifixion, or can you? If Jesus was not killed, was ignored, and people were not worried about what he was saying, he would have disappeared without leaving a mark; not even a trace would have been there. But because he was killed, because he was raised on a cross, he became very, very significant. The death became the seal. When he was killed it proved that he had something very significant to say, otherwise why kill him?

The Hindus are cleverer. They didn't kill Buddha; on the contrary, they accepted Buddha as one of the incarnations of God. I would like you to know the story of how they manipulated the whole thing. They were against Buddha, they were against his ideas, against his revolution, but they accepted Buddha as an incarnation of God. Just as Rama is an incarnation, Krishna is an incarnation, Buddha is also an incarnation. But they played a trick with it.

The story is that God made the world, he made heaven and hell. Then millions of years passed and nobody went to hell because nobody was committing sin. People were pious, simple, innocent. Everybody would die and would go directly to heaven. And what about the management which was looking after hell: the Devil, and the Devil's disciples, the mini-devils, and the whole government? They became very tired, bored. Not a single entry! And they were sitting there in their offices, at their doors with their registers and files, and nobody was coming.

The Hindu story is...

The Devil's disciples went to God, and they prayed, "What is the point? Close this thing completely. Nobody has ever come for millions of years. We are tired; we are bored. Either send people, give us work and occupation, or close this thing."

Their problem was real, and God pondered over it. And he said, "Don't be worried. Soon I will be born as Gautam Buddha, and I will corrupt people's minds, and they will start going to hell."

You see the point? "I will corrupt people's minds. I will manage to confuse them, and once they are confused, hell will be overflowing." And that's exactly what it has been. Hindus say that since Buddha, hell is overcrowded. God has to come in the form of Buddha just to help the hell management.

Now they have done two things. One: they have accepted Buddha as God's incarnation, and also they have rejected his teaching because the teaching is a corruption; it is to corrupt. "To be a Buddhist is to be corrupted. To be a Buddhist is a guarantee for going to hell. So pay respect to the Buddha because he is an incarnation of God, but never listen to what he says. Never follow him. Be watchful, be alert!" They did the same with Mahavira; they ignored Mahavira. Not even the name of Mahavira is mentioned in any Hindu scripture. Such a potential being, such a powerful being, such a magnetic personality – and not even the name is mentioned. They ignored him; they played another trick: just to ignore him.

The Jews crucified Jesus and committed a grave mistake. They made Jesus very important. I am not saying that he was not an important man, he was, he was absolutely important. But if they had ignored him, there would have been no Christianity. Because they killed Jesus, Christianity took revenge – with vengeance! Down the ages, for two thousand years, Christians have been killing Jews in one way or another.

And the wound remains open. You cannot forgive Jesus. In fact, you cannot forgive yourself that you crucified this man. It has been the gravest error. Now there is no way to undo it. It is the Jew within you that will not allow you to understand Jesus.

You say: "As a Jew I could never accept his teachings." His teachings are nothing but the flowering of the Jewish tradition. The Jewish tradition has come of age in Jesus. It is the fulfillment of all the Jewish desires, ambitions and longings. It is the fulfillment of Moses.

But certainly the root of a tree looks different from the flower of the tree. They don't look alike. The root is ugly; the root is not beautiful. To be beautiful is not its function. Its function is something totally different: to nourish the tree, to nourish the leaves, the foliage, the fruits, the flower. And it hides underneath the ground, it doesn't come up, it doesn't show up. It remains there hidden underneath the ground and goes on working there. If you have seen a roseflower, and then you dig for the roots and put the roots by the side of the flower, you will be surprised. There seems to be no relationship. And yet, I say to you, the flower is the fulfillment of the root. And the root has existed for the flower, and without the flower the root was meaningless. Its existence would have been sheer wastage.

So is the case with Moses and Jesus. Moses functions like the root. Of course his statements are not as beautiful as Jesus' – they cannot be, his function is different: he is the lawgiver. He gives a pattern, a discipline, a code to the society. He makes the primitive society into a civilized society. He changes the primitive mind, the crude mind, into a more sophisticated, cultured mind. Because only in that cultured mind, the egoist mind, can Jesus be possible. The third mind arises out of Moses. Jews have become very egoistic: the chosen people of the world, God's special people. A special covenant has happened between God and the Jews; they are not ordinary people. They have God's book, and they are his representatives on the earth.

This ego was given by Moses. Only through this ego can the mind evolve. Yes, one day the ego has to be dropped, but you can drop it only when you have it. If you don't have it, it cannot be dropped. The dropping is utterly beautiful, but the dropping is possible only when you have it. And you have to have it so much that it becomes anguish and you *have* to drop it. Moses gives the ego, the definition, the identity to the people. And then comes Jesus as a fulfillment and he wants you to surrender, he wants you to drop the ego. He gives you love. Moses gives you law. And they are different, they are really different.

In many ways they are opposite. Love is beyond law, and when love is there, no law is needed. So whenever Jesus says, "It has been told to you of old that you take an eye for an eye; and if somebody throws a brick at you, you have to throw a rock at him – this is justice. But I say unto you 'Love your enemy. Love those who hate you and persecute you. And if somebody hits you on your face, give him the other side too. And if somebody takes your coat, give him the shirt too. And if somebody forces you to carry his load and burden for one mile, go for two miles with him.'"

Now, this is different, utterly different, a new vision. But this new vision is possible only because Moses has cleared the ground. Moses has gone underneath as the root, and now Jesus comes as a rose-flower. He looks different, he looks opposite. Do you know? Roots go downwards and the flowers go upwards. They are opposites. Their dimension is different, their direction is different. Roots go downwards, deeper into the earth in search of more water. And the flower goes upwards in search of light, more sun, more air. They go diametrically opposite. To understand that they are one, needs great clarity. To understand that Moses and Jesus are one, needs meditation. To understand that the Vedas and buddhas are one needs insight, great insight – a radical change in your mind.

You say: "As a Jew I could never accept his teachings." It is your Jew, not you. You can understand, but the Jew cannot understand. The Jew is the one who has killed Jesus – how can he understand? If the Jew understands Jesus, then there will be great repentance, and he will never be able to forgive himself, because he has killed. So the Jew has something like an investment in not understanding Jesus. If the Jew understands Jesus then how will you be able to forgive yourself? You will not be able to forgive yourself and your forefathers. Then your whole tradition will be condemned, your whole heritage will be criminal. This is too much!

Just for one man, this fragile-looking Jesus... Just for one man you cannot condemn your whole race and five thousand years of existence. It is better to condemn this man and accept your heritage: a five-thousand-year-old race, rich history, meaningful incidents. That's how it goes on in the mind. You cannot understand Jesus because there is great investment in not understanding him. And the conditioning goes very deep. The conditioning becomes your blood, your bone, your marrow.

The other day I was reading an anecdote...

Schwartz and Pincus, complete strangers, were sitting across from each other, nude, in the steam room.

"I never met you before," said Schwartz, "and yet I'll bet you were born in Brooklyn."

"That's right!" said Pincus.

"In fact," said Schwartz, to his naked companion, "you're from my old neighborhood, Bensonhurst, and you went to the Seventy-ninth Street Synagogue, and your rabbi was Nathan Nussbaum."

"Amazing!" said Pincus. "You can tell all that just by looking at me?"

"Of course," said Schwartz, "Rabbi Nussbaum always did cut on the bias."

It goes deep. It goes into the blood, into the bones, into the marrow. You are not brought up as a man. You are brought up as a Jew, as a Hindu, as a Christian. You don't know who you are. You know only your conditioning, you know only the mind that has been put inside you from the outside. And that mind won't allow you to understand Jesus. That mind will have to be dropped.

"Never before did I think of him as an enlightened being, as I think about the Buddha." It is easier. You can open yourself for Buddha. He has not uttered a single word against the Jews, so you can open yourself towards him. He does not hurt your ego in any way. In fact, you can enjoy him very much because he is so much against the Hindu scriptures.

"When I first came in contact with Buddhist teaching in Nepal, I felt an immediate affinity towards it." And they are the same. Jesus had come to India and had lived in a Buddhist monastery, Nalanda. In fact, Jesus' whole teaching is more Buddhist than anything else. The language is different, he talks like a Jew, but the message is the same. But for that you will have to be really unprejudiced. It is good that at least you can understand Buddha and love Buddha. Love Buddha, go deeply into Buddha, and soon you will be surprised that from this understanding you will be able to learn much about Jesus too.

If you can love one enlightened person, sooner or later you will understand all the enlightened persons of the world because their taste is the same. Languages differ, their words are different. Buddha speaks a totally different language – naturally, he was talking to a different kind of people. And Jesus was talking to a different kind of people. Jesus had to speak the language of those people. Wherever Buddha says *truth*, Jesus says *kingdom of God*, but they mean the same. Wherever Buddha says, "Be a nobody. Drop the ego. *Anatta*, be a no-self," Jesus cannot say that because nobody will understand.

He says, "Drop your will, surrender your will to God's will."

Buddha never speaks about God. Jesus brings God in – but the strategy is the same. Whether you drop your will just by looking into it and into the misery of it, or you surrender it to a certain God who is there – Jesus says "My Father in heaven," and that father in heaven is just an excuse – the whole point is to drop the ego, to drop your will. Once the will is dropped you become one with the whole. Whether God exists or not does not matter. But Jesus had to speak in a Jewish world, in the Jewish way, in the Jewish language, and he had to use the metaphors, the parables of the Jews. Otherwise, he is a buddha.

"Here now in Pune, Jesus' sayings are becoming comprehensible and acceptable. Yet still doubts persist." They will persist while the Jew persists in you. Just as the Jew cannot understand Jesus, so the Christian cannot understand Moses. Only a man who has no ideas, who is simply like a mirror, can understand everybody and can become very much enriched by it.

If you can understand Buddha, and Jesus and Moses and Mohammed and Mahavira and Zarathustra and Lao Tzu, your richness is growing. Lao Tzu will bring a new breeze into your being which only he can bring because he opens a door which nobody else can open. He is a master, a master technician. He knows how to open a certain door, and at that door nobody else is more skillful than him. Zarathustra opens another door into your being. And your being is big, enormous! It is not finished with one door. You can have millions of doors in your being, when you come into each door you have a new taste, a new vision; a new treasure becomes available to you.

Now people are unnecessarily poor. When I see a Christian, I see a poor man. When I see a Hindu, I see a poor man. When I see a Jew, I feel great compassion. Why be so poor? Why not claim the whole history of man? Why not claim all the enlightened people as yours? That's my work here. That's why one day I speak on Buddha, another day on Jesus, another day on Lao Tzu – I go on changing. My effort here is to make you enriched, to make you available to all the joys possible in the spiritual world, to make you capable of all kinds of ecstasies. Yes, Buddha brings one kind of ecstasy: the ecstasy that comes through intelligence. And Jesus brings another kind of ecstasy: the ecstasy that comes through love. Krishna brings another kind of ecstasy: the ecstasy that comes through action. And Lao Tzu brings another kind of ecstasy: the ecstasy that comes through inaction. These are very different paths, but they all come into you, and they all meet you in your innermost core.

Be simply a man, a human being, with no Jewish, Christian, Hindu ideologies hanging around you. Drop all that dust and let your mirror be clear, and you will be in continuous celebration because then the whole existence is yours. Why go on worshipping one flower when all the flowers can be yours? And why go on putting only one flower in your garden, when all the flowers of the world can flower there? Why not be rich? Why have you decided to be poor?

"Yet still doubts persist. Why did he say it all in such a round-about way?" No, he has not said anything in a roundabout way – it is just that in two thousand years the languages have changed. Now, one thing has to be understood: Buddha's language is still modern for a certain reason, because Buddha was so logical, so rational. His approach is of intelligence. The world can still understand him; the world is still becoming intelligent, still becoming rational. In fact, science and the explosion of science have made people more capable than ever of understanding Buddha. That's why Buddha has a certain appeal for the modern mind. Buddha is very contemporary. He talks with logic, with rationality, with utter intelligence, the way that intelligence can understand. The world has become more intelligent, so Buddha has a certain affinity.

But Jesus has fallen very far back for a certain reason: the world has grown into logic; the world has not grown into love. That is the trouble. That's why Jesus looks roundabout, because the language of love has disappeared from the world. Love? Yes, it creates a sound in the ear, but no meaning.

I have heard...

Two hippies were sitting in front of a church, just outside in the garden. And then the ambulance came and the priest was brought out on a stretcher. And those two hippies were sitting there for hours, just sitting there, doing nothing. They suddenly became alive, and one hippie asked the other, "What's the matter? What happened to this priest?"

And the other hippie said, "They say he slipped in his bathtub and has broken his leg."

The first one brooded for a while and then said, "What's a bathtub?"

The second hippie said, "How am I supposed to know? I am not a Catholic."

Now, a hippie is a hippie. He may never have been in a bathtub. That word is meaningless. He says, "How am I supposed to know? I am not a Catholic." As if a bathtub has something to do with Catholicism.

It depends. Jesus' language is no longer relevant because man has fallen very far away from his heart. He is more in the head, and there, Buddha is the master. Buddha is the supreme master there, the incomparable master there. If you want to argue, then Buddha is the right person to convince you. He will never say a single thing which cannot be proved logically – not that he remains confined to logic, he goes beyond it, but he goes through it. He takes you to the very end of logic and then helps you to jump out of it – but he is never against logic. He goes beyond logic, but he is never against logic. You can walk with him with perfect ease, he will not create any trouble for you. He will not talk about the "Father who is in heaven." You cannot say to Buddha that this is father-fixation – he never talks about the Father. Freud can walk with him perfectly at ease, so can Marx; there is no trouble. Einstein can have a good conversation with him, and there will be no conflict.

But with Jesus it is difficult. He bypasses logic. He is illogical. Love is illogical. Only lovers can understand his language, otherwise it will look very roundabout. Have you listened to lovers talking to each other? It looks very roundabout what they are saying. To a rational person it looks absurd. And they go roundabout and roundabout. And one who is not in love will simply be bored: "What are they doing? Why do they go all 'gaga' – why not be pertinent, to the point? If you want to go to bed with the woman why not simply say, 'I want to go to bed with you'? Why talk about the stars and the moons and the flowers, and poetry, and all that nonsense – and finally you go to bed? So why not jump directly? This looks very roundabout: 'I love you' and looking into each other's eyes – for what? Come to the point! Be direct!" To the logical person that will be the right thing.

Yes, Jesus is roundabout, but he is roundabout because you have forgotten the language of love. He speaks in parables, he speaks in stories, he speaks in metaphors. He is metaphoric because he is poetic. In fact, no comparison exists. Jesus' words are so potent, so full of love, so full of poetry that no comparison exists. I have not come across such potent words. Buddha's words are very balanced, direct, mathematical; he never exaggerates. Jesus' words are over-flowing; exaggeration is not the exception there, but the rule. Love exaggerates because love has enthusiasm, because love has zest, gusto, and love speaks in metaphors because love is a poetic approach towards reality.

"Why did he say it all in such a roundabout way, especially considering that he was talking to the common people?" Yes, that's why, precisely that's why – because he was talking to the common people. And common people are the people who can understand love more easily than logic. He knew how to communicate with the common people.

The common people have always known the language of love. The common people can understand Shakespeare very easily. They cannot understand Albert Einstein that easily. It is said that while Albert Einstein was alive, only a dozen people in the whole world were capable of understanding him rightly. Of course, he speaks very math-ematically, he is very particular, he never goes roundabout. But only a dozen people capable of understanding him? What is the matter?

Down the ages love poetry has been understood by everybody; even the primitive person understands love poetry, understands the song, the music. Absolutely unsophisticated, not knowing anything of philosophy, but he can understand tears and laughter, and can under-stand a dance, a song, can understand the whispering of two lovers.

Jesus speaks to the common people. He is not a philosopher. That's why he speaks in metaphors, in parables. A parable is a beau-tiful way of saying tremendous truths, because a parable can be understood on many levels. A parable can be understood by a child; he will understand it on his level. The parable can be understood by an ordinary man; he will understand it on his level. The parable can be understood by a philosopher, by a logician, by a poet, by a very cultured person, by a wise man. They will all understand on their own levels. The parable can easily have as many meanings as there are people trying to understand it.

Mathematics has one meaning: two plus two is four. There are no other levels in it. It is simple, direct. The metaphoric language has many levels, and that is the beauty of Jesus' sayings. Read those sayings today, and mark which sayings appeal to you. Then meditate for a few months, and read them again. And you will be surprised: now the meaning has changed. Now you don't mark and underline the same lines, now you choose something else to mark. Something else has become important. Meditate for a few months more, and then go to the Bible. And you will be surprised again and again. And that is so with the Gita, and that is so with the Koran, because they are all metaphorical treatises. One can go on reading them again and again – they are never exhausted.

You cannot read a logical treatise again and again. Once understood it is finished, then there is nothing else in it. If you have understood Albert Einstein's treatise on the theory of relativity, once understood it is finished. Now you cannot go on reading into it, there is nothing else.

But you can go on reading Jesus' sayings every day – morning, evening – and always there is something new coming up, something new surfacing, because you are changing and your insight is growing deeper. Your life experience is becoming more mature, you will be able to see more every day. Because you grow, the scripture will grow with you: it can go as deep as you can go. And for lives together one can go on and on. It has an eternal quality to it, endlessness, and a depth which knows no bottom. It is abysmal.

"It doesn't make any sense to me, and I won't feel completely at ease with Jesus as I do with the Buddha, until this question is resolved." It is not only a question to be resolved, it is an insight to be evolved. You have to see the point that it is the Jew that is disturbing you. Drop the Jew and then look again, and you will find great harmony arising between you and Jesus. And I am not saying become a Christian. If you become a Christian – you drop being a Jew and become a Christian – then you simply change your disease. Then you have fallen from one disease into another, from one prison you have moved into another prison. Maybe while you are changing from one prison to another, for a few moments or a few hours in between you will be under the open sky, that's all. Sooner or later you will be in another prison, and again the same misery will start.

Never be a prisoner to any mind. And all minds are prisons. Beware of the mind and remain always above the mind. Remain always unprejudiced, remain without an ideology, and then the whole world and the whole world's treasures are yours.

The second question:

Osho,
Does a master's responsibility towards his disciples cease upon
the physical death of the master? What did Jesus mean when he
said, "And know that I am with you always, until the end of the
world"? With this assurance then, how come the infant church
received Paul instead of Peter, whom Jesus appointed as the head
of the church?

The first thing about the question: a master has no responsibility
at all – responsibility as you understand the word. He is responsible,
but he has no responsibility at all, it is not a duty. Duty becomes
a burden, duty becomes a tension, duty creates concern, anxiety. A
master has no responsibility, although he is responsible. The difference is great. When I say he is responsible, it simply means he is
loving, he is compassionate. If you ask for help, the help will be
given. But he has not taken it on his shoulders that he has to redeem
you somehow. It has not become a burden on him that you have to
be redeemed. It is not his anxiety.

He is available. If you ask, it shall be given; if you knock, the
door shall be opened unto you; if you seek, you will find. If you are
ready to partake, the master will pour his whole being into you. But
it is not a kind of responsibility. He is not a missionary. He is not
after you. He is not bent upon redeeming you. That's why I say he
has no responsibility. He is responsive. Whenever you are ready to
take, you will always find him ready to give.

But there is no anxiety in his mind. If you decide to be ignorant it
is perfectly your freedom. If you decide to remain in the world, if you
decide to remain in the imprisonment, it's perfectly your choice. It is
not his ambition to free you. Nobody can free you against your own
will; only you can free yourself. Yes, you can partake of all kinds of
help that a master makes available...

So the first thing: "Does a master's responsibility towards his
disciples cease upon the physical death of the master?" Even while
he was alive he was not burdened by any responsibility. But the disciple's mind always creates such kinds of bondages. The disciple
would like the master to be responsible so that the master becomes
answerable, so that the disciple can claim: "If I am not redeemed

yet, *you* are responsible!" This is a trick of the disciple to protect himself and to throw the responsibility on the master's head. And then you can go on living the way you want to live because what else can you do? You have accepted Jesus as your master, now it is his responsibility.

This is not the way to become free. This is not the way towards nirvana or *moksha*. This is not the way towards liberation. You are playing tricks even with your master. And the disciple would like that the master remain in a kind of contract – even when he is dead he has to look after you. And what have you done? What have you done on your part? You have not done anything. In fact, you are trying to do everything to hinder, to obstruct. You are clinging to the prison, and the responsibility is the master's. Don't befool yourself.

The question is from Chintana. She has been a nun and that mind goes on lingering around her. Christians have done that. Millions of Christians are thinking in their minds that they can do all kinds of things, whatsoever they want, and finally Jesus is going to redeem them. On the Day of Judgment he will be standing there, and he will call to all his Christians, "These are my children. Come and stand behind me." And all the Christians will be standing behind Christ and will enter heaven with flying flags. And obviously all others will go to hell. Those who are not with Christ will go to hell.

That is everybody's idea. The Mohammedan thinks the same: only those who are Mohammedans will be saved – the prophet will come and save them. These are stupid ideas. If you go on living the way you are living, nobody can save you – no Jesus, no Mohammed.

You will have to change your quality of life, you will have to change your vision, and then you are saved. You can learn the art of changing your vision from Jesus, from Mohammed, from Krishna, from Buddha; from any source you can learn how to change your vision. But you will have to learn the art and you will have to practice the art. Nobody else is going to transform you – nobody can do that. And it is beautiful that nobody can do it. If it were possible for somebody to transform your being, then you would have been a thing, not a person. Then you wouldn't have any soul.

That is the difference: a thing can be made. You can make furniture out of wood, you can make a statue out of stone, but you cannot make a soul out of a man. You cannot create enlightenment out of a man. If somebody from the outside can do it, that will be very insulting; it will be below human dignity. And what kind of freedom will it be which has been created by somebody else? If that somebody else changes his mind, then he can create your slavery again. It won't be much of a freedom. Freedom is freedom only when you have attained it.

So the first thing to be understood is, learn from Jesus, learn from me, learn from any other source that appeals to you. But remember, you are responsible for your life, nobody else is responsible. And don't go on befooling and kidding yourself. Don't go on believing in such beautiful dreams and consolations.

"Does a master's responsibility towards his disciples cease upon the physical death of the master?" In the first place there has never been a responsibility. The master was sharing – not out of responsibility but out of compassion. He was sharing because he had so much that he had to share. He was not obliging you; he was sharing just as a flower shares its fragrance to the winds – what else can it do? Just like a rain cloud shares its rains with the earth – what else can it do? When a master has come home, has become full of light and fragrance, he has to share it. But it is not a responsibility. That word *responsibility* is not a beautiful word; it is not some kind of duty that he is fulfilling, it is his joy to share.

Don't throw your responsibility on anybody. Remain responsible for yourself, otherwise you will become lethargic, lousy, and you will become dull and dead. You will lose your vitality because then you will be simply waiting. The Last Judgment Day will come and Jesus will save you. You have turned your whole life into an ugly affair.

Transform yourself. Learn from any source that appeals to you. Learn from all the sources. Become as rich as possible but change your life, transform your life, and don't wait for the Day of Judgment. There is no Day of Judgment. Each moment is the moment of judgment. Each moment we are facing our God because each moment we are living our lives. Let each moment be decisive. Let it be lived with art, awareness, skill.

"What did Jesus mean when he said, 'And know that I am with you always until the end of the world'?" He was perfectly right. He is with you until the end of the world, but are you with him? That is the point. The sun is there, and it is always there, but if you are sitting with closed eyes, what does it matter whether the sun is there or not? You can sit inside your room with all the windows and doors closed, with a blindfold on your eyes – you will be living in darkness. When Jesus says, "Know that I am with you always until the end of the world," he is simply saying, "Whenever you want, you can partake of me. I am available."

Once a being has become enlightened he is available forever. Forever! Because he has become part of foreverness, he has become part of eternity, he has become part of existence. Where can he go?

Raman Maharshi was dying, and somebody started crying and asked, "Bhagwan, are you really leaving us? Will you leave us?"

Raman opened his eyes and he said, "What nonsense you are talking! Where can I go?" And closed his eyes and died.

The last words were: "Where can I go? I will be here!" Raman has become part of that foreverness. Where can he go? He is part of eternity – nowness. If you are available you can drink of him. His fountain is flowing there.

But don't think in terms of the law and the courts, don't think in terms that when you go to God you will make him feel guilty. You will say: "Look at this man Jesus. He has said that he will live forever with us, and we were stumbling in darkness and he never came. We were committing this and that and he never came to stop us. We did many wrong things and he never prevented us."

No, he cannot prevent you, he cannot change you. He is just like the sun, the light. Open your eyes and it is there, close your eyes and it is not there. And when Jesus says: "I will be there forever with you," he does not mean: "I will be there in opposition to Buddha, I will be there in opposition to Krishna, I will be there in opposition to Moses." No he simply means: "I will be there as part of Buddha, Krishna, Moses, Zarathustra." They have all disappeared as persons, they have become oneness.

"With this assurance then, how come the infant church received Paul instead of Peter, whom Jesus appointed as the head of the church?" I have never said that he appointed Peter as head of the church. He had simply said, "You will be the foundation," not the head. He was not creating an organization. He was not making Peter the head, the boss, the chief, the chairman, no. He was simply saying, "Peter, I call you Peter." Peter means rock. "I call you Peter because you are rock-like, because you have attained to that consciousness which is rock-like. If on that consciousness one makes one's house, it remains forever. Be the foundation." He is simply saying in a metaphor: "Let awareness be the foundation of my church."

But, a nun is a nun, Even if she is an ex-nun, even if she has become a sannyasin, that past is there. Head of the church...! Peter was not the head. He was not meant to be the head, he was meant to be the foundation. A foundation disappears into the earth like roots. You cannot see the foundation – the foundation is invisible. So is awareness invisible.

And you ask, "Then how did it happen?" The question is a complaint. She is saying: "Christ says, 'I will be with you, and I will remain responsible,' then how come he didn't help his own church, the infant church, and allowed Paul to dominate it, instead of making Peter the head of it? Where is he, and what is he doing?"

He has committed a breach. He has betrayed, he has not been true to his word. He has not even helped his own church – and the church was infant. That's why she makes it clear: "infant church" – helpless. His help was needed!

"With this assurance then, how come the infant church received Paul instead of Peter whom Jesus appointed as the head of the church?" Paul was a politician and politicians dominate everything. Paul was a dangerous fellow, murderous. First he was trying to destroy Christianity – he was against Jesus, the arch-enemy – he was going to the Holy Land to persecute Christians. And then, on the road towards the Holy Land, the miracle happened that he heard the voice of Jesus calling him: "Why? Why do you persecute me? What have I done to you?"

It came from his own unconscious. Let it be clear. It was not coming from Jesus. Jesus had never asked, even of the real persecutors who were persecuting him when he was alive, "Why do you persecute me?" He wouldn't come to Paul to say this on that lonely road. It was his own unconscious because his conscious was full of hatred for Jesus, because he was full of enmity, jealousy, anger, rage.

The unconscious is always against the conscious; they move like polar opposites. If you love a man through the conscious, you hate the man through the unconscious. That's why you love and hate the same man, the same woman. In the conscious, he was full of hatred, but in the unconscious there must have been love, because only then could the hatred exist. They exist together. Love never exists alone, and so hate never exists alone; they always exist together. If you ask psychoanalysts, they say, "Love-hate is one relationship." *Lovehate* is one word. Even the hyphen that joins them is not needed; they are one word. From one side it is love, from the other side it is hate.

So in the conscious there was hate, in the unconscious was love. And when the hate was too much, extreme... The swing of the pendulum to the other side, and his unconscious asked, "Why? Why are you persecuting me?" The unconscious became the voice of Jesus.

He fell on the ground; he could not believe it. This was a miracle, and he was converted by this miracle. He turned and became a Christian. But he remained the same person. First he was trying to persecute Christians, then he started putting his energy into converting people to Christianity – but the same energy, the same aggression. First he is there to destroy Christianity, now he is there to create Christianity. It is the same man.

And another miracle happened: he became a Christian and destroyed Christianity by becoming a Christian. He created the church – that was the best way to destroy it. If he had been on the same road and if he had remained the same person, hateful against Christ, there would not have been so much harm. Because this aggressive man, this violent man became a Christian and became a missionary, he started converting people and changed the whole quality of Christianity. Christianity is no longer related to Christ. It is Pauline – it is related to Paul!

Chintana is asking, "Why didn't Jesus interfere?" Jesus never interferes. Buddha, Krishna or people like them never interfere. They give you total freedom. They give you as much freedom as God gives you. God never interferes. Even if you are going against God, he does not interfere. He can easily interfere – he can stop your breathing. When you are going to steal, he can stop your breathing: come home and you breathe again. Go to steal and it stops. You are going to murder somebody and you stop breathing. God can do that but he never does it; he never interferes.

Freedom is respected. If people wanted to create a church, if people wanted to create a church which goes against Jesus, then let it be so – that is their own decision. If people want a Christianity like this, then let them have it. If they don't want to choose the right, they have the choice to choose the wrong. Freedom is the ultimate value.

The third question:

Osho,
Why is there so much hurry in the West while the East seems to be so relaxed?

Different time orientation! The East thinks in terms of eternity, in terms of many, many lives, incarnation after incarnation, one after another. The time span is very big, so there is no hurry. In the West the time span is very small, so there is hurry – only one life. Only one life? And life is slipping by; it is going down the drain. If you live sixty years, twenty years will be lost in sleep; twenty years will be lost in some stupid job; fifteen years will be lost eating, defecating and things like that – what is left? And whatsoever is left will be lost sitting before a TV – finished! Fear arises, one becomes very frightened. Something has to be done before it disappears: there is a great, hectic hurry! The East thinks in a very, very infinite span: one life after another, the wheel of life goes on moving. If you miss in this life, there is no worry; you can do it in the next life – when you are here next time round. There is no hurry, so the East moves very slowly.
I have heard...

A surgeon was telling his patient: "Here we believe in getting the patient on his feet as soon as possible after the operation. So, the very first day I want you to get out of bed and walk around your room for five minutes. The second day you'll walk ten minutes. On the third day you must walk around for a full hour. Okay? Any questions?"
"Yes, Doc," pleaded the patient, "Do you mind if I lie down for the operation?"

This must have happened somewhere in America. The East has a different vision, attitude.
I have heard...

An American was going from Delhi airport to Delhi city. The taxi was moving so slowly and he was getting very worked up; he was becoming very restless: so much time lost. So he asked the cab-driver, "Can't you go a little faster?"

And the cabdriver, the *sardarji,* said, "Yes, I can, but I am not allowed to leave the cab."

It is different in the East. Nobody is in a hurry. The whole thing depends on the time orientation. The Western religions, Christianity, Judaism, Islam are all offshoots of Judaism – they all believe that there is only one life. That has created the trouble. The Eastern religions, Hinduism, Jainism, Buddhism, are all offshoots of Hinduism – they all believe there are many, many lives to live. Many you have lived, many you will be living. There is no hurry; infinite time is available. You can go as slowly as you want. In fact, there are only two religions: Judaism and Hinduism, only two standpoints.

Christianity and Islam are offshoots, and so are Jainism and Buddhism. The basic difference is in their time concept. Both concepts have something good about them and something bad too. The West has become very tense. Great anxiety, fear – the anxiety of "Am I am going to make it or not?" because this is the only time. So the West is very ill with anxiety and the East has become very slow, dull, lazy. Nobody seems to be interested in doing anything. "Why worry? Next time... We can wait."

The West has become very rich because something has to be done right now! And they have been doing many things. The East has become very poor because with such a time span you cannot be very rich. Both have their good points and both have their bad points. Something new is needed – something more like a synthesis, something which makes you very much alive to the moment, very active, alive, vital, and yet does not create tension in you. Both the visions have failed because they are half-half. Something better is needed.

An earthworm meets a centipede. "How are you?" inquires the earthworm.

"Not so good," sighs the centipede. "My feet won't do as much as they used to. You are lucky you don't have any."

"Ah," sighed the earthworm, "if you had my slipped discs, you wouldn't talk like that."

And that's how things are. The West has suffered, the East has suffered – both have suffered. Now that they have come very close there is a possibility of a third attitude. The West lives with the idea of one life; the East lives with the idea of many lives. One has a small time span; another has a big time span. But both are time orientations.

My vision is: live in eternity – neither one nor many. Live in eternity. And the only way to live in eternity is to live now because now is part of eternity. Don't live in the future. If you have a big future you will become lethargic, poor. If you have a small future then you will become very restless – rich, but very anxiety-ridden. Forget it! The future has no meaning; it is eternity, not one life, not many lives. We have always been here and we will always be here, so there is no need to worry about it. Now the only thing is how to live in this moment. We are not going anywhere. Remember Raman: "Where can I go?" We are not going anywhere. We are part of this existence, we will be here. Nothing is ever destroyed, all remains. Only forms change.

But to live, there is only one way: to live this moment *now* and *here.* And live relaxedly because there is no hurry. Time is never going to be finished. You cannot finish it, so live totally in the now, and live relaxedly, because there is no end to time.

The last question:

Osho,
Why was Jesus not born in America?

They could not find three wise men there.
Enough for today.

the phenomenon of
unconsciousness

John 4

Then cometh he to a city of Samaria, which is called Sychar,
near to the parcel of ground
that Jacob gave to his son Joseph.

Now Jacob's well was there.
Jesus therefore, being wearied with his journey,
sat thus on the well:
and it was about the sixth hour.

There cometh a woman of Samaria to draw water:
Jesus saith unto her, give me to drink.

(For his disciples were gone away unto the city to buy meat.)

Then saith the woman of Samaria unto him,
How is it that thou, being a Jew, askest drink of me,
which am a woman of Samaria?

For the Jews have no dealings with the Samaritans.

Jesus answered and said unto her,
If thou knewest the gift of God,
and who it is that saith to thee, Give me to drink;
thou wouldest have asked of him,
and would have given thee living water.

The woman saith unto him,
Sir, thou hast nothing to draw with,
and the well is deep:
from whence then has thou that living water?

Art thou greater than our father Jacob,
which gave us the well, and drank thereof himself,
and his children, and his cattle?

Jesus answered and said unto her,
Whosoever drinketh of this water shall thirst again:

But whosoever drinketh of the water that I shall give him
shall never thirst;
but the water that I shall give him
shall be in him
a well of water springing up into everlasting life.

Man's consciousness is just the tip of the iceberg; otherwise his whole being is drowned in darkness, in unconsciousness. And the little bit of consciousness that man shows is very fragile, very tentative, very accidental. It arises out of the pressure of circumstances; it is not a constantly flowing well in him. If there is danger, man becomes a little bit more conscious. If the danger disappears, he relapses back into his unconsciousness.

This unconsciousness is very deep and the consciousness is very shallow. And whenever there is a conflict between the unconscious and the conscious, the unconscious wins. The conscious can win only as a servant of the unconscious. This is the misery of man. All his pretensions of being conscious, alert, aware, are nothing but pretensions. This awareness is not even skin-deep. Scratch the man a little bit, and you will find a dark continent within him. Scratch yourself a little bit, and you will find a dark night of the soul. People don't go inwards because of the fear of this darkness.

The masters go on saying: "Know thyself!" The masters go on invoking, challenging: "Enter into your own being. Go inwards!" People listen, but they never follow, because of the fear of this inner darkness. Whenever they look in, there is nothing but darkness. Outside there is a little light; inside there seems to be no light.

Have you ever closed your eyes and sat in silence looking inwards? The moment you are really broken away from the outside, you will fall into darkness, into sleep. And the well of that darkness is very deep. Just on the surface a little consciousness exists, and that too not constantly. There are moments when it is there, and there are moments when it is not there. And it is very rarely there; more often it is not there. It is delicate and fragile.

That's why I say, "Handle it with prayer" – it is very fragile. And unless you grow deep into your consciousness, you will never know anything of truth, of freedom, of godliness, of bliss. Those words will simply remain words; they will never become alive in you, they will never bloom in you. You will never experience what they mean. *God* is an empty word unless you are conscious. *Christ* is an empty word unless you are conscious. Buddha is a myth, and all those talks of super-consciousness, nirvana, *samadhi*, the kingdom of God, are just parables – they don't mean much. They can't mean much, because the meaning has to come through your consciousness. The words are empty of content; you have to put the content in them. Only then will they start beating with life, only then will they start moving, dancing with life. Only then will flowers come and fragrance be released.

This is one of the most fundamental things to be understood about man: that man is only partially conscious. And that consciousness is more or less dependent on outer circumstances, not on you. It is not even *your* consciousness; it is not rooted in you, it is not centered in you, it is not coming out of you.

This is the whole problem that religion has to face. The whole science of religion is nothing but alchemy, an art for transforming darkness into light. The seers of the Upanishads have been praying down the ages: "Lead me from darkness to light. Lead me from death to deathlessness." In darkness is death. In darkness you are already dead. In darkness you don't live, you can't live. Only in light is there life – and life eternal, and life abundant.

Before we enter into this small parable, try to focus yourself on this phenomenon of unconsciousness...

A motorist who had broken down on a quiet country road opened the bonnet and inspected the engine.

"The trouble's in the battery," came a voice from behind him.

The motorist turned round, but the only thing in sight was a horse watching him from a field. This completely unnerved the man and he set off down the road.

After about ten minutes he came to a garage and told his story to the owner. "You mean to say that there was nobody near the car except a horse?" asked the garage proprietor.

"That's right."

"Was it by any chance a white horse with a black patch on its head?"

"Yes, it was!"

"Well, ignore him. He doesn't know a thing about cars."

The unconscious man is never surprised by anything. He takes life for granted. He knows nothing of surprise. He knows nothing of wonder. He knows nothing of the mysterious, the miraculous. And the miraculous is all around and the mystery surrounds you. But because you are unconscious, you go on moving in this mysterious world, dull, dead, fast asleep. You are not surprised by anything. If you are alive, conscious, each and every thing will surprise you. The grass leaf in the morning sun – and you will feel like worshipping. The roseflower in the moonlit night – and you will feel like kneeling down and going into prayer. The stars, and the people, and the children, and the animals and the birds – each and every thing will surprise you, each and every thing will challenge you. When life is a mystery only then are you religious.

But why is life not a mystery? – because you are so dull. Such dust has gathered on your consciousness that you go on pulling yourself along somehow, mechanically. You are not living life; you are simply dragging. One thing leads you to another, one thing pushes you towards another, and you go on, stumbling, till you die. If you look at an ordinary man's life from birth to death, it is nothing but stumbling from one accident to another. One goes on stumbling and finally stumbles into one's grave.

This is not life – not life as Jesus would like to define life, not life as I would like to define it. Life starts only by being conscious. And if you start being conscious you will not take anything for granted. You will not take your wife for granted, or your husband for granted. Small things will reveal their mystery to you. A bird will come and sit by your windowpane, and will start singing a song, and you will be thrilled and excited and ecstatic. Nothing thrills you right now. Nothing gives you excitement, nothing gives you ecstasy. You are insensitive. The insensitivity is always in the proportion that you are unconscious. The sensitivity comes only with consciousness.

The windows of the car parked in a lay-by late one dark night were well and truly steamed up, when the couple on the back seat heard the voice of the law outside the car saying, "Hello, hello, hello! What's going on here then?" The policeman opened the car door, gave the couple a two-minute lecture about the laws of the country, and then shone his torch on them as he informed them that he was going to report them.

"But officer," protested the man. "This lady is my wife. I was driving along the road in the pouring rain when I saw her walking along with a raincoat over her head. So I stopped to pick her up, and after a while we pulled in here to have a rest."

"Then why on earth didn't you tell me it was your wife instead of letting me lecture you?" the policeman demanded.

"Well," said the man, "I didn't know it *was* until you shone your torch on her."

Man is really unconscious. And life goes on, and you go on living – but that living is so lukewarm that nothing really happens. There is no passion in it, no intensity in it, no fire in it. Consciousness is fire. When consciousness is there you will be consumed in that fire, the ego will be consumed in that fire. And when you are not, and there is nothing but pure consciousness left, that is what godliness is, that is what nirvana is.

The whole effort of the masters down the ages has been one, singularly one: how to help you to become a little more sensitive, a little more conscious, a little more aware. A little more attention and things start changing, and you start moving in a new dimension.

These are the only two dimensions: either you live unconsciously or you live consciously. And to live unconsciously is to waste this great opportunity. It is immensely valuable that you *are*. It is immensely valuable that existence has given you a gift. It is a great opportunity. Don't miss it. It can be transformed into a greater opportunity: it can become eternal life.

Jesus says again and again, "If you come to me, I will give you life in abundance, life that can never be exhausted, life that goes on, life that knows no death, life that is forever." But you will have to jerk yourself a little bit out of your unconsciousness. And the unconsciousness is ancient. You have remained unconscious for many lives, for millennia. Yes, on the surface you appear conscious – you go to town, to the market, to the office, to the factory – you do certain things, but those are all habitual, mechanical. You have learned to do them and now you go on repeating them. You need not be conscious about them; you have become automatic, you have become an automaton.

Gurdjieff used to say to his disciples, "My whole approach is how to de-automatize you, how to bring again a non-mechanical life in you." Watch yourself how you react. You have reacted that way a thousand and one times; it has become a set habit with you. Now you are not needed for it; it is programmed in your brain. You need not be at home, and it will answer. You can go on sleeping, and it will answer. Somebody insults you; watch what you do. Somebody appreciates you; watch what you say. Are you really saying it? Are you there while you are saying it? Or are you not needed at all – is it a programmed thing in the mind and the mind repeats it?

A motorcar manufacturer designed a completely new car of the future, and advertised for a motorist who would drive it for six months and give it a thorough testing.

The successful applicant sat in the driving seat of the car, and the designer sat next to him in the passenger's seat.

"You'll find this car to be completely different from anything that you have ever driven before," said the designer. "There is no engine, no battery, no gears, no accelerator, no brake. In fact, there's nothing to go wrong at all. The only mechanism – if you can describe it as such – is a small black box, no bigger than a match box, which is located under the driver's seat. It is, in fact, an electronic computer which reacts to the sound waves it receives from the driver's voice. It has the added advantage that it can be set to receive code words of the driver's own choice, thus making it impossible for anybody to steal the car. Now to make the car go, all you have to say is 'Flippin' 'eck' because we have set it for that at the factory."

So the driver said, "Flippin' 'eck" and the car started to move forward. "How do I make it stop?" he asked.

"By the same principle," answered the designer. "Just say 'Hocus-pocus.'"

So the driver said, "Hocus-pocus" and the car stopped. He tried it a dozen times and it never failed. "Flippin' 'eck," and the car moved forward, "Hocus-pocus," and it stopped.

After driving the car round for several weeks, he took his girl-friend to the coast in it, and she was very impressed. As night was falling, she whispered to him in a romantic voice, "Let's stop on the edge of that cliff; there's a lovely view."

Nearing the cliff edge, the driver said, "Hocus-pocus," but nothing happened. "Hocus-pocus!" he shouted, but the car still moved forward toward the cliff edge and a sheer drop into the sea. "Hocus-pocus!" he screamed, and the car stopped about an inch from the edge of the cliff. Breathing a sigh of relief, the driver said, "Flippin' 'eck!"

That's how your mind functions – absolutely unconscious. Yes, it is perfectly capable of doing the ordinary things of life; it is perfectly good for the market place, for day-to-day life. But if you want to grow, if you want to go deeper into being, into existence, if you want to fly into the infinite freedom of divine being, then it is not enough. It is perfectly programmed for the ordinary world; it is not at all capable of the other reality. And the other reality is the real reality. This so-called reality is just so-so, it is a kind of dream that you are seeing with open eyes.

And you are lost. Everybody is lost. Have you ever thought about it: you are lost, you don't know from where you are coming, you don't know why in the first place you are coming, you don't know what you are, and why you are there, you don't know where you are going, and for what.

You move round and round like a wheel. Again and again the same thing. Again and again the same repeated experience. Naturally you are tired. Naturally you are bored. Boredom is so heavy in people's eyes. When I look into somebody's eyes I see only clouds and clouds of boredom. But this is natural because how can this repetitive, mechanical life give you joy? You know that nothing more is going to happen, and all that has happened was not of worth.

Sometimes sit silently and look backwards. Can you remember any moment when you really were in joy – really – not pretending, not consoling, but really, authentically in joy? Have you known a single moment of which you can say with your whole heart that it was a blessing, a benediction? No, you have only been hoping that day will come sometime, that moment will come sometime; but it is all hoping. And it cannot come the way you are moving, because that moment comes only to those who are really conscious, deeply conscious, because without consciousness there is no benediction.

A Londoner drove up to the Midlands without incident. But once he reached the Birmingham area, he found himself hopelessly confused in the complex of new underpasses, overpasses, and roundabouts, which had been built in connection with the junction of the M1, the M5, and the M6 motorways. Finally, he pulled up alongside a man who had a woman and two children in the car with him.

"Can you help me out?" implored the Londoner. "I've been trying to get on the Wolverhampton road for two hours, and I always finish up here."

"You're asking the wrong man," the other driver replied wearily. "I haven't even got home from my honeymoon."

And he has two children! But this is the situation: you always end up in the same place again and again. You have never been home for long – for centuries, for millennia you have not been home. And by and by, because you have been lost and wandering so long, you start thinking that this wandering is your life or this is all that there is to life.

Now, if this man continues in this way in his car, after a few years he will have many more children, and he will not have reached home. By and by, he will forget the whole idea of ever reaching. He will even forget that he is trying to reach home. He will start thinking that this car is his home – he has always been in it! And what to say about the children who are born in it? They will grow in it, of course.

They will fall in love, they will get married, and they will find them-selves from the very beginning in the car. That will be their home. That will be their life.

That's the actual reality. Your parents were lost, your parents' parents were lost – since Adam that has been the case. Since Adam you have not been home. And home is not far away either; the home is just within you. The home is very close by but you go on searching outside. You have lost track of only one thing, and that is your inner core. You rush from one outside thing to another out-side thing. Sometimes you are searching for money, sometimes for power, and then sometimes you start becoming religious and you start searching for God – but still outside. Whenever you look at the sky and pray to God, you are still looking outside.

The only real prayer looks inside. The real prayer is possible only when the eyes are completely closed to the outside and you are moving inwards, sinking in your own being, drowning in your own being – but fully conscious. In sleep you drown, but you are uncon-scious. In meditation, in prayer you drown into your being, but you remain conscious, you keep alert, you don't fall asleep on the way.

If you can reach to your own inner core alert, aware, then you have arrived. You start laughing at the whole ridiculousness of it: the home was inside, God was inside. And that is the message of Jesus, a continuous repetition from Jesus: "The kingdom of God is within you."

> Then cometh he to a city of Samaria, which is called Sychar,
> near to the parcel of ground
> that Jacob gave to his son Joseph.
>
> Now Jacob's well was there.
> Jesus therefore, being wearied with his journey,
> sat thus on the well:
> and it was about the sixth hour.
>
> There cometh a woman of Samaria to draw water:
> Jesus saith unto her, Give me to drink.
>
> Then saith the woman of Samaria unto him,
> How is it that thou, being a Jew, askest drink of me,
> which am a woman of Samaria?

for the Jews have no dealings with the Samaritans.

Jesus answered and said unto her,
If thou knewest the gift of God,
and who it is that saith to thee,
Give me to drink;
thou wouldest have asked of him,
and he would have given thee living water.

The woman saith unto him,
Sir, thou hast nothing to draw with,
and the well is deep:
from whence then hast thou that living water?

Art thou greater than our father Jacob,
which gave us the well, and drank thereof himself,
and his children, and his cattle?

Jesus answered and said unto her,
Whosoever drinketh of this water shall thirst again:

But whosoever drinketh of the water that I shall give him
shall never thirst;
but the water that I shall give him
shall be in him
a well of water springing up into everlasting life.

A beautiful incident. Move slowly into it, meditatively, comprehending, tasting every single word.

Then cometh he to a city of Samaria...

Jesus was a wanderer, wandering from one place to another. His life was a short life because he was murdered when he was only thirty-three – very young. And those few years that he lived were devoted to his own inner search. Thirty years of his life were devoted to his own inner work. He was in Egypt, he was in Kashmir, he was in Bihar, and there are stories that he was even in Tibet. Those thirty years he must have been a great wanderer. He wandered almost all over the known earth. He went in search of masters, of teachings, of devices. And he went to all the places where mystery schools existed. Egypt was one of the places; one of the most ancient traditions existed there. They knew many secrets. Jesus was initiated in the mystery schools of Egypt. But that was not the whole thing. Something was missing. He had to come towards the East.

In Kashmir he must have come across Buddhists. He learned a little more. He became a little more alert to the meditative techniques of Buddha. He had learned through the Egyptian masters, but those methods were more indirect. They were all towards meditation, but they were more indirect. In Kashmir he must have come across Buddhist teachings, Buddhist masters – he learned more direct methods. And then he became really interested in Buddha's philosophy and he traveled to the very center of the heart of Buddhist teachings – Nalanda. It is said he stayed there for at least two years. There he became a perfect master of meditation because there is no other school in the whole of human history which is as scientific about meditation as Buddha's school. It is totally dependent on intelligence.

But still Jesus felt that something was missing – the love part was missing. He had learned all about the path of awareness, but it seemed a little bit dry. It seemed like a desert where no trees grow. It is beautiful; the desert also has a beauty of its own. The silence of a desert, the vastness, the expanse of a desert is all is beautiful but it is dry, monotonous. So Buddha's path is dry, monotonous. One achieves very directly, but there are no juices – juices of love – flowing in it.

He traveled to Tibet because in those days Tibet was not yet Buddhist and the ancient religions in Tibet were still alive; they were love religions. Later on they disappeared because Buddha's religion became too dominant. Jesus traveled to Tibet to learn something of the path of love. Once he had learned both paths, he became one of the most evolved masters of both paths. Thirty years went into traveling, searching, and only three years were given to him for his ministry. Only for three years did he function as a master. That's why Christians don't have any stories about Jesus because those thirty years were spent in mystery schools in secrecy. And those thirty years have nothing to do with Christianity. Christianity has no stories about those thirty years, as if Jesus had not existed. And those were the most potential years, the most important years, because whatsoever

Jesus said later on was learned in those thirty years.

Christianity only has stories about the three years. In those three years he was again a wanderer. First he was seeking the truth for himself, and now he was searching for seekers. Now he was in search of those to whom he could deliver whatsoever he had attained. First he was in search of those from whom he could get, and then he was in search of those to whom he could give.

Then cometh he to a city of Samaria, which is called Sychar,
near to the parcel of ground
that Jacob gave to his son Joseph.

Now Jacob's well was there.
Jesus therefore, being wearied with his journey,
sat thus on the well:
and it was about the sixth hour.

There cometh a woman of Samaria to draw water:
Jesus saith unto her, Give me to drink.

Now this well of Jacob must have been an ancient place in Samaria – very famous. Some ancient, named Jacob, had made that well. It must have been a source of nourishment to the whole surroundings, and people still had great respect for Jacob because it was he who had discovered that well. That is on one plane.

On another plane, the meaning is that Jesus is saying: "The well of tradition that comes from the ancients can help you only so far." The well of tradition, scripture, knowledge – the well that you get through heritage – can help you only so far. It can quench your thirst for the time being, but again the thirst comes back. Unless you find a well in your own being, no outer wells are going to help.

Look in the Vedas – that is Jacob's well. Look in the Old Testament – that is Jacob's well. And now you look in the New Testament – and that is Jacob's well. Every well finally becomes Jacob's well. Look into the scriptures and you are trying to find something through tradition while the living truth is within you, not in tradition. And only the living truth can satisfy you, and satisfy you forever.

Beware of Jacob's wells. Use them, they are perfectly good as far as they go, but don't become dependent upon them forever. And don't think that they are going to lead you to the ultimate. Scriptures can give you thirst not truth. Knowledge can help you seek in a better way, but it cannot become the substitute for truth. Beware of all that you gather from others. Don't become too attached and identified with it, otherwise you will never come to your innermost source, and that is where God resides.

There cometh a woman of Samaria to draw water... On one level it is a simple story: a woman comes, and it is Jacob's well... But I would like you to feel the story on another plane also. I say Jacob's well means the well of tradition that you get through heritage. You are a Christian by birth, or a Hindu by birth, or a Mohammedan by birth – that is you sitting at Jacob's well.

And then there comes a woman of Samaria. Now that too has to be understood on a second plane, on a higher plane. Why a woman, why not a man? A woman is more past-oriented than a man. That's why you will find your churches, temples, full of women. A man looks to the future, is more future-oriented. A woman looks to the past, is more past-oriented. Why does the woman always look to the past? – because in the past there is more security, more safety, more certainty. About the past, things are clear: all has happened; things are finished. There is no fear of the new. With the future all still has to happen. Whether it will happen according to you or not, nobody can be certain of and there is no guarantee. It is groping in the dark, it is moving in the unknown.

A woman always chooses security, safety – that is the feminine mind. It is so for a certain biological reason. She has to become a mother; she has to look for security, safety. If a woman becomes interested in you, she wants to get married to you. She is very interested in marriage – that is a biological necessity. She is afraid. If she gets pregnant – then what? Who is going to take care of the child? For months together she will be incapable of doing anything. And when the child is born, for years together she will have to take care of the child. Somebody has to take care of her too, otherwise life will become unnecessarily difficult, will become a nightmare. She wants safety; her motherhood needs a certain safety.

This biological phenomenon has also made a certain pattern in her mind; it has given a certain structure to it. It is very rare for a woman to become an adventurer – she is not interested in that. It is very rare for a woman to move into the unknown. Even if sometimes she is existentially ready for it, it is difficult for her to move into the unknown. The fear of the unknown, the uncertainty of the unknown...

So the feminine mind is traditional. But in some other sense also it is significant and is needed. If you go on searching for the new and there is nobody to take care of it, it will be lost. So there is a certain division of labor: man goes on searching for the new, and once it has been sought and found out, the woman becomes the protector. Somebody is needed to protect it too, otherwise what will be the use of searching? Just the search cannot be the meaning of it. You have found a treasure and once you have found it, the man – the male mind – is no longer interested in it. His whole interest is in conquering. He has conquered the treasure, now he is no longer interested in it. He is interested in some faraway land; he wants to go to the moon. Once he has reached there he is no longer interested in the moon either, now he wants to go to Mars.

The man goes on searching; somebody is needed to take care of that which has been sought and discovered, somebody has to maintain and protect. The woman has the mother's instinct to protect, to help, to take care of that which has already happened.

So, on a second plane, the story is meaningful. A woman from Samaria came to draw water. The woman is the protector of the tradition, of the past, of all that has happened before – of Jacob's well. She comes again and again to Jacob's well. She goes to the church, to the temple, she reads the Bible, she reads the Gita; she teaches her children. She brings water from Jacob's well for her family, for the future, for the children who are going to grow.

The mother is the cradle of all religions. It is through the mother that religion enters you. It is through her religiousness that you become acquainted with that quality called religion. The man, if allowed, will create science but will not create religion. And even if he creates religion, he will not be able to protect it. He will not be able to keep it intact for the ages to come; he has no instinct for it.

A woman comes to draw water and ...*Jesus saith unto her, give me to drink.* Now, something very valuable has to be understood. This has been my observation: it is difficult for people to love, but there is one thing which is even more difficult than to love, and that is to receive love. To love is difficult, but to receive love is almost impossible. Why? – because to love is in a way simple, and one can do it because it is not against the ego. When you love somebody you are giving something, and the ego feels enhanced. You have the upper hand: you are the giver and the other is at the receiving end. You feel very good; your ego feels enhanced, puffed up. But when you receive love, you can't have the upper hand. Receiving, your ego feels hurt. Receiving love is more difficult than giving love. And one has to learn both: to give and to receive.

To receive is going to transform you more than giving can do, because in receiving love your ego starts disappearing. Have you watched it in yourself? If not, then observe. When somebody gives love to you, you become a little resistant, you protect. You create a wall – a subtle wall; you look as if you are not interested. You are interested – who is not interested in love? Love is such nourishment but you don't want to show that you need it. You pretend that it's okay: "If you are giving, I will oblige you by receiving, otherwise I don't need. I am enough unto myself." You may not say so, but that's what you pretend. That's what your eyes show, your face shows. You become a little resistant, you withdraw.

This always happens to couples. If the woman is very loving, the man starts withdrawing. If the man is very loving, the woman starts withdrawing. Couples come almost every day to me, and it is one of the basic problems that if one is too much in love, the other starts escaping. What is the matter? It is very rare that a couple comes to me who are both in love and nobody is withdrawing. It never hap pens. It is so rare.

Why can't it happen? – for a certain basic reason. If the woman is too loving the man becomes afraid: "Now she is gaining the upper hand." And if he shows love then he will become dependent, then he will become a slave. And she is so maternal that she will surround him from every side, she will become a prison to him, and he will not find any escape. He starts escaping before it is too late. He starts managing how to get out of it, or at least to keep a little distance, a little space, so that if the time arises he can escape. And the same happens to the woman. If the man is too loving and surrounds her from everywhere, she feels suffocated. She starts feeling that something is wrong, that she is no longer free, that this man is too much.

Both want love, both need love, but the ego does not allow you to receive. And if you become incapable of receiving, you will become incapable of giving – that is a logical corollary. If you become incapable of receiving, if you are so afraid when somebody is giving love to you, a natural consequence will be that you will become afraid of giving, because now you know how people become afraid when somebody gives love. When somebody gives love to you, you become afraid. Now you know that if you give too much love the other will become afraid. You don't give too much: you become a miser. You become a cripple, a paralyzed person.

This story is beautiful. It starts by Jesus asking ...*give me to drink.* This is the beginning of love: Jesus asking ...*give me to drink.* And you will see how the story unfolds and brings subtle messages.

(For his disciples were gone away unto the city to buy meat.)

Then saith the woman of Samaria unto him,
How is it that thou, being a Jew, askest drink of me,
which am a woman of Samaria?
For the Jews have no dealings with the Samaritans.

In christ consciousness there are no distinctions, no divisions – no distinction of caste, no distinction of creed. Christ consciousness means a sky which has no boundaries. Now there is nobody who is a Jew and nobody a Samaritan. Now there is no question of nationality and all those stupid things which divide people: of color, creed, tradition. In christ consciousness no distinctions exist. It is a unitary consciousness. For a christ, the whole existence is one.

But the woman says: ...*thou, being a Jew, asks drink of me...?* First, Jews used to think that they were the highest people, the chosen people of God. Samaritans were poor people, and not the chosen ones. Jews used to treat the Samaritans just as brahmins use sudras in India – untouchable. It is impossible to see a brahmin going to an untouchable woman and asking for water. It is impossible; the woman cannot even be touched. You will be surprised to know that in India this foolishness has gone to its very logical end.

In the South, not only is the untouchable, untouchable, but even his shadow. If the shadow of the untouchable falls on your body, you have to take a bath. Shadow! When some untouchable has to pass through a town, he has to shout, "I am passing by here. If a brahmin is around here, please let me pass. Avoid my shadow." Because he will not touch you – that is impossible – but sometimes in a crowd, in a market-place, his shadow may touch you, and that is enough of a crime. Now foolishness can go to very great extremes.

And these are the people who go to the West, to the world, to teach – these brahmins, brahmin sannyasins, these Hindus. They go to the whole world, and they have the idea that they are the greatest religious people in the world, and it is to them that God is looking to transform the whole world.

I have heard...

Dr. Sarvepalli Radhakrishnan, who was once a president of this country, went to America on a tour. He lectured in many places. In one university he talked the way Hindus talk – that they are the highest people in the world and they exist only to serve the world and to transform the whole world.

A young man stood up and asked, "Sir, if you say that Hindus are so great and they can help the whole world, why don't they help themselves?"

And do you know what stupid answer Radhakrishnan gave? He said very arrogantly, "The great Christ was born to help others not to help himself. India was born to help others not to help herself."

This idea is very egoistic, but the same was the attitude of the Jews. Jews and Hindus are very similar. You will be surprised to know that these are the only two religions in the world which don't convert, which never allow anybody to convert. You can only be born a Jew, or born a Hindu – there is no other way. The only way is to be born a Hindu or to be born a Jew. Hindus and Jews don't allow any conversion. Why? – because nobody is worthy enough to be converted. How can you be converted to be a Hindu? Your blood, your bones, your marrow, your skin are all non-Hindu. Just by making you go through certain rituals, how can you become a Hindu? Your blood cannot be changed, your bones cannot be changed. So a Hindu can only be a born Hindu. So a Jew can only be a born Jew. Both religions are very egoistic, and that's why both have suffered. That suffering has come as part of the ego. It has been created by the ego itself.

This woman, this poor woman of Samaria, must have been surprised that Jesus, a Jew, was asking for water from a Samaritan –

which was unthinkable. But for Christ there are no distinctions. And if you are a religious man there cannot be any distinctions for you either. That's why I say again and again that a religious man cannot be a Hindu, cannot be a Jew, cannot be a Christian. A religious man can only be just a religious man and that's enough. He cannot have any adjective to his life – Hindu, Jew, Christian. To be religious is enough. If it is not enough and you need to be a Christian, and a Jew, and a Hindu, then you don't know what religion is.

> ...*How is it that thou, being a Jew, askest drink of me,*
> *which am a woman of Samaria?*
> *For the Jews have no dealings with the Samaritans.*
>
> *Jesus answered and said unto her,*
> *If thou knewest the gift of God,*
> *and who it is that saith to thee, Give me to drink;*
> *thou wouldest have asked of him,*
> *and he would have given thee living water.*

Now you know. Jesus asks: ...*Give me to drink*... so that he can give something to the woman.

If you want to give something, you have to be ready to receive first, particularly with love. First be a receiver, and only then can you give. Because then in your giving there will be no ego. And when there is no ego, only then can love be given; otherwise the ego can destroy even the purity of love and the beauty of love, and can make it ugly.

...*If thou knewest the gift of God*... And Jesus says: "Look at me. I am standing before you. Can't you see me?" That's what I mean when I say man lives in unconsciousness. Even if Jesus comes to your home and knocks on your door, you will not recognize him. You will not be able to see who has come to you because you have not even recognized yourself. How can you recognize anybody else? You have not seen your own being, how can you see this divine being who is confronting you?

Now, this woman must have been a woman just like you, just like everybody, just an ordinary human being. Jesus is asking for water, and she cannot see the man who is standing there. She cannot feel him. And she is thinking, "He is a Jew." She has her categories; her mind is full of her prejudices. And a light is standing in front of her – life itself is standing in front of her. But that moment is being missed.

Jesus says: ...*If thou knewest the gift of God*... What is the ...*gift of God?* There are only two gifts – love and awareness. If you love, then you will recognize Jesus; or, if you are aware, then you will recognize Jesus. And these two things are God's gifts. They are already there inside you but you have not used them. Because they have not been used for many lives, they have lost their functionality. That faculty of love has become paralyzed, and that faculty of awareness has become paralyzed because you have not used it.

Don't use your eyes for three years. Go into a dungeon and sit there in darkness for three years. When you come out you will be blind. Don't speak for three years, and when you would like to speak, it will be difficult. You will have lost the quality, the faculty. You will have to learn from *ABC* again. Don't walk for a few years, and you will not be able to walk. And for thousands of lives you have not loved, and you have not been conscious. So it is not something to be surprised about that we have lost those qualities.

And Christ can only be recognized either through love or through awareness.

Don't think about the woman that she was ignorant. Don't think, "That poor woman who did not know who was standing before her." The same is the case with you. You may have passed Christ, you may have passed a buddha. It is almost impossible that in so many lives you never came across a master. You must have come across one many times, because you have been here. While Buddha was here, you were here. While Krishna was here, you were here. While Zarathustra was here, you were here. You must have come across, but you could not recognize, you could not see. You are blind. You only appear to see, but you are blind. Would you not call this woman blind? Will you not call this woman dead?

Jesus answered and said unto her, If thou knewest the gift of God... Jesus says, "I am a gift of God to you. I have come as a gift. If you accept me, if you allow me a little corner in your heart, it can become a transformation. This little spark can bring a great fire in you, can make you a flame with God." A gift from God – but the woman is thinking only that he is a Jew. People only see bodies. It is natural because they think about themselves that they are bodies. They never have any vision of themselves as something beyond the body. Jesus is there as the body and as the soul. But how can you see his soul? And that is the *gift of God.* The body is as human as anybody else's body, with all the limitations of human bodies, but the soul which is just hovering there, which is just there like an aura, needs eyes to be seen.

...If thou knewest the gift of God, and who it is that saith to thee, Give me to drink... God himself is asking for a little water, and God is asking so that God can give to you. God is on the receiving end so that when he gives to you, you can also accept it; otherwise it will be difficult and resistance will be created.

This is a constant problem with masters. They want to give to you, they have immense joy to share, but the problem arises that if they simply go on giving to you and you are not allowed to give anything to them you will not be able to receive. The master has to create devices in which he can make you feel that something which you are giving to the master is immensely valuable too. It is not one-sided. It is a communication; it is a dialogue. The master has to create those situations in which he can make you feel important, in which he can make you feel needed, in which he can give you the feeling of significance, so that when he starts pouring his being into you, you can receive it. You know that you can also give something to him, so there is no problem in receiving; otherwise you will be too obliged, you will be too burdened. So a master has to find small ways in which he can take something from you. It may not be anything meaningful – Jesus just asks for a little water.

He says, "I am thirsty, give me a little water to drink." *...and who it is that saith to thee, Give me to drink...* If you had known the gift that is there just ready to be delivered to you... But the woman is blind – as everybody is blind. *...thou wouldest have asked of him...* Jesus says: "If you had looked at me, if you had seen me – even just a small glimpse of who I am then you would have prayed to me: 'Give me something from your well. Give me something to drink so that I will never feel thirsty again.'"

Jesus was there, those beautiful eyes were there, that vibe was there which could transform the woman, transport the woman from the ordinary reality to the other reality, from this shore to the other shore. But the woman was too concerned about water, the Jew, the Samaritan – about the nonessential.

The woman saith unto him,

Sir, thou hast nothing to draw with,
and the well is deep:
from whence then hast thou that living water?

Now, the woman seems to be very logical – as everybody is logical. Logic goes perfectly well with stupidity. There is no conflict between logic and stupidity; there is no conflict between logic and ignorance. They go perfectly well – hand in hand, they are great lovers, logic and ignorance are married to each other.

Now, the woman is being logical and her logic is perfectly okay. That's what a scientist will do, a professor will do, a pundit will do. The woman rises to the occasion. She says: "Look sir, what are you talking about? What nonsense are you talking about? You don't have anything to draw with, and you are thinking to give me water? And the well is very deep."

The well is deep and ...*thou hast nothing to draw with*... Now she is very scientific, logical, rational. ...*from whence then hast thou that living water?* "And what are you talking about? About what living water? From whence? I see you tired, covered with dust, alone, weary, thirsty – I can see it in your eyes. And look at the pretension... And you are saying that you can give me water. From whence?"

Art you greater than our father Jacob...? That too has been asked again and again. Whenever a new being is born into christ consciousness, whenever a new being becomes a buddha, this is the question asked again and again. That's what the Jews were asking Christ: "Are you greater than Abraham? Are you greater than Moses? Are you greater than our own prophets? Are you greater than our past?" That's what Buddha was asked again and again: "Are you greater than the Vedas and the Upanishads and the *rishis* of old? Are you greater than all of them put together?"

That's what has always been asked because you know about the past. When Buddha happens, Christ happens, he is so new, he is so fresh. You don't know anything about him. You know about your past; he looks like a pretender. He looks as if he is distracting you from the path, because he says, "I say unto you... If Moses has said this to you, forget about it. I have brought a higher dispensation; I have brought a new message from God." If Moses says, "Hate your enemy," I say to you, "Love your enemy." If Moses says, "It is just to punish the criminal," I say to you, "Forgive him. Judge ye not. Don't become a judge to anybody. Drop all judgments, condemnations. Let God be the only judge. Don't interfere."

Naturally, the Jews must have said, "What are you talking about? Are you greater than Abraham, Moses?"

And the woman says:

Art thou greater than our father Jacob,
who made this well, gave us this well, and drank thereof himself,
and his children, and his cattle?

"And where is your well? What well are you talking about? You don't have anything to draw with, and I don't see any well."

She is being logical. Remember, when you are being logical, you will miss Jesus, you will miss Buddha, you will miss Krishna, because they cannot be understood through logic, they can be understood only through intuition. You will have to put your reason aside, otherwise their statements will look illogical. If you put your reason aside, only then can you see the truth of their statements. Their statements are not arguments, they are simply declarations of truth.

Jesus answered and said unto her,
Whosoever drinketh of this water shall thirst again...

You can go on drinking from tradition and the well of tradition – Jacob's and others – but you will thirst again. It is not going to really satisfy you because unless you know, you don't know. Unless you realize, nothing is going to change. If God becomes your own experience, only then does the thirst disappear. Otherwise the thirst will come again and again. You can postpone it for a few days... You can postpone it, that's all; you can delay it, that's all. But it will never be gone, it will come, and it will come with a vengeance.

...Whosoever drinketh of this water shall thirst again:

But whosoever drinketh of the water that I shall give him
shall never thirst...

But look, Jesus says to the woman, "Here I am, ready to pour something into you – something of the eternal, something of the timeless, something that once tasted, fulfills and fulfills forever."

...but the water that I shall give him
shall be in him
a well of water springing up into everlasting life.

Once christ consciousness has touched you, the spark has entered you and your own fire has started burning. Then it will be a constant source of light, life. Then there is no end to it.

The only question is of the first spark. You are carrying great potential but the spark is needed. That spark jumps from the master to the disciple. It can jump only in deep intimacy and closeness. It can jump only when there is no wall between the two, when their hearts are open to each other, when there is great trust. Then, in a certain moment, in a certain closeness, in a certain attunement, the spark reaches the disciple. And once the spark has reached, there is no need, then the disciple is on his own. Now he himself is a christ.

That's what I mean when I say, "Unless you become a christ, you cannot understand him." By becoming a Christian you cannot understand. Becoming a Christian is just a poor substitute. Become a buddha not a Buddhist, become a christ not a Christian. And you can become a christ because you are carrying the potential for christ consciousness, that fourth state of consciousness: *turiya*. It is there, it needs only to be provoked. It needs only to be brought to your consciousness, or your consciousness has to be brought to it. The treasure is there, you are there, but you are not bridged.

The master can only show you the way. Once the way has been seen, there is no problem, then you start moving. You cannot do otherwise. Then you have to move. When you have seen that the treasure is within you – the joy of joys and the eternal well, and the well from which you can attain to immortality – you will start moving towards it. In fact, you have been searching for it – searching in wrong directions. Now you will search in the right direction. That right direction comes from the master – that spark...

Jesus is talking about that inner experience. The woman is thinking about the outer well, the woman is thinking about outer water. And Jesus is talking about the water of life – the living water.

Jesus answered and said unto her, whosoever drinketh of this water shall thirst again: but whosoever drinketh of the water that I shall give him shall never thirst: but the water that I shall give him shall be in him a well of water springing up into everlasting life.

Let this parable become an insight in you. Meditate over it because I also am here to give you something of the eternal. If you recognize it, only then can it be transferred. If you go on living in your limited logic, then you will miss. And only you will be responsible, nobody else. The spark is here ready to jump into you. Just don't obstruct. Take the risk. Be a little adventurous.

Yes, that water is confronting you again. If you drink of it your thirst will disappear forever. But don't be like that woman of Samaria – and all are like her.

These incidents are tremendously significant if you meditate over them. But don't think that they happened some time in history, think of them as incidents that always happen. Whenever there is a master, these are the incidents that go on happening. And don't think of them as past. If you think of them as past you will miss the meaning of them.

It may be that they are happening to you. It may be that you are the woman at Jacob's well, and Christ is standing before you and you are too occupied in your own logic. And remember, the woman's logic is perfect. There is nothing wrong with it as far as logic is concerned. She is perfectly right; she is being very realistic, pragmatic, empirical. She says, "Where is the well? Whom are you trying to kid? And where is anything that you can draw with from this well? And this well is deep!" The woman has not said – maybe out of politeness, otherwise that would seem to be very logical to say – "If you can give me water, then why are you asking water from me? If you have that water that which quenches the thirst forever, then why are you looking so weary and thirsty? Then why in the first place are you asking me to give you water?" Natural, logical! But then you go on missing. Jesus has only asked you to give something to him so that he can give something to you. He is simply preparing the ground.

And that's what I am doing here. Somebody I put in the garden, and I say, "Work in the garden." Somebody I have put in the office, and say, "Work in the office." And somebody I have put in the kitchen, and I say, "Work in the kitchen." I am simply saying, "Give something to me, so that I can give something to you," because only when you give will you be ready to receive. If you give me some-thing, the door opens to give, and that is the moment when I can enter into you. Certainly, if you want to give something to me, you will have to open your door to give to me. And when the door is open is the moment that I can sneak in.

That's what Jesus is saying: "Give me water." When the woman pours water into Jesus' hands is the moment he can enter the woman, when the spark can jump into her. And this too I would like to remind you of, that only a woman can receive the spark.

By woman, I don't mean just a biological woman. A man... But he will have to be in a state of femininity, only then can he receive, because all receiving is possible only when you are receptive. This woman at Jacob's well is very symbolic because only a woman can receive. Only the feminine mind can receive because it is non-aggressive. And only a woman can come in deep trust and inti-macy; a man remains afraid. And remember, I am not saying that men will not be able to receive, but they will be able to receive only when they also become feminine.

The disciple has to be feminine – whether man or woman doesn't matter. The disciple has to be feminine because the disciple has to receive the spark, the disciple has to become pregnant with the spark. That's why the woman at the well has been chosen. Whether it happened historically or not is irrelevant, but it has always been happening. It has happened with Buddha, it has hap-pened with Zarathustra, with Lao Tzu, with Christ. It is happening right now, here! Meditate over it.

Enough for today.

you are a mystery

The first question:

Osho,
Your last words at this morning's talk were: "Meditate on this."
What do you mean? How does one who only knows how to think
about things learn to meditate on things?

Knowing what thinking is, is the beginning of knowing what
meditation is. Thinking is the negative part; meditation is the
positive part. Thinking means mind in turmoil; meditation
means mind in silence. But the turmoil is the beginning of silence,
and only after the storm is there silence.

If you can think, you are capable of meditation. If a man can be
ill, he can be healthy. Health becomes impossible only when you
cannot even be ill. Then you are dead. Only a corpse cannot fall ill.
If you can fall ill, then there is still hope. Then you are still alive. And
so is the case with thinking and meditation. Thinking is the mind which
is ill: not at ease, not reconciled with itself, disturbed, fragmented,
divided. Meditation means the division no longer exists, the fragments have disappeared into oneness – you are at ease, at home.

It is the same mind: divided, it becomes thinking; undivided, it becomes meditation. If you can think, you are capable of meditation although meditation is not thinking. Thinking is an ill state of affairs, pathological. But one can transcend it, and the transcendence is easy; it is not as difficult as you think. The difficulty comes because you don't really want to go into meditation. In meditation not only is thinking going to disappear; you are also going to disappear. Only an ill man *is*, a healthy man disappears. In health you are not; you exist only in illness, you exist only in pain, in suffering, in hell. You can't exist in heaven because to feel one's existence means to feel pain.

Have you not observed it? When you have a headache, then you have a head. When the headache disappears, the head disappears too. If your body is perfectly healthy and everything is running smoothly, humming smoothly, you don't feel the body at all; you become bodiless. In the ancient Indian scriptures, health is described and defined as bodiless-ness: you don't feel your body. How can you feel your body if it is not ill? Only illness creates knowledge; self-consciousness is created by it, self is created by it.

So meditation is not difficult if you really want to go into it. It is the simplest thing possible, the most simple, the most primal. In your mother's womb you were in meditation. There were no distracting thoughts; you were not thinking about anything, you simply *were*. To regain that state of in the womb is what meditation is all about. When you see a person meditating, what do you see? He has disappeared into the womb again, he has made his whole body like a womb, and he has disappeared into it. Buddha sitting under the *bodhi* tree... What is he doing? He has moved back to the source. He is not there. There is nobody sitting under the *bodhi* tree. That's what a buddha means: there is nobody sitting under the *bodhi* tree.

When Jesus goes to the mountains away from the multitude, where is he going? He is going inward, he is trying to make contact again with the original source, because from that original source is rejuvenation. From that original source there is again freshness, vitality, and the waters of life are flowing again – one is bathed, one is resurrected.

In the world, thinking is needed. In your inner being, thinking is not needed. When you are communicating with somebody, thought is a must. When you are just communing with yourself, what is the need of thought? Thought will be a disturbance.

Try to understand why thinking is needed and what thinking is. When there is a problem, thinking is needed to solve it. You have to go round about, look from every angle of the problem, think of all possible solutions. There are many alternatives, so one has to choose which one is the right one. And there is always the possibility of error, and there is always fear and anxiety – that is natural – and still there is no guarantee that you are going to succeed in finding the solution. One gropes in the darkness, one tries to find a way out of it. Thinking is the confronting of a problem. In life there are millions of problems and thinking is needed.

I am not saying thinking is not needed. When you relate to the outside it is needed. But when you are facing your own being, it is not a problem; it is a mystery. And let it be very clear what a mystery is. A problem is something that can be solved; a mystery, by its very nature, is something that cannot be solved. There is no way out of it, so there is no question of finding the way.

You are a mystery. It is never going to be solved, because you cannot go behind yourself. How can you solve it? You cannot stand outside yourself and tackle yourself as a problem, so how can you solve it? Who is going to solve whom? You are the solver, and you are the problem, and you are the solution. There is no division at all. The knower and the known and the knowledge are one – this is mystery.

When the knower is different from the known there is a problem. Then there is something objective; you can think of a way out, you can find out something which becomes knowledge. But inside yourself you are facing the eternal – the beginningless, the endless – you are facing the ultimate. You cannot think. If you think you will miss. Only through non-thinking will you not miss. You can see into it – with awe, with great wonder. You can go into it deeper and deeper, you can dive into it. You can go on digging, and the more you dig, the more you will understand that this is a mystery to be lived, not a problem to be solved. So thinking is irrelevant. And when thinking is irrelevant, meditation arises. The failure of thinking is the arousal of meditation.

Science is thinking; religion is meditation. If you think about God it is philosophy; it is not religion. If you live godliness, then it is religion.

If you are looking at a lotus flower and thinking about it, then it is science, philosophy, aesthetics. But if you are simply looking at the lotus flower... The look is pure, uncontaminated by any thought, and the lotus flower is not thought to be a problem but just a beauty to be experienced... You are there, the lotus flower is there, and there is nothing in between, just emptiness, nobody is standing between you and the flower – it is meditation. Then the flower is not outside you because there is nothing to divide as the in and the out. Then the lotus flower is somehow within you and you are somehow within the lotus flower. You melt into each other; divisions are lost, boundaries become blurred. The lotus starts touching your heart, and your heart starts touching the lotus. There is communion. It is meditation.

Whenever thought is not functioning it is meditation. Listening to me sometimes becomes meditation to you. I say "sometimes" because sometimes you start thinking and then you lose track. When you are just listening, not thinking at all about what is being said – neither for, nor against, not comparing with your past knowledge, not being greedy to accumulate it for your future use, not trying to justify, rationalize, not doing anything at all... I am here, you are there, and there is a meeting. In that meeting is meditation, and then there is great beauty.

You ask me: "Your last words at this morning's talk were: 'Meditate on this.'" Yes. Whether I say it or not, that is my message every day – in the beginning, in the middle, in the end. That's what I am saying: meditate on this. Meditate.

The English word *meditation* is not adequate for what we in the East mean by *dhyana*. *Meditation* again carries some idea of thinking. In English, *meditation* means to think about, to meditate upon something. *Dhyana* does not mean to meditate upon something. *Dhyana* simply means to be in the presence of something, just to be in the presence. If you are in the presence of a tree it is meditation on the tree. If you are in the presence of the stars then it is meditation on the stars. If you are here in the presence of me then it is a meditation. And when you are alone and you just feel your own presence, it is meditation.

From *dhyana* came the Chinese word *ch'an*; from *ch'an* came the Japanese word *zen*. They are all derivations of *dhyana*. *Dhyana* is a beautiful word. It is not translatable into English, because English has words like *meditation, contemplation, concentration* – they all miss the point.

Concentration means concentrating on one thing. Meditation is not a concentration, it is an absolutely de-concentrated state of consciousness – it is just the opposite. When you concentrate there is a tension, you start focusing, there is effort. And when you concentrate on one thing other things are denied, then you are closed for other things. If you concentrate on me, then what will you do with this plane passing by, and the noise? Then you will close your mind to it, you will focus on me, you will become strained because you have to deny this roaring airplane. You have to close your mind to it; then your mind is not open. A bird starts singing – what will you do? You will have to close yourself. That's what is being taught in the schools and the colleges and the universities. It is concentration.

Meditation is not concentration; it is just openness, alertness, presence. You are listening to me, but you are not listening to me exclusively. You are simply listening. And the airplane goes roaring by – you listen to that too. And the bird starts singing and you listen to that too. There is no division; you don't choose. All that happens in the surroundings is accepted: it becomes part of your listening to me. Your listening is not exclusive; it is inclusive of all.

So concentration is not meditation. Then the word *meditation* itself is not meditation, because in meditation somebody meditates on Jesus, somebody meditates on the Bible, somebody meditates on God. Again it is not meditation. If there is a God as an object and Jesus as an object, then there is a distinction between the knower and the known; there is duality. And in duality there is conflict, and in conflict there is misery. In non-duality conflict disappears, and when conflict disappears, hell disappears. Then there is joy.

So meditation is not meditating upon something, meditation simply means a different quality of your inner being. In thinking your mind goes on weaving, spinning thoughts. In meditation your mind is simply silent, utterly silent, not doing anything at all – not even meditating! Not doing anything at all. Sitting silently, doing nothing and the grass grows by itself. The spring comes, and the grass grows by itself. Meditation is a natural state of silence. It is not contemplation either.

In contemplation you think about "high thoughts," spiritual things – not about mundane things, not about the market, not about the family, but high values, truth, beauty, bliss. But you contemplate on these. You try to think about these high values of life – then it is contemplation.

But meditation is not even that. Meditation is a state of stillness. And this state of stillness has not to be forced because it cannot be forced. If you force it, it will not be the right stillness. If you force it, *you* will be there forcing it; it will not be natural, it will not be spontaneous. So what has to be done?

One has to understand the ways of thinking. One has to understand the stupidity of thinking. One has to understand that thinking creates conflict, division, struggle; that thinking fragments you, that in thinking you start falling apart. One has to see what thinking does to you. In that very seeing arises meditation. In that very understanding, suddenly you feel breezes of silence coming to you. For a moment everything becomes still, utterly still, a standstill. And the taste of it will bring more of it. By and by you will know the knack of it. Meditation is a knack. It is not science, it is not even art – it is a knack. You have to learn it slowly, slowly, through your own experience. So when I say: "Meditate on this," I mean don't think upon it. Just close your eyes, be in silence. Let it be there.

For example, Jesus' story: Jesus and the woman of Samaria are standing at that well, Jacob's well, and Jesus is asking, "Give me some water to drink" – the dialogue that ensues, just let it be there.

Be utterly silent in front of this parable. Let this parable be like a lotus flower – it is! Just let it be there, throbbing, pulsating with a beating heart. Let it become alive in front of you, and then become silent. What can you do? You can only be silent. Let this drama be enacted in front of you. In deep silence you see it, and that will reveal to you the meaning of it. And that will reveal to you all the dialogues that have happened between any enlightened person and the disciple. And it will become not only Jesus' parable, it will become a parable between you and me too. It is happening every day. That's what I mean when I say: "Meditate upon this."

The second question:

Osho,
When you speak of the need for trust in order to let go of the ego,
I feel that's where I'm stuck, for my distrust is a tangible thing.
It feels painful, but I can't let go of it. Early this year, for a brief
period, I felt high energy and with it, open, loving and trusting.
But now that energy has gone, and with it, the openness.

Always remember that when I am saying something, I am not

giving you an order to do it. If you take it that way you have already missed the point. I am simply making it clear to you. Don't be in a hurry to practice it. Whatsoever I am saying has nothing to do with practicing it. You just have to understand it. Around me, the only thing that is going to help you is clarity, transparency.

When I am talking about the ego, don't jump ahead. Don't start thinking, "How to drop this ego? Yes, Osho is right. This ego is creating the trouble, so how to drop it?" You have not attained to clarity; you have gone into greed. You have become ambitious. Rather than understanding what was being said to you, you made it a desire. And now you will be in trouble. While I am talking about the ego, listen meditatively and totally. Just see the point of what is being said. There is no hurry; there is nothing to be done, nothing to be practiced. Don't bring tomorrow in, don't even bring the next moment. Don't bring in the future because with the future comes the desire, and with the desire all hell is let loose. While listening to me, if you start thinking how to do it: "Yes, it looks beautiful. And if I can do it there will be great joy in me. How to do it?"... And while you are thinking how to do it, I am talking about the ego, and you are not listening any longer.

The ego can be dropped only when your clarity is complete, entire. *You* cannot drop it. You *are* it! How can you drop it? But while listening totally, silently, meditatively, you are not – there is clarity. In that clarity something will click. You will see it so one hundred per-cent that the very seeing will become a transformation. Not that tomorrow you will have to drop it. No, tomorrow you will not find it there. Not that the next moment you have to go home and practice how to drop the ego...

I am not teaching you yoga exercises. These are not yoga postures that you have to prepare and rehearse and practice and discipline yourself with. What I am doing here is sharing my enlightenment with you, my clarity with you. I have a clarity, I am inviting you to come and share in my clarity. In that very sharing something will change in you, that sharing is alchemical. Next moment you will be surprised: the ego is not there. Not that you have to drop it. You understood the point, you understood the foolishness of it, the ridiculousness of it, the absurdity of it; now, what is there to leave and what is there to renounce? Ego is not some entity in you that you have to drop. It is not something like cancer that you have to operate on or be operated for. It is just an illusion.

It is as if you see a rope on a dark night and you think it is a snake. And you become very frightened and you start running, and you are breathless and perspiring. Then I come across you, and I say to you, "I know perfectly well it is not a snake; it is a rope. Come along with me." And you go on asking or thinking, "How to kill that snake?" I am saying, "It is not a snake. Come along with me and see. Here is the light and the lamp; we will go together and have another look. And I know, I have been there; I have known that rope. Once I also used to know it as a snake, and I also used to get very frightened just like you, so I understand. I am not laughing at your misery, I feel compassion because I know; I was in the same situation myself. But come along with me."

You are asking, "Osho, how to kill that snake? Should we take a gun with us, or will just a stick do? Or – there are rocks around – can we use the rocks and kill the snake?" I am constantly saying there is no snake, there is only a rope. But you are not listening, and you ask, "When we have reached there, what are we to do?" Even if you are not saying it in so many words, deep inside you are thinking it. You are still afraid, and you are not walking courageously; you are hiding behind me. You say, "Who knows? It may be a snake after all. How can I trust this man? Maybe he is mad, because I have seen it with my own eyes. It is a snake and a very dangerous one." This is the situation when I say the ego is a shadow. You have certainly seen it, but it is not an entity. You have certainly suffered from it, yet it is an illusion.

I can understand your problem. You say, "How can one suffer from something which is not?" It looks very logical: how can one suffer from something which is not? If one suffers, then the logical mind says the cause of suffering must be there because the effect is there. But can't you suffer from a rope, thinking it a snake? Have you not suffered in your dreams? Have you not suffered through your own delusions, projections? You *have* suffered. Many a time you have suffered from a cause which doesn't exist, but which can create the effect.

You can fall ill if somebody says that the water you have drunk just now is poisonous – you can start vomiting. And if so many people say that yes, it is poisonous, if the whole town says it is poisonous, if the whole world says it is poisonous, then... Then your illusion is supported, nourished more and more.

This is what is happening! You are suffering from an illusion called the ego. The whole world says, "Yes, it is there." And not only the world – your so-called religious people, mahatmas, saints also say, "It is very dangerous, this ego. It has to be dropped, it has to be crushed and killed. It is the enemy." And they devise techniques, strategies to kill it. The whole world believes in it. The people who are worldly believe in it and the people who are called spiritual believe in it. Somebody follows it, somebody fights with it, but they both believe in it. As far as the belief is concerned, they both agree.

What I am doing is a totally different thing. I am saying: "The ego exists not." I am not saying that you drop it. How can you drop it? It is not there in the first place. And if you start dropping a thing which is not, you will be in trouble. You will not be able to drop it, and so you will become very miserable. And you will make hard efforts to drop it, and you will again and again find that you have not dropped it. Then, more and more frightened, more and more miserable, you will start feeling very inferior: you cannot do a simple thing – dropping the ego?

Nobody has ever been able to drop the ego. Let it be remembered: nobody has ever been able to drop the ego. What do I mean by it? Has Buddha not dropped it? Has Jesus not dropped it? No, not at all! They have only understood that it is not. They have seen through and through and they laughed. They were simply running from something which is not there. In that understanding it disappears. Many times it disappears in your life too – in spite of you. Sometimes in deep love it is not. Hence, the joy of love. It is not really the joy of love, it is the joy of the disappearance of the ego. Sometimes in prayer, sometimes in meditation, sometimes seeing nature – watching the sea or sometimes just looking at the stars – it happens, and there is great benediction. One is showered.

But it comes only for moments because you don't understand even then what is happening. Again it is lost. When it is lost you become very miserable, and you start thinking how to get it again, how to go into that space again. It was not that you had gone into that space. It was simply that, because you became so enchanted with the stars, for a moment you forgot your old obsession: the obsession of the ego. You became so enchanted with the stars that you forgot the rope and the snake. It was just forgetfulness. But how long can you remain enchanted with the stars? Sooner or later you will have to come back, and the rope is there – waiting as a snake! Again you are frightened.

Sometimes in love with a woman or a man, looking into the eyes of a beloved, it disappears. But for how long? The honeymoon cannot be very long. Sooner or later… You know those eyes, you know that woman, you know that man, and then by and by you start settling back into your old so-called reality – and the rope, which looks like a snake to you, is there. This is the situation.

You say – the question is from Bodhiprem – "When you speak of the need for trust in order to let go of ego…" You misunderstand me. You are saying: "When you speak of the need for trust in order to let go of the ego…" You are saying that I say to you: "Trust so that you can drop the ego!" I am not saying that. I am saying that if you trust, the ego is dropped. It is not like cause and effect – that your trust will be the cause, and the ego will be dropped as an effect. I am saying that the moment you trust, the ego is not there. In trust the ego is not found.

But you are so concerned with the ego that you say, "Okay. If you say in trust it is not found, I will trust in order that the ego is not found." You are bringing in that "in order." Please be very careful, because what is being said to you is immensely significant. Don't change it. Don't interpret it. Let it be as it is said to you. I am not saying: "Trust in order – so that – the ego can be dropped"; other- wise your trust will be a means and the dropping of the ego will be an end. Naturally the end will be in the future, and the means has to be practiced. You will have to practice for years or for lives, and when you really have come to gain trust, then you will be able to drop the ego. No!

I am saying that this very moment, if trust is there, the ego is not there! They don't exist together. It is as if the room is dark and I tell you, "Take this lamp." And you say, "If I take this lamp into the room, how long will it take for the darkness to disappear? If I go into the room and practice light there, how long will it take for the dark- ness to disappear?" You need not practice anything. Simply take the light there and you will not find darkness. They don't exist together.

What is trust? It is the highest kind of love. It is the purest love. It is uncontaminated love – uncontaminated by any desire. If you trust me with a desire, it is not trust. Then you are using me. If you think by trusting in me you will attain to nirvana, *moksha*, the kingdom of

God, then you don't trust me. You are using me; you have made me a means. That is not very respectful. If you trust me, this is your kingdom of God – this trust. There is nothing else, there is nowhere to go. This is your nirvana. In this very trust, darkness has disappeared, and the light is burning bright.

Bodhiprem says: "When you speak of the need for trust in order to let go of ego…" Now he is creating a great problem. "…I feel that's where I'm stuck." You are stuck because of your misunderstanding, unclarity. It is not the ego that is obstructing you; it is the unclarity. It is because you have not been present to me; it is because you have not been listening to me without desire. It is not the ego that you are stuck with, it is your unintelligence.

Now that will hurt you because it is okay to be stuck with ego, but to be stuck with unintelligence? That will hurt very much: "Am I unintelligent?" You can accept the idea that you are an egoist, but to accept the idea that you are unintelligent is very difficult. Your ego will say, "You – and unintelligent, Bodhiprem? You are the most intelligent person in the world!" That's what Bodhiprem must be saying right now.

But be patient; try to understand. We are stuck because of our unintelligence. Call it sleep, call it ignorance, call it whatsoever you want to call it, but basically it is unintelligence. An intelligent person… And I don't mean that there are intelligent persons and there are unintelligent persons. Every unintelligent person carries the potential of being an intelligent person. Unintelligence is just the seed which has not broken its shell yet. Once the shell is broken and the seed starts sprouting, it becomes intelligence. So unintelligence is not against intelligence; it is the very womb that intelligence arises out of. But let me tell you that a spade is a spade. Even if it hurts, one has to understand it. It is unintelligence which hinders us. Intelligence becomes freedom. You have not understood me. Out of your unintelligence you are creating desires.

"…for my distrust is a tangible thing." It is not distrust because you have not even known trust, how can you distrust? Let it be very clear to you. Distrust is possible only when you have known trust. You have not known trust, so distrust is impossible. So what is it then? It is untrust, not distrust – and that is a different thing. It is untrust. What is the difference?

Untrust simply means you have never tried trust so you are

afraid, frightened. Everybody is frightened when there is something new one is going to do, when one enters an uncharted sea, or goes into a jungle where there are no longer any maps available, no milestones. And there is every possibility that you will never come across any other human being that you can ask where to go and how to find the way.

I have heard, it happened in a jungle...

A man, an explorer, was lost for three days – hungry, almost going crazy, running from this place to that and reaching nowhere. Early in the morning on the fourth day he saw another man sitting under a tree. He was overjoyed; he forgot all those three days of suffering, when in the night he could not sleep because of the wild animals. And in the day searching and searching and there was no way to find out how to get out of this jungle. It had appeared endless.

Naturally, if you were that explorer you also would have been overjoyed, you would have become full of joy at seeing another human being. Now...

He rushed, hugged the man, and said, "I am so happy!"

And the man who was sitting under the tree said, "For what?"

And this explorer said, "Just seeing you because for three days I have been lost."

And the man said, "So what? I have been lost for seven days!"

Now, even if you can find a human being – who is himself lost – what is the point of finding him? Now you will both be lost together, that's all. Maybe even more lost because now there will be two persons continuously conflicting. Up to now you were alone, at least free to move on your own. Now you have a marriage partner, now there are going to be more problems because he would like to go north and you would like to go south – each will create fear in the other: "Maybe the other is right and I am going wrong?" And each may create guilt in each other.

It is a natural fear of the unknown that creates untrust; it is not distrust. Distrust means that you trusted and you were cheated; you trusted, and because of your trust you were deceived, then distrust comes. But trust has never cheated anybody, it cannot. And I am not saying that through trust people cannot cheat you. Remember, I am saying trust never cheats anybody. Sometimes it has happened that a disciple has become enlightened because he trusted the master, and the master himself was not enlightened. This strange thing has been happening down the ages many times.

It happened in a Tibetan mystic's life...

The mystic went to a master who was a fraud – and frauds exist in the world of spirituality more than anywhere else, because there it is very easy to cheat since they deal in invisible things you cannot see. They say, "Here is God. Look into my hand." If you don't see, they say you don't trust. If you see, they say, "Then, perfectly okay." Can't you see? And you say, "Yes, sir," and you are *not* seeing. When you deal in invisible goods it is very simple to cheat. In the marketplace there are frauds, but not so many. There cannot be so many because they deal in visible goods. There is some way, some criterion to judge whether the thing is right or wrong. But in religion there is no way to judge. So out of one hundred, ninety-nine percent are frauds. It is the best way to cheat people, nothing like it.

This mystic went to the master, and the master was a cheat. But this young man trusted – trusted utterly. He thought his master was enlightened, and whatsoever the master said, he followed one hundred percent. It was rumored around the place that the master was such a great man that even if you repeated his name and walked on the water, you could walk. Nobody had tried it before. And even if somebody had tried, he must have sunk. Then there is always the rationalization that your trust is not total, so you cannot catch hold of the master: "Your trust is not entire, that's why you sank."

This young man walked on water – and he really walked. It became his usual thing. When you can walk on the water, who bothers to go to the bridge, or things like that? People started coming to see him and the other disciples – particularly the senior ones – became very disturbed. They tried in secret but they all sank. So, even the master was puzzled. One day, in secret, the master himself tried, thinking: "When my disciples can walk on the water just by trusting in me, then what can't I do? I can do anything! I am the greatest master in the world, my disciples are walking on water. Jesus used to walk on water and my disciples are walking on water, so I must be greater than Jesus!"

So he went – in secret of course because he was afraid. He had never tried: "Who knows?" And he knew perfectly well that he was a fraud. The disciple had deep trust in him but he had no trust in himself. How could he have any trust? He knew perfectly well that he went on deceiving people. He walked and sank.

Then he called the young man and said, "How do you do it?"

He said, "I simply say your name – 'Master, I want to go to the other side' and you take me. And recently I have started flying from one peak of the mountain to the other because I said, 'When it is possible on water, why not in air?' So one day I tried and said, 'Master, take me from this side to the other side,' and you took me. Now I can do anything. Just your name…"

The master had to fall at his feet. He said, "Initiate me; you know the secret. I am an ordinary man, and last night I tried walking and I sank."

It has happened many times, because it is not really a question of whether the man you trust is cheating you or not, the question is that trust never cheats. You cannot be cheated because of your trust. If the trust is infinite you are impossible to cheat. Nobody can cheat you. Your trust will protect you. Your trust will become your very experience. Your trust will become your boat. Your trust will take you to the other shore, but remember, what you have is not distrust. You can't have distrust; you have never trusted. Distrust can come only as an experience that trust failed. But trust never fails, so *distrust* is just a word; untrust is true.

You have never tried, so only just a little courage is needed to try. Give it a try. Be a little courageous. Slowly, slowly go beyond the limitations that you have created around yourself – step by step. And the more you go beyond the barriers that you have created around yourself, the bigger you become, the more expansion comes to your consciousness. Then you will see that you can go as far as you want because every move beyond the limitation brings more joy, more freedom, more being.

"…for my distrust is a tangible thing." It is not distrust; it is only fear which is tangible. "It feels painful, but I can't let go of it." There is no need to let go of it. Meditate on it; see exactly what it is. We go on giving names to things, which we have not even watched correctly, and once you give a wrong name you will be in a trap. The wrong name will never allow you to see the thing as it is. Don't be in a hurry to name a thing and categorize a thing and pigeonhole a

thing. There is no need. Just watch what it is. If you watch, you will
find it is untrust, not distrust. If you watch, you will find it is simply a
lack of courage – fear, not distrust and tangible, no.

Then things will be different. When you know it is fear, when the
disease is known rightly, a right medicine is possible. When you go
on calling your TB cancer, then you go on treating cancer and the
TB is never treated. Diagnosis is far more important than medica-
tion. And this is the problem: people don't worry about diagnosis
and they are simply ready to jump upon any medicine. They are
ready to take any medicine without bothering at all what exactly
their disease is. That is ninety percent of the problem; medicine is
only ten percent. Diagnosis is needed and that's why a master can
be helpful: to diagnose things.

I would like to remind you that it is untrust not distrust, that it is
fear and, in a way, natural. It exists in everybody. So don't start
feeling yourself a coward; it is natural. The fear of the unknown
exists in everybody. And one has to go slowly, slowly beyond the
known – just a few steps, so that if it becomes too much you can
come back. But once you have started going...

It is the same fear as that of a new bird which is ready to go into
the sky and is afraid, sitting just on the edge of the nest. The wings
are there, he can fly, but he has never flown before. So an untrust –
not distrust, untrust: "Maybe I cannot make it, maybe I will fall; can I
really go into this beautiful sky?" He flutters his wings, tries to gather
courage, and still remains there, hanging. And the mother pushes
him. The mother goes on flying around the nest to show him: "Look,
I can fly, why can't you? You come from me, you are just like me.
Look at my wings – you have far more beautiful wings. My wings are
old, yet I can fly. Your wings are young. You can go far away, farther
than me. You just see!" And the mother goes on flying, comes back
to the nest, looks into the eyes of the child, pushes him, nags him.

That's what I go on doing – nagging. Sometimes, if it is really
needed, she really, physically, pushes him, throws him out of the
nest. And he starts, in a haphazard way of course because he has
never done it before, not in a very skillful way, not very aesthetic,
not very artistic – it is natural. Just a few seconds fluttering around
and he comes back to the nest. Still the fear is there, but now trust
has started to come. Now he knows that he is not very skillful but
he has wings; then skill can be learned. Now, next time he will not

need the mother's push. Next time he will tell the mother, "Just sit here and watch, I am going to take a trip!" And he takes off, first around the nest, then around the tree, then he starts going to other trees, and then one day he has gone.

This is the way a disciple moves. It is fear and is natural. I understand it. Don't be worried about it, and don't misname it otherwise things will be difficult. You will go on fighting with distrust and the problem is fear, not distrust. And you will go on fighting with ego, and the problem is unintelligence, not ego.

"Early this year, for a brief period, I felt high energy and with it, open, loving and trusting. But now that energy has gone, and with it the openness." Now, understand something. It has happened to you that you have been out of the nest; you have been on a small trip. Maybe it was very small, but you have tasted it! Now, watch how it happened that time and why it is not happening now.

There are a few things. First: when it happened for the first time you were taken unawares; you were not waiting for it, and it happened. Now because it has happened, you are waiting and desiring. That desire may be one of the barriers. These things come on their own; they are happenings. Happiness is a happening. You cannot bring them by force, by coercion, by violence; you cannot bring them into your life. They come on their own. You just have to be open for them to come. Your door should remain open; when the breeze comes, enjoy it. But you cannot go out and force the breeze to come in.

The first time it happened. It is always easy the first time and the second time it is difficult. It is not only so with you, it is so with everybody. When people come here come for the first time they are not expecting. They don't know what is going to happen, they are simply open. They only know that something may happen: "So keep the doors open." When for the first time they come and fall in love with me, there is a kind of honeymoon. They are utterly in tune with me, shocked into a new kind of awareness, feeling a new hope; again feeling alive – dullness has disappeared – again a door opens. Otherwise they were thinking that there is nothing in life, there is no meaning. The poetry has disappeared long ago. Again they start pulsating, again there is hope, again they can feel that there is still some possibility. They become expectant.

Without any expectation, just expectant, something is possible.

What, they don't know. And with the first impact their mind is not able to cope with it, so the mind becomes silent. The thing is so new that they cannot control it: meditation, listening to me, and the whole family around here dressed in orange... The whole vibe simply turns them on and things start happening. The moment things start happening, the problem arises. They start desiring more, and the moment you desire, things stop. When the "more" comes, the mind has come back; the greed has come back. You are no longer in the present, you have moved into the future. And when you ask that the same thing should be repeated again and again, you are hanging with the past. Now you are no longer here.

Listening to me, by and by their mind becomes knowledgeable; they become great knowers. That too becomes a barrier. Listening to me, become more and more unknowing. That is the whole effort here. I want to take all your knowledge away from you. I want to destroy it. I want you to be ignorant, innocent, because in innocence all is possible. With knowledge, nothing is possible. But listening to me again and again and again, you become knowledgeable – even about these things: that one has to be ignorant. It becomes your knowledge. Not that you become ignorant, you start teaching others to become ignorant. "One has to be innocent"– this becomes your knowledge. You don't become innocent; you become knowledgeable about innocence. You start talking about innocence, what innocence is and how it should be brought about. You become experts. But you miss the point. And then things close. The honeymoon is over and the dark night of the soul starts.

Bodhiprem is in the dark night of the soul. But try to understand it, and in the very understanding it will start disappearing. The morning is not far away. Next time when it happens... And it will happen, it will happen only when you are tired of your desire and you forget about it. It will happen only when the past is so far away and distant that you start thinking: "Maybe it had never happened in the first place. Maybe I was dreaming. I was in a kind of hallucination." Or, "I had read it in a book, or maybe I got deceived by Osho, or something. I was hypnotized." When it becomes so distant that you cannot really think it had happened to you, you will lose the grip on the past.

If it had not happened, what is the point of desiring more of it? How can you desire more of something which has not happened to you? Then the future will disappear. This dark night of the soul becomes darker, darker, darker... A moment will come when all hope disappears. And with that disappearance of hope, and of the past and of the desire for the future, all that you have gathered around here – the knowledge – will look meaningless. You will think, "So it doesn't work. It is meaningless." You will start dropping that knowledge too.

Then – the morning! Then, suddenly, one day you see it is there again. The sun has risen and the fragrance is coming from many, many unknown flowers. You are full of it again. And the second time it will be deeper than the first. Now, I would like you to remember, when it happens the second time don't make the same mistake that you made the first time. Next time when it comes, enjoy it, feel thankful and grateful, and when it goes, say "Good-bye" and don't be bothered by it. It will come and go many times before it settles permanently. It will come and go many times. So it is not going to be solved within two or three times; it may come many times. And if you go on making the same mistake again and again, then it may go on coming and going for many lives. Next time, be a little more alert – don't desire, don't expect. When it comes feel thankful because you have not earned it; it is a gift.

A gift cannot be desired; a gift cannot be earned. It comes to you as a gift. But it happens with gifts too. If somebody gives you a gift every birthday and now your birthday is coming, you are thinking, "Now what is he going to give me?" And naturally you desire more than the last time. The last time he had given you a bicycle, now you want a car. And if the car does not come, you will be very angry. In fact, if a bicycle comes, then too you will be very angry: "What to do with the bicycle? One is enough. Now again a bicycle?" And if even the bicycle does not come, you will be in a rage. You don't understand the point that it was a gift. You cannot expect it – it was a gift. When it comes you have to be thankful, when it does not come you cannot demand it. Gifts cannot be demanded.

Godliness comes as a gift. Light comes as a gift. Love comes as a gift. Life itself is a gift! You cannot demand it. That's what you did, Bodhiprem; deep down you started demanding it. And hence you missed it. Next time it comes... This dark night of the soul will not be forever; the morning is coming closer. But when the morning comes closer, the night becomes darker and darker. And one has to pass through it. When it comes this time, just enjoy it. And if you just enjoy it, it will become long. It may never go. If you have learned the secret of enjoying a gift it may never go. I am not saying that it *will* never go. I am simply saying that if you have learned the art of not desiring, not clinging, not demanding, it *may* never go. But if it goes, then don't ask, then accept. Then relax into the dark night of the soul again.

It happens many times because man goes on committing the same mistake again and again. But slowly, slowly the understanding dawns, and one day one sees the point that God is available if you don't desire. God is available in desirelessness. If you desire, you lose.

The third question:

Osho,
Why are there so many religions?

Because there are so many people, because there are so many languages, because there are so many types of people – and because there are so many ways to approach God. It is a rich world. It would have been a very poor world if there was only one religion. Just think of a world where only the Bible exists, and no Vedas and no Gita and no Koran. Think of a world where only the Koran exists.

Now, one friend goes on asking every day why I don't speak on the Koran. I don't speak for a certain reason. The Koran is a beautiful song, the music of it is ultimate, but there is nothing in it to discuss. In that way it is poor. You cannot sing Buddha's message, but you can discuss it. In that way it is rich. Buddha's message can be discussed. You can go on, layer upon layer, deeper and deeper and deeper, and there is no end to it. But you cannot sing it. In that way it is dry. You cannot put it to music, you cannot make a melody of it, but it has great philosophical insight. The Koran is beautiful as a song. It has to be sung to be known. But as far as insight is concerned, it is poor; there is no insight in it. That's why I don't discuss it, because there is nothing to discuss in it.

If I have to discuss it, I will have to say many things against it, because the Koran is not a pure religious book. It has politics, it has sociology, society, law, marriage. It is the whole code. Only five percent of it is religious; ninety-five percent is about other things because it is the only book of the Arab people.

It is just like the Vedas. Only a few sentences here and there reach to the peak, other sentences are ordinary because it was the only book the Aryans had, it was their all. Their science was in it – whatsoever of science existed in those days – their religion was in it, their philosophy was in it, their poetry was in it, their business was in it, their economics was in it, their agriculture was in it. There was everything – it was their *Encyclopedia Britannica*. And so is the Koran. It is the only book. The Arab people had no other book, so the Koran functioned as their all. It talks about marriage – how many wives a husband should have; it talks about food – what you should eat, what you should not eat, it talks about prayer, the ritual – how you should do it.

Now you will not find things like that in Buddha's sutras. That will look so absurd: Buddha talking about how many wives you should have. What has Buddha to do with it? You can have as many as you want, and a wife can have as many husbands as she wants. What is the point of talking about it? Buddha is not giving a social code; he is giving the science of spiritual evolution. So when you talk about Buddha, there is so much to talk about and go into. Each word can become a deep well and you can draw infinite water out of it. But the Koran is rich in another sense. It is a poor man's book for unedu-cated people – not philosophic, not theological – but people who loved life, who loved the small things of life. It has great song in it.

If some day I decide to share the Koran with you, then the only way is that somebody will have to sing the Koran, and you will listen and I will also listen, because there is nothing to speak about. If one has to speak about something, then there are far more beautiful things. The Koran should be sung and listened to. It is music, it is pure music. It should not be discussed logically, it should not be analyzed logically. Then it looks very poor.

You don't analyze music. If you analyze music it loses its beauty. You don't analyze poetry. If you analyze poetry it becomes prose – something has disappeared from it, then there are ordinary words. You can have all the words that are in Shakespeare, you can have all the words in a box, but not in the same order as they are in Shakespeare, then you will not have poetry. The whole art of poetry is that those words are put in a certain order, and because of that certain order something transcendental descends. Those words simply create a net to catch hold of the transcendental. You need not look at the net at all. If you start analyzing the net – if you cut the net and you see what the net is made of, you will not catch the transcendental in it. The fish of the transcendental will escape. You need not cut and dissect the net; the net has only to be used.

So is the Koran: it is music, it is poetry. And it is good, I say, that Buddha exists – that is a different approach; that poetry and the Koran exist – that is another approach; and that the Bible exists. And there are Moses and Zarathustra and Jesus; different people bring different angles into the world, they open different windows into godliness. It is perfectly good that there are so many religions; nothing is wrong with it. If something *is* wrong, then it comes from arrogance, not from so many religions. Then it comes from the arrogance of a Hindu when he says, "Only my religion is right," or when a Jew says, "Only my religion is right," or when a Christian says, "Only those who go through Jesus will reach, nobody else." This is arrogance, this is stupidity; this should be dropped. There are many languages and different ways of expressing things.

Two patients at an asylum passed the swimming pool early in the morning. A nurse, thinking she was unobserved at that hour, was bathing in the nude. As she climbed out, one inmate said to the other, "Boy! Wouldn't she look good in a bathing suit!"

There are different visions.

"Hey man," one hippie said to another, "Turn on the radio."
"Okay," the second hippie answered. And leaning over very close to the radio, he whispered, "I love you."

Now that is a hippie's way of turning things on. Beware! Don't say this to Pankaja. If you say this to her in her ear, whisper, "I love you," you will turn her off, not on. She is very afraid of somebody saying to her, "I love you." She is afraid of love. She is afraid of being turned on: the fear that if you are turned on, then you don't know where you are going and what is going to happen.

Just few days ago she came to me to tell me about her fear, and I told her and the people who had gathered for that evening's darshan to spread the rumor, that whosoever comes around Pankaja should just come close to her and say in her ear, "I love you." She simply gets shocked when you say, "I love you." Even when *I* said to her, "I love you," she was shaken. Just the very idea of love, the very word... What to say about the experience? The very word pierces her heart.

Now, there are people who are waiting for somebody to come and say "I love you," and there are people who are afraid – different people, different approaches, and each has its own validity.

Now she cannot move on the path of prayer because there God comes and whispers in your ear, "I love you." Now that is not for her. She has to go through meditation. Buddha will be her way, not Christ, because Christ says: "Love is God." That will be difficult for her. It is just an example of what I am talking about. Everybody has different visions, different dreams, different pasts, different experiences. God cannot come alike to everybody, and it is very good that there are so many religions. That means that everybody can have his own way, everybody can choose. This is a rich world. It is not monotonous.

The problem is not that there are many religions, the problem is that people are arrogant, stupid. A really religious person is one who loves his way towards God, and who loves your way towards God too, howsoever opposite to his it may be. And remember, I am not saying that he tolerates your way. *Toleration* is a very intolerant word! When you say, "I tolerate Mohammedans" – toleration? Mahatma Gandhi used to teach toleration in India. Toleration is very intolerant. It gives you a feeling of superiority; that you are a man of tolerance, as if the other is not worthy. But still you tolerate: that the other is very low, but still you tolerate because you are such a liberal man. Such compassion is in your heart, you tolerate. Of course, you know that the other is not as right as you are, but still you tolerate because you believe in democracy. You believe that if somebody wants to go wrong, he has to be given freedom: "Okay, go."

Toleration is not a good word and I don't want you to become tolerant. I want you to become lovers. You love your way, you are moving on your way; love those who are moving on their ways, and their ways too because all ways are moving towards God. Tolerance is not a right thing. Love! Don't have any notions that you are higher than and superior to others. That's what is happening in the world.

There are people who cannot bear the presence of the other: Christians who cannot bear the presence of the Jews, Jews who cannot bear the presence of the Christians. These people are thought to be very orthodox, conventional, out of date. The modern mind says, "This is not right." The modern mind says, "We tolerate." Christians say: "Yes. Hindus are also right – not as right as we are, but still right, better than nothing, better than not being religious."

Mahatma Gandhi used to write books, articles proving that the Koran is also right, that the Bible is also right. But the way in which he proves it is very cunning. The way he proves it is through the "right thing": the criterion is the Gita. Now whatsoever corresponds with the Gita in the Koran is also right. Whatsoever corresponds in the Bible with the Gita is also right. And what about that which is against the Gita? He never talks about it. The real problem arises there. There is no problem if the Gita says one thing and the same thing is being repeated in the Koran; then it is only a question of a language difference. You can simply say that the Koran is also right; it is saying the same thing as the Gita. It has been decided that the Gita is right; now, whatsoever corresponds with the Gita is right. This is a cunning approach.

What about the things in which the Koran is against the Gita? I say then too the Koran is right! And what to say about the Bible where it is against the Gita? Then too, I say, the Bible is right. The Gita has no monopoly; the Gita is a path. And whatsoever the Gita says is right on that path. It is as if you are going in a bullock cart. Somebody else is moving in a car. Now what do you say about these two vehicles? Something is right in the bullock cart: the wheels of the bullock cart are right on the bullock cart. The bullock cart will not move without those wheels. But those same wheels are wrong on a car. If you put those wheels on a car, the car will not move at all. Those wheels are right on the bullock cart; the bullock cart has its own unity. And the mechanism that is in the car is right in the car – it has its own organic unity.

Each religion is an organism. My hand is right on my body, it may not be right on your body – it may be too short, or too long. Lenin had very small legs. It was very difficult for him to sit on chairs because they would never reach the ground, so special chairs had to be made for him. Somebody asked him, "What do you think about your legs?"

He said, "I am not in any trouble. They are perfectly okay for me. I can move, I can walk. They are perfectly right in my organism – small or big is not the point – but on somebody else's body they may create trouble. Your head is perfectly right on you, on somebody else's body it may not fit. It may be ugly, they may not go together."

Each religion is an organic unity. You need not tolerate it. You have to love it; somebody is moving on that way. Somebody is going by bullock cart and you are going in your car. Can't you just say, "Hello"? Do you have to tolerate the bullock cart? Can't you say, "Hello! I am also going"? Somebody enjoys the bullock cart, and the bullock cart has its own joys which no car can have. The bullock cart moves more naturally, in tune with nature. The car goes too fast to appreciate nature. The airplane goes so fast that it is not a journey at all. From one point to another you jump so fast that you have missed the whole journey. And somebody is walking – not even in the bullock cart – he wants to enjoy walking. That too is perfectly good.

To me, all religions are perfectly good because every religion is an organic unity. Its goodness is in itself; it is not comparable to anything else.

The fourth question:

Osho,
Can't a religious man be a politician?

Never heard of it! It is impossible because religion is love, intelligence, awareness, meditation, desirelessness, non-ambition. And politics is just the opposite: ugly ambition, violence, aggression.

Politics is the desire to rule over others, and religion is the desire to free oneself from others and to free others from oneself. Religion is freedom. Politics is a kind of slavery. When you seek power, what in fact are you seeking? You are seeking power over others; you want to reduce them to nobodies. You want to reduce them to slaves, serfs. When you are searching for religion, what are you searching for? You are simply searching for a way out of your imprisonment into freedom. Those who love freedom, make others free also, and those who love slavery and want others to make others slaves, become slaves to their own slaves.

Politics is cunningness; religion is innocence. They can't go together. Yes, politicians pretend to be religious, because that helps; that is part of their strategy. But don't be deceived by it.

Three politicians – one English, one German and one Indian – all died and went to heaven at the same time. On their arrival, St. Peter asked the Englishman how many lies he had told during his professional career. The Englishman admitted to twelve lies and was told that he had to run round heaven twelve times. When asked the same question, the German politician said that he could remember telling twenty lies, and he was told to run round heaven twenty times.

St. Peter then turned to the Indian, Gandhian, politician, only to find that he had disappeared. "Where's he got to?" he asked an angel standing nearby.

"Oh, he's gone back to get his bicycle," said the angel.

Now the Gandhian politician is trying to be religious in politics, and they have proved to be the most mischievous people in the whole history of world politics – the ugliest. Because of the mask of being religious, they can go on playing all sorts of nonsense behind the mask. Remember that the very desire for power is an ugly desire. It makes you ugly. In a religious consciousness there is no desire to have any power over anybody. That brings beauty; it brings freedom not only to you, but freedom for others too.

The politician is interested in the ordinary world; the religious person is interested not in the ordinary world, but the extraordinary that is hidden in the ordinary. The religious person is searching for the invisible in the visible, for the soul in the body, for godliness in matter. Their searches are different, utterly different.

A poet can be religious. A religious person can be a poet. But a religious person cannot be political, and a political person cannot be religious – they exclude each other. And if by chance somebody is really religious and is in politics, he will never succeed. He will be a failure, an utter failure; you will never hear of him. Only people who are cunning succeed in politics. People who can cheat, and can cheat with smiles on their faces, people who can kill, and kill "for your own sake." People who can kill, exploit and still can manage to prove that they are serving their people – they succeed.

The last question:

Osho,
What is presence of mind?

This story…

A woman was driving her car at about sixty miles an hour in a built-up area when she noticed in her rear-view mirror that a motor-cycle policeman was following her. Instead of slowing down, she thought that she could shake him off by increasing her speed to seventy miles an hour.

Looking through her mirror again, she saw that there were now two motor-cycle policemen following her. She stepped up her speed to eighty miles an hour and, when she looked again, there were three policemen on her tail.

Suddenly she saw a garage up ahead and, pulling into it, she got out and dashed into the ladies' toilet. Ten minutes later she ventured out, and there were the three policemen waiting for her. Without batting an eyelash, she said coyly, "I'll bet you thought I wouldn't make it."

Enough for today.

About Osho

Osho defies categorization. His thousands of talks cover everything from the individual quest for meaning to the most urgent social and political issues facing society today. Osho's books are not written but are transcribed from audio and video recordings of his extemporaneous talks to international audiences. As he puts it, "So remember: whatever I am saying is not just for you... I am talking also for the future generations."

Osho has been described by *The Sunday Times* in London as one of the "1000 Makers of the 20th Century" and by American author Tom Robbins as "the most dangerous man since Jesus Christ." *Sunday Mid-Day* (India) has selected Osho as one of ten people – along with Gandhi, Nehru and Buddha – who have changed the destiny of India.

About his own work Osho has said that he is helping to create the conditions for the birth of a new kind of human being. He often characterizes this new human being as "Zorba the Buddha" – capable both of enjoying the earthy pleasures of a Zorba the Greek and the silent serenity of a Gautama the Buddha.

Running like a thread through all aspects of Osho's talks and meditations is a vision that encompasses both the timeless wisdom of all ages past and the highest potential of today's (and tomorrow's) science and technology.

Osho is known for his revolutionary contribution to the science of inner transformation, with an approach to meditation that acknowledges the accelerated pace of contemporary life. His unique OSHO Active Meditations™ are designed to first release the accumulated stresses of body and mind, so that it is then easier to take an experience of stillness and thought-free relaxation into daily life.

Two autobiographical works by the author are available:
Autobiography of a Spiritually Incorrect Mystic,
St Martins Press, New York (book and eBook)
Glimpses of a Golden Childhood,
OSHO Media International, Pune, India

OSHO International Meditation Resort

Location

Located 100 miles southeast of Mumbai in the thriving modern city of Pune, India, the OSHO International Meditation Resort is a holiday destination with a difference. The Meditation Resort is spread over 28 acres of spectacular gardens in a beautiful tree-lined residential area.

Uniqueness

Each year the Meditation Resort welcomes thousands of people from more than 100 countries. The unique campus provides an opportunity for a direct personal experience of a new way of living – with more awareness, relaxation, celebration and creativity. A great variety of around-the-clock and around-the-year program options are available. Doing nothing and just relaxing is one of them!

All programs are based on the OSHO vision of "Zorba the Buddha" – a qualitatively new kind of human being who is able *both* to participate creatively in everyday life *and* to relax into silence and meditation.

OSHO Meditations

A full daily schedule of meditations for every type of person includes methods that are active and passive, traditional and revolutionary, and in particular the OSHO Active Meditations™. The meditations take place in what must be the world's largest meditation hall, the OSHO Auditorium.

OSHO Multiversity

Individual sessions, courses and workshops cover everything from creative arts to holistic health, personal transformation, relationship and life transition, work-as-meditation, esoteric sciences, and the "Zen" approach to sports and recreation. The secret of the OSHO Multiversity's success lies in the fact that all its programs are combined with meditation, supporting the understanding that as human beings we are far more than the sum of our parts.

OSHO Basho Spa

The luxurious Basho Spa provides for leisurely open-air swimming surrounded by trees and tropical green. The uniquely styled, spacious Jacuzzi, the saunas, gym, tennis courts...all these are enhanced by their stunningly beautiful setting.

Cuisine

A variety of different eating areas serve delicious Western, Asian and Indian vegetarian food – most of it organically grown especially for the Meditation Resort. Breads and cakes are baked in the resort's own bakery.

Night life

There are many evening events to choose from – dancing being at the top of the list! Other activities include full-moon meditations beneath the stars, variety shows, music performances and meditations for daily life.

Or you can just enjoy meeting people at the Plaza Café, or walking in the nighttime serenity of the gardens of this fairytale environment.

Facilities

You can buy all your basic necessities and toiletries in the Galleria. The Multimedia Gallery sells a large range of OSHO media products. There is also a bank, a travel agency and a Cyber Café on-campus. For those who enjoy shopping, Pune provides all the options, ranging from traditional and ethnic Indian products to all of the global brand-name stores.

Accommodation

You can choose to stay in the elegant rooms of the OSHO Guesthouse, or for longer stays opt for one of the OSHO Living-In program packages. Additionally there is a plentiful variety of nearby hotels and serviced apartments.

www.osho.com/meditationresort
www.osho.com/guesthouse
www.osho.com/livingin

More Books and eBooks by
OSHO Media International

The God Conspiracy:
The Path from Superstition to Super Consciousness

Discover the Buddha: 53 Meditations to Meet the Buddha Within
Gold Nuggets: Messages from Existence

OSHO Classics
The Book of Wisdom: The Heart of Tibetan Buddhism.
The Mustard Seed: The Revolutionary Teachings of Jesus
Ancient Music in the Pines: In Zen, Mind Suddenly Stops
The Empty Boat: Encounters with Nothingness
A Bird on the Wing: Zen Anecdotes for Everyday Life
The Path of Yoga: Discovering the Essence and Origin of Yoga
And the Flowers Showered: The Freudian Couch and Zen
Nirvana: The Last Nightmare: Learning to Trust in Life
The Goose Is Out: Zen in Action
Absolute Tao: Subtle Is the Way to Love, Happiness and Truth

The Tantra Experience: Evolution through Love
Tantric Transformation: When Love Meets Meditation

Pillars of Consciousness (illustrated)
BUDDHA: His Life and Teachings and Impact on Humanity
ZEN: Its History and Teachings and Impact on Humanity
TANTRA: The Way of Acceptance
TAO: The State and the Art

Authentic Living

Danger: Truth at Work: The Courage to Accept the Unknowable
The Magic of Self-Respect: Awakening to Your Own Awareness
Born With a Question Mark in Your Heart

OSHO eBooks and "OSHO-Singles"

Emotions: Freedom from Anger, Jealousy and Fear
Meditation: The First and Last Freedom
What Is Meditation?
The Book of Secrets: 112 Meditations to Discover the Mystery Within

20 Difficult Things to Accomplish in This World
Compassion, Love and Sex
Hypnosis in the Service of Meditation
Why Is Communication So Difficult, Particularly between Lovers?
Bringing Up Children
Why Should I Grieve Now?: facing a loss and letting it go
Love and Hate: just two sides of the same coin

Next Time You Feel Angry...
Next Time You Feel Lonely...
Next Time You Feel Suicidal...

OSHO Media BLOG
http://oshomedia.blog.osho.com

For More Information

www. **OSHO** .com

a comprehensive multi-language website including a magazine,
OSHO Books, OSHO Talks in audio and video formats, the OSHO
Library text archive in English and Hindi and extensive information
about OSHO Meditations. You will also find the program schedule
of the OSHO Multiversity and information about the OSHO
International Meditation Resort.

http://OSHO.com/AllAboutOSHO
http://OSHO.com/Resort
http://OSHO.com/Shop
http://www.youtube.com/OSHO
http://www.Twitter.com/OSHO
http://www.facebook.com/pages/OSHO.International

To contact OSHO International Foundation:
www.osho.com/oshointernational,
oshointernational@oshointernational.com